Y0-DNC-400

RECOLLECTIONS OF A NY PUERTO RICAN

Best wishes to
Mr. Ralph A. Leal

Filux A Santiago
June/2003

RECOLLECTIONS OF A NY PUERTO RICAN

A Memoir

Fidel Angel Santiago

Copyright © 2003 by Fidel Angel Santiago.

Library of Congress Number:		2003090267
ISBN:	Hardcover	1-4010-9273-X
	Softcover	1-4010-9272-1

All rights reserved. No part of this book may be reproduced or transmitted in any form or by any means, electronic or mechanical, including photocopying, recording, or by any information storage and retrieval system, without permission in writing from the copyright owner.

This book was printed in the United States of America.

To order additional copies of this book, contact:
Xlibris Corporation
1-888-795-4274
www.Xlibris.com
Orders@Xlibris.com
17793

CONTENTS

PART I
The Early Years

Chapter 1: Searching for a theme 13
Chapter 2: Logic Reasoning 17
Chapter 3: The City and its public schools 19
Chapter 4: Reading for Pleasure 22
Chapter 5: The Model Airplane, and The Movies 24
Chapter 6: Caguas, Puerto Rico 27
Chapter 7: A brief Encounter 30
Chapter 8: The Benitez Family 32
Chapter 9: A Digression: Thoughts Relating to Fate 34
Chapter 10: Biatriz: With My Uncle Cirilo and His Family 37
Chapter 11: Tio Cirilo 39
Chapter 12: A Brief Interlude 42
Chapter 13: Activities 44
Chapter 14: Corn, Apples, Oranges and the Plaza 46
Chapter 15: The Yegua, Teams of Bulls and The Foguera 48
Chapter 16: Recognition and Rewards 51
Chapter 17: Three Kings Day 53
Chapter 18: Developing The Calluses 55
Chapter 19: Tobacco, The Money Maker 57
Chapter 20: The Underlying Forces of Money 60
Chapter 21: Nature's Forces 63

PART II
The City

Chapter 22: The Arrival 67
Chapter 23: Uncle Domingo 70

Chapter 24: Philosophical Thoughts About Life 73
Chapter 25: Values and Principles of Behavior 76
Chapter 26: Remembered Sights 79
Chapter 27: Remembered Incidents 81
Chapter 28: Family Values 84
Chapter 29: The "Fair Lady" 86
Chapter 30: A Judgment on Self-esteem and Values 88
Chapter 31: A Bit of Poetry, and Real and Unreal Happiness .. 91
Chapter 32: Some Types of Reality 94
Chapter 33: Toys, Games, Holiday Rituals, and The Movies .. 97
Chapter 34: The intrusion of Society, and Tradition 102
Chapter 35: The City in The Early 1930's 105
Chapter 36: More about the City in the 1930's 110
Chapter 37: Reality, Passion and Reason 114
Chapter 38: The Fair, Stickball, Hockey and The "Silver King" ... 119
Chapter 39: Our Neighborhood 122
Chapter 40: "Skippy," and The Model Airplane 127
Chapter 41: A Learning Experience 131
Chapter 42: The Search for Variables in Our Lives 134
Chapter 43: Activities, and Fear of the Unknown 138
Chapter 44: Afterlife 144
Chapter 45: Amusements and Fashions 147
Chapter 46: The Young Teenage Years 151
Chapter 47: The Unexpected Factor 156

PART III
The War Years

Chapter 48: The Home Front 165
Chapter 49: An Alternative to Capitalism 171
Chapter 50: How An Alternative to Capitalism Can Work ... 176
Chapter 51: Boot Camp and School 181
Chapter 52: The Mexicans 188
Chapter 53: The Ship 194
Chapter 54: The Island 199
Chapter 55: Critical Thinking 203
Chapter 56: More On Logic Reasoning 208
Chapter 57: Manus and Leyte Islands 215

Chapter 58: Palawan Island 221
Chapter 59: In The Name of Patriotism 230

PART IV
The Post-War Years

Chapter 60: Some Observations 235
Chapter 61: Taking on Responsibilities 240
Chapter 62: The Expedition, and Leisure Activities 245
Chapter 63: ARINC 250
Chapter 64: A brief interlude 256
Chapter 65: Unfamiliar Surroundings 260

PART V
The Turbulent 60's

Chapter 66: A System's Error 269
Chapter 67: Searching For A Purpose 274
Chapter 68: Brief Notes On Music and The Guitar 278
Chapter 69: Observing, Listening, and Discovering 284

PART VI
A New Beginning

Chapter 70: Weather, and City Happenings 291
Chapter 71: Morocco and Spain 296
Chapter 72: Our Travels Continue 304
Chapter 73: Another Brief Encounter, and Fears 310
Chapter 74: A Mother's End 315
Chapter 75: Emotions, and The Ravages of Time 319
Chapter 76: The Bridgeport "Flight Service Station" 323

PART VII
A New Career

Chapter 77: Some Opinions On Public Schools 347
Chapter 78: The Past, Present, and A Racist Society 353

Chapter 79: The Relentless Passage of Time 360
Chapter 80: Defining Love 363
Chapter 81: Further Reactions Relating to The Public Schools 369
Chapter 82: Opinions 373
Chapter 83: Hazardous Work 379
Chapter 84: A Vacation 384
Chapter 85: Reactions to an Action 389
Chapter 86: The Vacation Ends 393
Chapter 87: Journey's End 398

PART I
The Early Years

CHAPTER 1

Searching for a theme

How does one channel, if you forgive the usage of this modernistic and perhaps pretentious word, the senses to focus on a theme in which both the writer and the reader relate to situations, settings and happenings which have occurred in the past, present and in all probability will happen in the future? A rather long sentence for starting a writing project, particularly in these times, where generally speaking, people tend to have very little time, patience and attention span for reading material that is lengthy, and which may be rather dull and boring, depending on their perspective in the world in which they live. Better to have said our world, and one which for us had a beginning and most certainly will have an end; and this end is the true reality of our lives. However, to get back on course, the long sentence has already been thought-out and put on paper, so, let's get on with the task, searching the mind for a theme to develop within the senses of this writer.

The search, however, may be difficult, and one which may lead the writer to, ultimately, select the easy-way-out, that is, choosing a subject he is totally familiar with, his being. In a clearer manner, the writing will involve situations, settings and happenings that have thus far occurred in his life. Further, he will, from time-to-time cast opinions and make judgmental analyses which may yield for the reader a sense of the writer's ideological point of view in terms of life as he has experienced it. More precisely, the writing will also encompass philosophical inquiries as to what may, or may not be the true reality of our lives.

A moment ago I spoke about the present world in which we live. This world appears to be populated with people whose only goal exist in how much wealth they can accumulate for the sole purpose of consuming materialistic objects within their lives span. Of course, this goal is wide in scope among the masses. Moreover, in reflecting momentarily on this matter, one realizes the enormous cleavage that persists between those who have, and the unfortunate, or the disadvantage who don't. This fact can be more clearly stated as the total inequality of life throughout the world that's prevalent today. The quality, furthermore, is based on the amount of wealth one can acquire as a means for becoming equal, or maintaining an existing condition, the status quo. One may now speculate a bit, equal to what, to those who have it? What I'm attempting to underscore is that this quality of life we have been psychologically conditioned to may be defined as the amount of materialistic wealth we can acquire during our lifetime. Never mind the spiritual wealth, in a capitalistic society such as ours, there is no room for this form of wealth. Plainly speaking, there's no money in it.

This quality of life concept raises serious questions. For example, why are we faced with the horrendous problems of drugs, homeless people, many of whom are on the streets panhandling for money, and the common lawlessness of individuals who prey on others by helping themselves to what does not belong to them; these individuals motivated, perhaps, by a need for money to buy hard drugs or alcohol which will bring them happiness. This may or may not be true, nevertheless, the fact is that the happiness is only momentary. To be sure, it is a transient experience, which gradually wears off leaving them to seek more money for regaining their happiness.

For some people, drugs are the means for experiencing this happiness. Nonetheless, the happiness, the well-being and the euphoric feelings are only temporary, and will dissipate once the drugs wear off. More to the point, the physical and mental effects of drugs, or the overall stimulation and happiness experienced is, indeed, the motivating factor for what today is commonly known as "doing drugs." In essence, what we must realize is that drugs are artificial in nature. In other words, the body reacts to a chemical stimuli that generates the momentary happiness. Furthermore, this momentary happiness is not the real thing; but what, in fact, is the reality of a situation when we relate it to drug abuse?

It may be the awareness of knowing the underlying circumstances that are causing the drug abuse problem. Having this insight may be a form of well-being for the person experiencing it. Better yet, it is having a sense of one's self in relation to what is happening and the causality for the happening in the drug culture. Further, dealing in drugs connotes for some individuals the acquisition of "easy money" with little or no manual labor involved in it. What makes the selling of drugs so lucrative is the great demand for a substance that has been declared illegal by the government authorities. I'm using the word substance to define a particular type of drug such as heroin, cocaine, or marihuana. There are other drugs of course, for instance, alcohol, which incidentally, bears the stamp of approval by the United States Government, thereby setting a double standard syndrome. More so, despite its addictive qualities, and its far-reaching harmful effects, the selling and consumption of alcohol is not unlawful in this country.

The point to highlight is that accumulating money and experiencing the momentary pleasures derived from indulging in drugs, whether they are the substance variety or alcoholic beverages, are directly related to our relentless search for a quality of life that will bring us happiness. The key question to ask ourselves is, will money as the means for acquiring material objects, and artificial transitory highs experienced by the consumption of drugs bring us the happiness we humans are constantly craving for; or are both these factors superficially shallow in nature, and not the profound experience we desire in the transient scope of our lives? Yes, life on this earth is but a temporary experience, in effect, a mortality that is persistently closing in on us from all directions with the passing of time. Therefore, why not pursue a goal which is on-going, or one In which the sole purpose will be that of seeking-out the reality of what is around us. Thus, we rip-out the veneer of the falseness and artificial trappings, beliefs and needs that have been imposed on us by society, our government and the media.

The reader at this point should keep in mind that I'm still searching for a theme to develop. Nonetheless, the foregoing observations have not been idle streams of consciousness and spontaneous ramblings from the writer's mind. Rather, they have been well thought-out concepts and beliefs of what he conceives to be the real and un-real aspects of our lives in the context of our environment. This milieu may be better described as a sense of powerlessness in so far as bringing about political reforms, which can eventually wipe-out the unfairness, injustice and blatant abusive power that a government can wield on its people. A prime example is our current political situation in which we are led to believe by President George Bush that the country should go to war in order to liberate Kuwait from the Iraqs. However, in applying our reasoning powers, we can realize that the underlying motive for the war is to preserve this country's vital dependence on Kuwait's oil resources.

Why can't we be more thoughtful and more analytical with our reasoning. We should be prepared at all times to question the validity of, or mass consensus of a situation, whether political or not, in order to arrive at what we believe to be "the true nature of the beast." Applying our reasoning powers, our logic and our common sense, we can then draw our own conclusion. We should, therefore, cast doubts on all systems, organizations, or individuals claiming to have knowledge on anything that matters to us. Let us become free thinkers, who rather than accept long held beliefs or doctrines, instead, become skeptics, non-believers, until we have had sufficient time to examine all data, all aspects and all evidence. Thereafter, applying logic reasoning, we can judge and draw our own conclusions as to what is right or wrong, who is the real enemy in a particular situation; and how we can achieve end results which will ultimately benefit us and our love ones.

CHAPTER 2

Logic Reasoning

Reflecting on this theme of thoughtfulness, a question that readily comes to mind at this moment is why are there so many homeless people wandering along the streets of New York City today. Strange as it may seem nowadays, when I was a young boy growing-up in this City during the height of the great depression, and before the advent of World War 11, I cannot recall seeing homeless people; or for that matter, individuals in the streets, on subways and in front of stores begging for "loose change." Ironically, the majority of the people in those times were struggling for just the bare essentials, enough money to have food on the table, to survive and sustain themselves. Yet, we didn't have the widespread robberies, muggings, and vandalism that we're now experiencing. Why is this happening today in our supposedly modern quasi-affluent society, and not during the depression of the 30s when people had a rightful cause, and were justified in seeking some form of assistance from others?

To be quite frank about the matter, I don't have any answers to this question. Nevertheless, logic reasoning tells me a substantial amount of our tax dollars, and lets face it, we're all aware of the large amount of dollars we pay-out for taxes, should be allocated toward helping these poor homeless individuals. Instead, the government appears to have disregarded this urgent matter, and has opted to involve us in a shooting war with the Arabs of Iraq. This issue is too wide in scope, and the implications are of a magnitude so large that it's impossible at this point to attempt any type of analysis on the situation. Nonetheless, because of its political and social impact, I will surely revert back to it during the course of the writing project. What I desire to do at this juncture is reflect back, or bring into focus that period of time in the mid 1930s during which I experienced as a young boy of school age what can best be described as a horrible hardship, the aftermath of which gave me the inner strength to come to grips with myself, to cope with and deal with any situational crisis on a rational level. Thus, from this point onward, a major portion of the writing will be based on what is define in an old Spanish proverb, "recordar es volver a vivir," literally meaning, to recall is to live again. This, indeed, will be the purpose, or the writer's intent, to re-live his life by recalling memories from the past.

CHAPTER 3

The City and its public schools

In the following chapters the reader will, no doubt, recognize the writing style as autobiographical in form, though I prefer the more descriptive style composed of happenings, observations, analyses and conclusions of a New York Puerto Rican. I have chosen this description seen that I consider myself a person who, having lived the very first years of his life on the Island of Puerto Rico, nevertheless has resided most of the years thereafter in the City of New York. Granted, there were the three years in the South Pacific during the second world war, and the four years living in Patchogue, Long Island in the early 60s, however, having lived most of my life in "the Big Apple," I'm an almost lifetime New York City dweller. I say this since the expectations are to live the rest of my life in this City, the City that has everything to offer its inhabitants and the tourists.

All things considered, and by this I mean that, having visited most of the capital cities in Western Europe, Rio, Caracas and Mexico City, I still have the opinion that "The Big Apple" surpasses all others. Perhaps not in its architectural beauties, but rather, it has what can be described as tourists delights. Among many other attractions, the City has its restaurants, too numerous to mention by name, theatres, two opera houses, concert halls, more than fifteen museums, art galleries, the largest library in the country, three private universities, one of which is an ivy league college, the statue of liberty, Harlem, and a mass transit system that serves the public twenty four hours a day, seven days a week. Needless to say anymore about what this City has to offer.

The name "Big Apple" strikes an odd chord despite its familiar reference to New York City. As much as I have tried, I still can only recall "the Big Apple" as the name of a popular dance of the late 30s and early 40s, and not that of the name for the City. In that long ago era of my childhood and early manhood years, the City was known as "Little Old New York," or "the City of eight million." George Gershwin vividly described it with musical tones that transcend the life and mood of the City with its eight million souls in his popular musical composition, "Rhapsody in Blue."

The early interest as a young boy, however, was not in music, which was to develop later in life, but instead, in movies and reading that occurred around the sixth grade level. Perhaps these self-interest evolved because of the loneliness experienced in my early years during which I had no close friends. This loneliness and feelings of isolation from everything and everyone whom I had desired to relate to may have been attributed, particularly during the first years of public schools, to the failure to speak and understand the English language. Good reading skills, which for a time were non-existent, added to my overall frustrations at a period in time when I had to compete with the great achievers of the day who were "the gifted students" of the New York City's public schools, the German refugee children. Further, at a time when I needed all possible nurturing as survival skills for overcoming the barriers of not knowing the country's language, I had no guidance, no mentors, no one to depend on except for my dear non-English speaking mother, and a stepfather who was a borderline English language illiterate.

The New York City's public schools in the mid 30s were staffed with predominantly Jewish teachers. For those teachers the German refugee kids represented the eminence of high scholastic achievements in the classrooms; and rightfully so, considering these children's previous excellent academic background developed in the schools of Germany. Bitter are the memories that seem to linger on from thoughts that not once did any of these "gifted" kids come forward and volunteer to help me with problems in school work I was obviously experiencing; nor for that matter, neither did the teachers or any of the other students

In the school's classroom in which there existed a clannish environment, were three distinct groups of students. The first group consisted of the high achievers, who, more likely than not, were the German refugee children. Native born Jewish kids from middle and high income families made-up the second group; and the third group of children, most of whom came from low income families, or families receiving public assistance, were labeled as the problem learners. I was considered part of this latter group, perhaps because of my English language disabilities. What surprised me was the lack of Black children in my classroom, and also throughout the school. Yet, the school, which was officially known as Public School 165, and located at 109th street between Broadway and Amsterdam avenues in the borough of Manhattan, was no more than seven blocks away from Harlem.

The school, not unlike many of the other schools in the White neighborhoods, had indeed established a defacto system which, in reality, served to preserve the school's white image by segregating the Black children from the public schools in the White neighborhoods. Teachers, moreover, contributed to the divisiveness structure by catering to the three groups according to the students' learning abilities. This had the effect of fostering a polarization climate among the three groups of children, in particular, during the classroom sessions. That this classroom structure was the forerunner of the infamous tracking system may be arguable among administrators, principals and teachers in today's public schools.

CHAPTER 4

Reading for Pleasure

Eventually, the academic obstacles creating a barrier in the learning process, particularly in reading comprehension, both in grade school, and to a lesser degree in high school, were overcome, and as a result, I gradually developed an interest in reading. Serious interest in music, however, did not appealed to me until much later in life. By serious interest I mean the desire to play a musical instrument, which actually began after well passed my 30th birthday. Listening and dancing to music, in particular, the type played by the swing bands of the thirties and forties were an early infatuation during the teenage years. Yet, on reflecting on this period in time, I realize now the infatuation was, to some extent, superficial in nature, and not a deep inner sense of appreciation for these diversions. Rather, this was merely my way of attempting to conform with my peers. I wanted, almost desperately you might say, to possess all their attributes, the way they thought, dressed, and to have all that was of interest to them.

The reader at this point may identify this behavior, and quite rightly so, as the innocence of youth. Why is it that we are unable to acquire our wisdom when we're young, instead of waiting until the twilight years of our lives before we finally attain it? However, I may be confusing wisdom with the physical process of a child maturing into manhood. Nevertheless, the likelihood of equating the maturing process in humans with that of gaining wisdom may be highly debatable. What prompts me to say this is the fact that all humans, barring any major physical misfortunes, mature to adulthood. However, do they all acquire wisdom? What I'm saying is that, in essence, maturing may be, for the most part, a physical action, whereas wisdom is an on-going mental process that appears to develop its very last stages only toward the end of our lives. As a final note associated with this line of reasoning, and one which may tend to instill some form of curiosity, just think how easier our lives' experiences would be not having to be subjected to the needless suffering and distress in our early years. This may have been possible if we had had the wisdom that we seem to attain in gradual stages as we grow older with age.

Reading, as I have already mentioned was one of my interest. Despite the difficulty with the English language, what brought on this interest, or prompted me to get involved in it, I don't rightfully know; the fact that I had no friends, except for my dear mother may have been the cause for the interest. Unlike other activities, reading is practiced most times in solitude without the needless distractions from others around us. I can still recall the satisfaction experienced in reading my first book from cover-to-cover. Though at this moment I cannot remember the author's name, the title of the hard cover book, by the way, this was before the advent of paperbacks, was, *Don Sturdy Among the Giants*. There were others that followed, most of which dealt with the adventures of young boys and girls. The series, Bomba the Jungle Boy, and the Nancy Drew series were some of the favorites. Also, there were the *"Big Little Books,"* which were small hard cover books, about five inches squared in overall, size in which most of the stories were about "comic strip" characters who had previously appeared in newspapers; some of the popular ones were "Dick Tracy," "Terry and the Pirates" and "Little Orphan Annie." I had barely scratched the surface in my new found pleasure. Still to come were the great works of Servantes, Shakespeare, Tolstoy and Dostoyevsky, two of which still are favorites of mine, War and Peace, and The Brothers Karamazov.

CHAPTER 5

The Model Airplane, and The Movies

Movies, and in particular, building model airplanes were two of my other interests. Building these small models were delightful pass times for me; nonetheless, the hobby, which I seem to have taken an immediate liking to when a boy in my class brought a model to school, proved to be a rather difficult task, especially in the beginning because of my difficulties reading the step-by-step instructions in the schematic diagrams. Further, the task of constructing these small models was, to a certain point, frustrating primarily for reasons that neither my mother nor my stepfather were capable of helping me. My stepfather had very little skills in understanding what he read, and my mother, though highly proficient in reading and writing in Spanish, was illiterate in English. Gradually, however, I developed the essentials, the know-how, by simply doing the process by "trial and error," which in my opinion is the most effective method of learning. I call it the hands-on experience.

The cost of a small flying model kit in those times, which was at the height of the depression, and about two years prior to World War 11, was a mere ten cents. Of course, during that era ten cents was a large expenditure for my mother, especially when it involved the purchase of what she perceived to be only a toy, rather than the more practical investment of buying a quart of Grade (B) milk for the price of another cent. To digress a bit, milk was sold in two grade levels, A and B, and naturally, grade (A) milk was the more expensive one. Often I wondered what criteria the dairy companies used to determine the grade levels. What was obviously clear to the keen observer was the fact that unlike grade (B) milk, the neck of a quart bottle of grade (A) milk appeared to contain only cream. But to get back on course with my topic after the diversion, the cost factor of a small model airplane resulted in my having to wait over a year before I was able to purchase a larger twenty five cents kit. These models, particularly the larger ones with their long wing spans, ribs and skeleton bodies built from balsa wood and covered with tissue paper of various colors, were magnificent sights to behold. To give it a non-wrinkled look, the tissue paper was sprayed with what was known as "dope," but in reality, was a clear Dupont chemical liquid with the strong odor of nail polish that when dried, stretched the tissue paper, thus giving it a smooth appearance. The power that enabled the model to fly was furnished by rubber bands attached from the propeller to the rear of the fuselage, or the body of the plane. Twisting the thick rubber bands around one another by moving the propeller clockwise provided the required tension for the propeller to rotate at a very fast rate when released. My ultimate goal, and one which was never achieved during my youth, was to have enough money to buy a small model airplane gas engine, and not have to rely on rubber bands to fly my models.

Movies were not a hobby like building model airplanes, but a favorite amusement instead. Though unlikely as it may seem, movies no longer have the appeal they once did when I was a young boy growing-up in the mid 30s and early 40s; most likely since there is really no need to escape from anything. During the depression years the movies were the means of distraction from the harsh realities of poverty. A fantasy world may be a way of describing this form of escapism, which was accessible to the masses because of its extremely low cost. The majority of the movie houses in the neighborhood offered two full-length features, a serial and animated cartoons for only ten cents. On certain days, bingo games, free dinnerware for the ladies and toys raffled off to children were offered as a strategy for enticing more customers into the theatres. The fantasy world was always there to be seen on a silver screen. Viewed by an audience confined in almost total darkness, they saw facial features on the screen, in particular those of the hero and heroine who appeared almost inhuman in their un-real made-up beauty, which can only be seen in movies. It was, indeed, an un-real world in which one often saw the Black actor always playing the role of servant, maid, or what may have been worse, the lazy good for nothing Black individual who was, more often than not, projected on the screen dozing-off. Moreover, perhaps for the purpose of re-enforcing the issue of differences in man, the studio heads had created a force of evil populated, especially in westerns with men of dark complexion who rode on black horses, in sharp contrast to the hero's horse, which of course was always white. To make matters worse, and what may have instilled a sense of shame or outrage in some people's sensibilities, Native Americans were relegated to playing the roles of villainous Indians. On a speculative note, this fantasy world may have had its origins from a philosophy imposed by the Federal Government on the studio heads who had the technology and human resources to de-sensitize the masses from the miseries of extreme poverty. A propaganda act created by the government with the aid of Hollywood may be another way of perceiving it; An act whereby the objective was to soothe the people from the harsh realities of poverty by subjecting them to a fantasy world of movies created by Hollywood. In a clearer sense, perhaps, Hollywood and not the government may have been responsible for providing people with the means for escaping from the reality of their situation.

Failure to comprehend the reality in a situation is a form of neurosis according to psychologists, furthermore, the disorder can eventually attack the nervous system. Therefore, our perspective should be one of striving to unravel the fantasy so that, ultimately, the reality of a situation can reveal itself to us. We mortal beings must function on reality. There are too many variables out there attempting to disguise for us the true nature of reality in our world.

CHAPTER 6

Caguas, Puerto Rico

The opinions, observations and reactions discussed thus far, in particular, the conditions in the New York City public schools during the thirties and early forties are not what I had originally intended as topics for the actual beginning of the writing project. This may have led the reader astray. Therefore, to make amends for the oversight, what I propose to do now is attempt another new start; only this time it will be from the very beginning, highlighting among many other incidents, my early and happy childhood years in Puerto Rico with my uncle Cirilo and his family.

Puerto Rico in the early 30s was a land that had a common denominator. This is to say that its population had a common culture, which was deeply rooted with that of Spain. Naturally, the national language was, and still is, Spanish; and virtually everyone was poor. The Island, which is shaped not unlike an Idaho potato, is approximately 100 miles in length and 35 miles wide became a Colony of the United States as a result of Spain's defeat in the Spanish American War of 1898. Its feudal system, similar to the one that flourished in medieval Europe from the 9th century until about the 15th century, allowed a man, his wife and siblings to live and raise crops on someone else's land provided they shared their crops with the owner of the land.

My uncle was one of these "share croppers" who with his wife and six children, and there were six more to come during the course of the following ten years, lived on his father-in-law's land in a rural area know as Biatriz The area, or actually the farm, was about 15 miles east of Caguas which was, and still is today the third largest City on the Island. As far as I can recall, my happiest times in Puerto Rico occurred on this farm where I lived with my uncle Cirilo and his family for almost two years, at about six months after mother left for the United States. However, the earliest recollections were not those ones which happened on the farm, but instead, the ones of an earlier times living in Caguas with my mother and her sisters Maria, the oldest, and Katherine, the youngest who was in her early twenties, and whom everyone called Nene.

I have often been curious in how far back in time a person can recall, especially after having already lived seventy years of his life. In general, according to psychologist, this inherent attribute we are all blessed with, if you can call it a blessing, varies solely with individuals. Some persons seem to remember more of their past, and at an earlier time, than others. My earliest recollections were not those of which my mother had reminded me: How she had fulfilled religious vows by carrying her infant son on her shoulder from door-to-door soliciting contributions for a sacred saint who, supposedly, had cured my dysentery. Rather, what I do, in fact, remember is a house in Caguas in which I was the sole child occupant living with my mother and her sisters. I must have been no more than four or five years of age at the time.

Various noteworthy incidents occurred during this period, some more significant than others, but surprisingly, some still remembered vividly. To begin, there was the time I was in an unknown building, and almost overcome with fright on realizing that after pulling on a dangling chain from an overhead box, I had caused the strange and loud sounds of rushing water coming from a large white upright object on the floor. My only thoughts were that I had broken the strange and expensive looking thing with the large opening on top shaped like a horseshoe. The incident may serve to underscore the innocence of a very young boy, and his initial encounter with in-door plumbing. Then there was the time I recalled seeing moving pictures projected on a large screen of men wearing hats with wide brims, somewhat like my uncle Cirilo's garrison hat, and riding on horses that were seldom trotting, instead, always galloping across the countryside. Escorted by my twelve year old cousin, Freddy, the experience, though a novel one was not memorable, and the only reason for mentioning it is that this was the first and last time I was in a movie theatre in Puerto Rico.

Why is it we can recall only certain happenings occurring in our past and not others? Indeed, our recollections are never total but fragmentary memories from our past. What we appear to remember from our very young years are those events that have some emotional impact on our being. A fact to consider is this, why is it we don't have total recollections of our past?

CHAPTER 7

A brief Encounter

The answer to the last question in the previous chapter must be left unanswered, seeing that I have absolutely no idea what the correct answer can be. I do know for a fact that I do have some recollections of my past, which leads me to, yet, another happening, and one that I like to refer to as the mango tree incident. Mother and I had gone to visit her uncle Pancho Rivera whose house was on the outskirts of Caguas in the town of Gurabo. Near the house, which was on top of a small hill overlooking a highway was an enormous tall tree literally covered with mangos, which were beyond my reach. My only recourse, therefore, was to find some object with which to attempt to knock down one of the delicious looking mangos. I remembered throwing the rock, and immediately thereafter, hearing a very loud "bang." Frightened about the noise I had caused after throwing the rock at the tree, I ran back to the house. Moments later there was a knock at the front door, and I must have had some premonitions what was about to happen, so I hid under a bed. I heard the argument that ensued between my mother's uncle and another man regarding a rock that had struck, not the mango I had almost desperately hoped for, but the man's vehicle, which was traveling along the highway at the time. What the final outcome of the argument was, I don't recall, however, what I do remember is receiving a loud verbal reprimand from my mother's uncle after the man had left the house.

Not too far from uncle Pancho's house, perhaps a half mile or so, there occurred at another house what can only be described in a literal sense, as a once in a lifetime happening. Some months prior to my mother becoming mentally and physically disabled as a result of a stroke, I spoke to her about the happening. She was amazed in how I was able to remember the incident, in particular, when I was only five years old at the time of its occurrence. I have heard people say they can remember as far back as when they were two or three years old. Having the traits of a skeptic, I tend to have doubts about these people's claims. To be sure, there is absolutely nothing in my life that I can remember before the age of four. This is a fact despite my mother's vain efforts in trying to help me recall my late breast feeding habits, and taking the bottle until the age of four.

The house was the same one where my aunt Nene passed away in her early thirties of what, I was never to find out; though there were rumors that she had died from "a mind disorder." This house had a uniqueness about it which I had never before noticed. All the ones I had previously known were structures constructed from wood. This house's front surface was covered with white cement, that is, had a stucco façade. It had three levels with a balcony on the second floor facing a highway. At the rear of the house, beginning at its third level, there was a winding stairway that led directly to a yard, which faced the highway. It was in this yard that I gazed at the man quickly descending the stairs and coming directly towards me. I can still remember distinctly his reddish gray hair, red complexion and his light brown suit. Quickly he picked me up, and smiling, held me on his chest and shoulders, all the while stroking my hair, and speaking to me words that at this moment I cannot recall their meaning. The incident came to an end quickly. Lowering me to the ground, he swiftly went on his way. This was the first and last time that I *saw and shared some brief moments with my father, Fidel Solano.*

CHAPTER 8

The Benitez Family

Monserrate was my mother's name, though everyone knew her as Monsita. The year may have been 1929 or 1930 when she left for the States. Thereafter, I was placed with the Benitez family who lived in the Mountain town of Cayey. Pedro Benitez who was a cousin of my mother was someone of an oddball, a tall man with bright red hair, which was odd for a Puerto Rican, and a thick red walrus mustache that made him appear different from the other men. He lived with his wife and his three grown-up children, two of whom were "the boys" in their late twenties, and a younger daughter about nineteen years old whom they called fat Sista because of her enormous weight. She must have carried on her body all of 300 pounds. Farmers they were not; instead, the family was involved in the lucrative business of bootlegging by distilling and selling illicit rum. Their only other means of livelihood was producing cigars. What may seem natural now, and indeed it was to them at that time, they all smoked cigars, including the women. Despite the questionable environment, which certainly was not conducive to a very young child's upbringing, I have no bad memories of ever being abused in any manner, nor neglected by any of them. As a matter of fact, I quickly became the house pet of the family, most likely since I was the only child in the household. In any event, I was happy and contented in my new home, and though mother had recently left me, I don't ever remember missing her, or for that matter, being lonely.

Two events come readily to mind during the period. The first one was the initial night visit to the still which had been purposely situated on a high mound in the woods some distance from the house as a precautionary measure against law enforcement people. Visits were always made at night seeing that was the time the still was in operation, and supposedly, safe from the eyes of the law. Vivid memories still exist of what I saw that first evening in the dark woods on a mountain top in the town of Cayey. There were the huge metal drums lined-up in small rows, and connected horizontally to each other at their mid-section with copper tubing. Fires fed by charcoal roared underneath the drums. Plumes of smoke drifting slowly upward from the drums giving them the appearance of angry monsters belching their fiery smoke and fire, and ready to devour me at any moment. What also added to that first frightening experience at the still was the foul odor emanating from the process of distilling the juices from the burnt sugarcane to produce the rum.

There are times when recalling past memories a pensive sadness pervades the soul in realizing that this event happened so long ago and so far away, and that it can never again happen. Nevertheless, I consider myself a fortunate man who at a ripe old age can still recall some events and scenes from his early boyhood years. The second event during this period can be described as a method used to lull myself to sleep at night times. Next to my bed was a large window, which enabled me to view the surrounding landscape. In the far-distant darkness there was a highway that I only noticed at night time when going to bed. It was there in my bed that every night, as a way of lulling myself to sleep, I counted the headlights of the on-coming cars as they drove along the highway and passed by my widow. In those long ago years, there was very little vehicular traffic on the roads, especially at night, and as a result, the count seldom went beyond ten before I was sound asleep.

CHAPTER 9

A Digression:

Thoughts Relating to Fate

M using on past joyful events tends to re-kindle a sensory awareness of the many experiences that have passed me by. It's like traveling on a train, and viewing the landscape made-up of all the past happenings. More to the point, it's coming to grips with yourself by realizing the train has indeed picked-up speed and is rapidly and relentlessly coming to the end of the line; but what sense can one make from these occurrences, and of a more puzzling factor, could they have been ordained by fate? For a start, you begin to re-assess the purpose of your life, the purpose of your being, and the realization that, after all the many years of striving to attain your desires, you become aware that, in fact, you do have the power to make things happen with discipline, perseverance and reliance in yourself. You come to realize that, yes, you do have a sense of worth about yourself, and of equal significance, you take pride in your Spanish culture, rather than strip yourself of it because of the desires of others. Getting back to the question of the purpose of our lives, I have yet to draw any sensible conclusions about it. However, we can perhaps envision the purpose as a personalized mission in which we are the sole actors, and all else revolves around our being. This can be comparable to the wheel in which, which we represent the hub, and all the spokes are the happenings in our lives; but once the hub breaks down, as it's destined to do sooner or later, the spokes collapse causing the wheel to cease to function.

Relating this to the element of time, can this personalized

mission be one that has been pre-determined for us by fate? And at times I wonder if the blueprint for my son who has completed 12 years of his life has already been drawn, so that every moment and every happening of his future life is on fate's blueprint? On the other hand, what if curiosity should get a hold on us and we begin to speculate as to what may happen if, rather than obey our instincts and our reasoning, we instead, act-out the opposite behavior in order to release ourselves from the powers of fate, that is, if there are any such powers in fatalism.

Fatalism can be defined as a belief that all human events, or happenings are pre-determined regardless of our efforts to prevent them from happening. In other words, no matter how we try to modify our behavior, what is destined to happen will indeed happen. Thus, all events, therefore, are inevitable, and are pre-determined by fate. As non-believers, nevertheless, can we observe, examine and measure the belief in order to detect the presence or absence of fate? Can we, in fact, as non-believers prove to ourselves and to others that the powers of fate are non-existent? This proof, however, may be beyond our reach. We can, nonetheless, make observations, rationalize and draw our own conclusions. Let us say, for instance, that there is free will, and we have the option to choose what has not been pre-determined by fate. How then do we explain that this free will can be manipulated with rewards or punishments? We may, therefore, conclude that free will is subject to manipulations and is not really free. On the contrary, rational considerations can cast some doubts on what I have just said. The fact that we have human virtues leads me to believe that moral and ethical behavior acted-out by our free will, or what may be a controlling factor to ward-off the powers of fate, cannot be influenced by rewards or punishments. Whether fate exists or not has yet to be proven. As a result, we may realize that based on what was instilled in us by our parents, culture, religion and education, we can, indeed, manipulate our environment to improve our future means of existence.

A final note to consider, and one which may or may not instill or re-enforce a belief in fatalism. All forms of living matter conform to a common lifecycle, depending on the species of course. If we observe this cycle in humans, particularly during the maturation phase, we notice the behavior develops into similar patterns, as though guided by a guideline or some frame of reference which appears to have been pre-selected. The behavior naturally starts with the beginning of life. I'm referring, not to learned behavior, but rather, to instinctual behavior in which the infant without any prior learning begins to crawl, walk and finally run. Similar are the infant's speech patterns that begin initially with crying sounds, babbling, saying individual words, and ultimately with speech patterns having a grammatical structure. Can we define this as merely the process of maturation that is a common trait in all human life? And what begins the process? What, in essence, is the stimulus that arouses these actions. Is fate the correct answer to these questions. At this point I'll let the reader be the judge of this. Suffice to say, all living matter follow what may be defined as pre-ordained, or destined to happen, and we seem to have absolutely no control in the process. Hence, we can conclude that the maturation process, the physical progression to manhood in us behaves according to a pre-determined order. Therefore, fate may play an active role, at least during our growing-up period.

CHAPTER 10

Biatriz: With My Uncle Cirilo and His Family

My stay with the Benitez family in Cayey was a brief one lasting perhaps no more than a year. The happy and carefree young life, nevertheless, continued, during which I lived with my uncle Cirilo and his family in Biatriz, a farm district about Five miles from Caguas. Apparently, my uncle had known about the Benitez family's occupational background and offered to take care of me until his sister had the financial means to send for her only child.

The house where we lived was extremely small, having but one bedroom, a living room, or the parlor, and the kitchen, which was the largest one of the three rooms. Dwelling on this now, it seems odd that such a small place accommodated my uncle, his wife, their six siblings ranging in ages from six to fourteen years old and myself. The house was situated on a slope, almost a quarter of a mile from a running brook, which was our only means for obtaining fresh water. It rested on wooden piles about five feet above ground. All the wood framed houses were built in this manner, which gave the farm district a distinct appearance of a community made-up of large and small houses resting on stilts. The style was introduced in the 16th century by a Spanish Field Marshall, Don Alexandro O'Reilly to protect the houses against the flash floods, which were always the aftermath from the torrential rains during the rainy season. Another advantage from this style was the height of the houses above ground protected their occupants from the intense tropical surface heat, particularly, during the months of June, July and August.

In the corner of the kitchen was an immense rectangular shaped black table whose top appeared to be a distance not too far from the ceiling. Its height was a prevented measure against the smaller children coming too close to what rested on top of the table, and what can best be described as a primitive cooking stove. On top of it there was a set of four triangles formed with three large stones for each one of the triangles. Within the stones were the fires fueled with charcoal or wood. In effect, the stones were there to support the pots and pans above the fires. A thick layer of sand covered the entire tabletop's surface area to its outer edges, which were enclosed with a wooden border to prevent the sand from falling to the floor. Obviously, the sand had been placed there to prevent the large wooden table from catching fire.

We had a white cow, which my uncle milked in the mornings and evenings when he arrived home. Also, roaming around the large backyard were goats, pigs, chickens, roosters and guinea hens; and we had our house pet, a big and strange looking skinny brown dog that was named Tigere, (Tiger) because of the ugly black stripes all over his body.

Wonderful things happened during this period, some of which I will described with the intent of giving the reader a notion of happiness as experienced by a young boy living on a farm. Bear in mind, of course, that happiness may be an elusive event for some of us, and can have various meanings, depending on our individuality. More sharply defined, our meaning is based, or associated with the culture in which we were raised. Our beliefs, attitudes and what we consider intelligence are the results of this culture.

CHAPTER 11

Tio Cirilo

My hero, and the person I had aspirations to be like, and to have all his good attributes when I grew up, was Tio (uncle) Cirilo. I had the greatest admiration for Tio Cirilo as only a child of five or six years of age who had no father could have had for a caring relative. No matter how tired, or exhausted might be a more suitable word, he may have been after a day spent plowing the tobacco fields of his father-in-law, Tomas Vasquez, he never ignored me by showing favoritism toward his own children. Always, he had the time to greet me by rubbing my head gently and asking me about some of the things I had done that day.

His profession was that of a plowman. He had developed the professional skills required for not only guiding the plowing tool in straight rows, or furrows along the earth, but also in handling the two huge bulls that pulled the plow. There were those happy occasions when I was sent by Tiodora, his wife, to bring him his lunch so that I was quite familiar with the type of work my uncle did. Vividly, I can still remember approaching the field from a distance where I had no visual sight of him; yet, I was able to hear his loud and distinct, "Hah, hah, hah" voiced sounds he made to keep the bulls moving at a steady pace along a pre-determined path in the field being prepared to plant tobacco. There were times the animals ignored his sounds, and he had to resort to his long shiny black whip, which he snapped at the bulls, but never struck them with it. The snapping sounds from the whip were always effective in keeping the bulls moving.

Tio Cirilo, who had a gold capped front tooth, which gleamed

39

beautifully when he smile, always wore a hat, similar to the ones worn by forest rangers, and large brown boots. On arriving home evenings, he always had the gleaming black whip curled in a circle dangling from his waist. The evening ritual on arriving home never varied for him. He would remove his boots and socks and soak his tired feet in a basin of warm water before having his supper. Adding to my fondness for him, he was gifted with a unique physical feature that I have yet to see on any other person. Tio Cirilo had six fingers on his right hand; the extra finger was alongside his pinky. Often, while soaking his feet, he wiggled this finger, which was about the same size as his pinky, to emphasize a point in the story he was narrating to us. He was a marvelous storyteller of tales always about animals and the forces of nature.

He taught me many wonderful things, among them, how to milk the cow, plant tobacco and sweet potatoes. Moreover, he showed me the intricate method of digging-up a sweet potato without injuring its outer skin. What is still clearly perceived in my mind, however, is the time Tio Cirilo allowed me the privilege of assisting him to slaughter a small pig. The occasion was to be a feast of roast pork and fricasseed goat meat celebrating the baptismal of the recent arrival in the family, a baby boy named Juan, who was later to be nicknamed Tute. Today he lives in Philadelphia with his wife and two daughters. and is still known only by his nickname. The method of slaughtering the pig involved a person, and at this moment I can't recall the person's name, except that it was not a child, who held the animal's front and hind legs while Tio Cirilo droved a long knife into the pig's neck. My task was to hold a basin beneath the animal's wound to catch the precious blood, which was later flavored with spices, poured over boiled rice and then used as stuffing for sausages. The animal, despite being held by its feet, was relatively quiet, and I was prepared to catch the blood in the basin the moment it appeared. However, I had absolutely no idea what followed the aftermath from the thrust of the knife into the pig's neck. No sooner had the knife pierced the skin, I heard the loud squealing sounds from the animal. As the warm blood gushed into the basin, I knew for a fact it was warm since the sudden and violent flow caused some of it to splash on my small hands. The squealing never ceased, and seem to go on forever, during which I collected the gushing blood into the basin. I doubt I will ever forget that unpleasant experience.

CHAPTER 12

A Brief Interlude

An incident such as the one just described can become all the more significant when we reflect on ourselves in relation to a happening from the past, which influences future traits in our behavior. To this day, I cannot tolerate the sight of blood, whether mine, or the blood of another living thing. Furthermore, memories of the hideous sight of the animal squealing, which can be associated only with severe pain has been a lasting experience resulting in my evading anything that may result in physical pain. These ethics of avoiding pain have had the effect of revealing the "moral smallness" in some people. For example, I have been labeled, and in fact, by more than one person a coward, an individual unwilling to participate in any physical encounters that may tend to cause pain. Yet, I have come to terms with myself in realizing that, indeed, I am not a coward, rather, I have the self-discipline that enables me to challenge others on my own terms, terms that do not include physical violence.

A clearer focus may be in order in how I have used the phrase on my own terms. More sharply defined, what is meant is applying a strategy, which will give me the upper hand, as the saying goes, in any situation. In dealing with situations in which people are involved, in order for me to achieve any moral, spiritual or monetary rewards from these situational encounters with individuals, I deal with them on their terms and not on mine. That is, I relate to their level of thinking, their beliefs and their values. More to the point, it is conforming to a philosophy in which you don't impose your beliefs and values on others in order to attain some form of success. Instead, you put yourself in their shoes, you adopt their ways, and you join them so as to become one of them, part of their group. Once you're accepted, then, and only then, can you be in a position to dictate to them, influence them, and instill your beliefs on them. On second thought, however, this ideology may not always be the suitable strategy for avoiding pain. Nonetheless, all things considered, the way to defeat your enemy may not be effective by applying physical force, but instead, by using the powers of psychology. If the enemy is master of the house, you obey him, and humble yourself to him for the sole purpose of gaining the master's confidence, learning his methods, and of most importance, seeking out his weaknesses. Thereafter, as soon as they have been discovered, then you are ready to exploit the vulnerable aspects of the master in order to acquire the means to your needs. The catalyst for part of this idealistic point of view may have been the incident of a young boy who witnessed at close range the killing and draining of blood from a helpless animal.

CHAPTER 13

Activities

Structural activities, or those that are pre-planned by adults, of whom there were only two in the household, Tio Cirilo and Tiodora, were virtually nonexistent. In fact, they were too occupied with fieldwork and house chores, and therefore had very little leisure time in which to be with us, specifically, during the daytime. The lack of having ample time for fun activities, nonetheless, was never a problem for the children. Activities were numerous, some of which were swimming in a part of the river called the black hole because of the water's color, galloping bareback, or without the aid of saddles, on Tomas Vasquez's horses, and fishing for crawfish.

Pleasant memories of fishing with my cousins in the shallow waters of a brook will never be forgotten. Quickly turning over the rocks where they hid, and literally trapping them with the opened palms of our hands was our method of fishing for them. On these special outings, Ismael the oldest one of the boys who was about eleven years old, always carried a small piece of glass and scrap paper, which were the tools for starting the fire to roast our catch. By Ismael holding the piece of glass against the scrap paper and toward the sun's rays, the paper quickly ignited and we had the start of our fire. There, alongside the flowing crystal waters of the brook, and shielded from the heat of the afternoon sun by the lush foliage, which was everywhere to be seen, my cousins and I indulged ourselves by munching on delicious roasted crawfish.

When our appetites were not for crawfish, there was always the abundance of tropical fruits to be had in the nearby woods. On our excursions into the woods in search of fruit, we often found trees and bushes bearing bananas, guavas, mangos and oranges. Unlike bananas, guavas and oranges, which grow on small trees or bushes, mangos grow on very tall trees. As a result of this, we were successful only in gathering from the ground the over-ripe ones, which had fallen beneath the trees. Over-ripe mangos are not edible seeing that they have an extreme bitter taste, unless they are boiled in water. For this reason, we brought them home to Tiodora, and at some future time she rewarded us with delicious desserts made from this fruit.

CHAPTER 14

Corn, Apples, Oranges and the Plaza

During harvest time, dry Indian corn, after their husks had been removed, was put through a slow roasting process. This was done by hanging with thin wires the ears of corn from the kitchen ceiling to about a foot above the low charcoal flames on the black wooden stove. After the corn had been thoroughly toasted, it was converted into brown corn flour. A primitive mill, undoubtedly a replica of the ones used by the Taino Indians, who inhabited the Island before the Spaniard's arrival, accomplished the task of converting the corn into flour. Actually, the mill had the appearance of s large two-layer cake made from two curved slabs of stones about the size of automobile tires. The upper moveable layer had a large hole in the middle where the corn seeds were poured. To another much smaller hole at the side of the upper stone, or layer, a long wooden pole was inserted, and its other end was firmly attached at the ceiling to a metal swivel. Grasping the pole close to the moveable layer enabled a person to rotate the heavy upper layer over the stationary lower layer, thus grinding the seeds into floor. At breakfast time, Tiodora mixed the corn flour with milk and brown sugar and served us the delicious tasting mush, or cereal might be a better way of describing it.

Not too far from the farm was the City's plaza where one evening Tio Cirilo bought us what I had never seen or tasted before, shiny red apples which were known as manzanas in Spanish. Apples, because of their need for cool weather, especially during the months of autumn are not grown on the Island. Instead, they are imported from the mainland, usually in late autumn when the fruit is harvest in the Northeastern States. In an enchanting plaza that evening, I had my first taste of a delicious American apple.

Puerto Rico, not unlike Spain, has a plaza in every town or city, and every one of these plazas has a chapel, church or cathedral, depending on the size of the town or city. Caguas' gothic cathedral with its imposing high twin towers appeared that evening to reach-up almost to the overhead gray puffy clouds. Its, façade, which was covered with lights reflecting from the small round windows looked like rows of lights one sees during the night on a cruise ship. The cathedral faced the plaza, with its outer edges or perimeter, lined with rows of what at first glance seem to be bushes, but were actually small trees, almost identical in height and shape. Each one of the small trees was decorated with twinkling colored lights, and literally covered with small oranges about the size of plums, and because of their bright colors seem almost artificial. Vendors were everywhere selling their wares, which were mostly small toys, and at various times, chimes were heard from the cathedral's bells. In that festive air, children frolicked, laughing, running and chasing one another throughout the plaza. That evening's holiday atmosphere in the plaza, I was later to find-out, was associated with the celebration of the coming of the Three Kings, "El Dia de Los Reyes," or the Island's Christmas, which is still celebrated annually on the sixth day of January.

CHAPTER 15

The Yegua, Teams of Bulls and The Foguera

Our toys were the home-made variety, some of which were made for us by Tio Cirilo, for example, the common swing strung-up with ropes from the sturdy branches of trees, the hammock and the yegua, which means mare in Spanish; others were actually made by the children. The yegua, because of its uniqueness as a toy, or better yet, as a special type of merry-go-round, should be described for the reader. Balsa wood, which grows in abundance all over the Island, was the material my uncle used to make our yegua. In effect, the merry-go-round was a (T) shaped affair in which the stem of the (T) was a thick balsa wood log about twelve feet in length partially sunk and secured into the ground with poured cement. The outer end of the part of the log that was above ground was then rounded-off. Another thick balsa log, about twenty feet in length, and with a hole gouged into its mid-section almost half way through the log, was to form the horizontal part of the (T). Thereafter, chunks of cactus, which when squeezed of their juices can be used as a lubricant substance, were stuffed into the hole. The log was then turned over and inserted at its mid-point, where the hole had been gouged-out, into the rounded outer edge of the partially sunken stem log, thus forming the completed (T). Our yegua, or our merry-go-round, was now ready for use. With hunched backs, thighs straddling the horizontal log and our small legs dangling in mid-air, we were ready for thrills one would hardly had ever imagined from such a primitive device. The log, which was equally distributed with children on both sides from the stem log was usually pushed around the stem, or base log, by an adult who had the required stamina to rotate it at fast speeds, even though at times there were at least ten or twelve children straddling the horizontal log. This was made possible by both the thickly lubricated mid-section with ground-up cactus, and because of the balsa wood's lightness.

Then there were the toys my cousins and I made, two of which, due to their novel aspects, may be worth mentioning. In the first one, bottles were what we used to build our teams of bulls. Actually, these were toys that had to be pulled along the ground to simulate the animals' movements. The bottles represented bulls, and a team consisted of a pair of bottles of similar length, with each bottle attached by its neck with cord to one of the ends of a piece of wood about the size of a twelve inch ruler. The wood served as the yoke, to which the bottles, bulls to our imagination, were harnessed too. My cousins and I competed with one another in search of bottles for the purpose of making as many teams as possible, fastening them in tandem with strings, and then pulling our teams of bulls along the ground.

The second, which rather than a toy was a fogon that we called foguera, or hearth in English, was used for making charcoal. As a matter of fact, our foguera was a much smaller version than the one made by Tio Cirilo that yielded the vital fuel needed for cooking, charcoal. First we dug a hole in the ground about three feet deep and four feet in length, which with its dimensions appeared to look like a small grave for a child. After the hole was dug, it was partially filled with kindling wood. Small logs spread-out and placed one on top of the other were then put over the hole, thus covering it completely. Thereafter, the logs were covered with a thick layer of grass giving the foguera the appearance of a large mound of grass shaped like the hump of a giant beetle. The next step was to saturate the grass thoroughly with water. The final phase in the building project was to light the kindling wood beneath the logs, and the foguera was now ready to make us some charcoal.

My cousins and I well knew from previous experiences that by the following day part of the logs would turn into charcoal, though the reason for this happening was unknown to us. We were only emulating what my uncle had built, never realizing that the limited supply of oxygen on the fire because of the wet grass covering the wood caused the logs to burn slowly at a rate producing partially burnt wood rather than ashes. After removing the black burnt portion from the wood with a machete, we proudly brought our charcoal to Tiodora knowing she would always reward us at the moment, or at a later time with cookies, an extra portion of bread at breakfast or making us, a especially prepared dessert solely for her small charcoal producers. Knowing for a fact that our endeavors would always be recognized, my cousins and I never loss the incentive for building fogueras.

CHAPTER 16

Recognition and Rewards

Recognition and rewards are what most likely instills the incentive in most of us. Awareness of this fact, mainly when dealing with people, should be part of our moral vision. To underscore the point, I once submitted a lengthy case study report to the Government Agency where I was employed thirty eight years before retiring. The report dealt with a detailed outline in how to achieve better and quicker results when training new employees. Weeks went by, and only after alerting my supervisor about the report did I get a response from "upper management" that "they would look into it." The result from the prolonged waiting period had the ill-effects of discouraging me from ever again submitting any of my ideas to the Agency.

At the risk of repeating myself, recognition in the form of some rewards, monetary or otherwise, is what tends to be the motivating force that moves us into action. Pavlov's dog can be the appropriate analogy to apply in comparing this dynamic human attribute, which is inherent in all of us with that of animals. Ivan Pavlov, who was a Russian physiologist, trained a dog to activate a lever that caused a bell to ring. Soon after the bell had been rung, the animal was given food. As the Russian doctor, in all probability, had suspected, after a few trial runs with the procedure, the dog learned to associate the sound of the bell with food. He then responded by pushing the bell anytime he came near it, knowing of course that his efforts would be rewarded with food. Indeed, by the same token, we will activate ourselves in some positive manner when we know our efforts will be recognized and rewarded. Only by being aware of this fact and acting on it accordingly, can leaders, managers and supervisors obtain more efforts, more work, and more ideas from their employees, or people, in general, who may benefit the State, City or the firm.

Recognition and rewards are two words, which in the most glaring sense, have meanings that can be associated with one another. The same may be said for Christmas and toys, particularly in the minds of children; though for most of us in this commercialism era, we may see it as money expenditures for the outlay of gifts, not only for our children and family members, but also for the people who provide us with services in our everyday lives. These people can be, among others, the caretaker of our building, the doorman, or the mailman who delivers our mail. Perhaps the business of rewarding people rather than only children with gifts has gotten out of control to the point where we give for the sake of giving, simply since it's the customary thing to do on this festive holiday. Too much giving, however, may be harmful in some respects. For example, the novelty of receiving can, in fact, wear off to the point were people can become jaded with the rituals of receiving gifts, specifically during the Christmas holidays. Nevertheless, like Pavlov's dog, we should be cognizant of the human factor, and that is, people will not go out of their way to push any levers, which in the context of these thoughts have the meaning of extra effort or extra work, unless they are rewarded with some form of recognition.

CHAPTER 17

Three Kings Day

Christmas in Puerto Rico was not celebrated with the arrival of Santa Claus on December 25th with bundles filled with toys for the children; At least, not in a particular year in the early 30s when I was under the care of my uncle who lived with his wife and siblings on a small farm. Instead, Christmas was celebrated on January 6th and known as, "El Dia De Los Reyes," or the day of the kings. Supposedly, in the minds of children, it was considered a special day when three kings traveling on camels from distant lands arrived on the Island bearing gifts for all the children. In effect, it was a traditional custom that originated in Spain, which symbolized the bringing of gifts to the new born Christ Child by three wise men.

Stockings were not hung-up by a fireplace in hopes of a Santa Claus filling them with toys. Shoe boxes were what we used rather than stockings hoping the three kings would fill them with toys. With the help of Tio Cirilo who took us to the Plaza where the shoe merchants were, we collected from them the used empty shoe boxes needed on the eve of the special day's arrival. Following Tio Cirilo's and Tiodora's instructions, the night before "El dia De Los Reyes," we put some grass in each of the boxes before placing them under our beds as a token of appreciation for the camels that, most likely, may have been hungry after their long journey.

The likelihood of waking up finding shoeboxes full of toys we had been advised was unrealistic thinking, and somewhat of a fantasy. Thoughtfully, my uncle had prepared us for the prospects of finding only one toy in each of the boxes because of the "Kings' lack of resources in those difficult times." However, the fantasy materialized about a week after "El Dia De Los Reyes when the family received a huge postal parcel from the States, which was a large cardboard box almost overflowing with what we children least expected; toys of every imaginable size and shape had been sent to us by my dear mother. My toy, in particular, merits mentioning, if only because of its bright colors, which I can still visualize at this moment. It was a large four wheels milk wagon painted white and hitched to six beautiful small woodened black horses. The wagon's shape was not unlike the horse driven carriages used today by the Amish people in Pennsylvania. Inside the wagon were small crates filled with tiny sized milk bottles made out of glass. Many were the carefree times I spent pulling my treasured toy wagon with the small six black horses around the house's yard making believe I was delivering milk.

CHAPTER 18

Developing The Calluses

The "difficult times" my uncle was alluding to were the depression years. Those years become all the more important now when I realize they may have served as the essential foundation, or learning experience, for fortifying myself against any adverse experiences, for example, the bad times that are sure to occur sooner or later in life. To emphasize the point, you develop a protective shield that enables you to deal with bad or unpleasant things in any situation so that at the end of the unpleasant encounter you emerge unscathed; Still strong of mind and body, you are aware and prepare for the next bad incident to happen.

Arguably, hardships, in whatever form they may appear, can be seen as a process of developing the calluses one needs to cope with them, to run barefooted on life's occasional rocky terrain. This may be pushing the metaphor a bit too far, nonetheless, the point to underscore is that, all things considered, the hardships we experience can give us the underpinnings, the inner strength needed to deal with most obstacles, most barriers, and in some ways, go on to achieve whatever goals we have set our minds on. Indeed, coping with any situation may well be one of the ways of attaining some success in our lives.

Continuing with this line of thinking, we can raise specific serious questions, for instance, why the mental breakdown in some people, their suicidal tendencies, their drug abuse, or their alcohol indulgences? Why do you suppose a prize fighter trains before a boxing bout, a baseball or football player practices before a game, and a musician rehearses before the performance? This training or rehearsal process may be seen as the essential "fundamental nature" we must endure before we succeed; and on another significant level, if we should fail in any manner whatsoever, we have been conditioned not to succumb to any mental or physical breakdown. It is this training process that perhaps the self-destructive people, the alcoholics or the drug addicts are lacking, and as a result, do not have the ability nor the inner strength to persevere, to struggles with all the barriers that sooner or later they will come upon along the path of their lives.

Critical reflections such as these readily come to mind when one focuses on the hardships people endured during the great depression of the 30s. The almost desperate need to have sufficient money to purchase the basic commodities of life, food, clothing and shelter was their only concern. In essence, very few people had a surplus amount of money in those days. I cannot ever remember seeing or handling paper currency as a young boy living on a farm in Puerto Rico. However, what may seem somewhat of a surprise to the reader, I do recall handling coins, lots of coins as a matter of fact.

CHAPTER 19

Tobacco, The Money Maker

The coins were the results of wages earned by working in the tobacco fields owned by my uncle's brother-in-law. Child labor was performed, not as one may have surmised, by planting or picking the valuable crop, but by removing worms from the tobacco plants. These small animal creatures about the length of an adult's index finger, with ugly little claws on both sides of their bodies, and as though protected by a nature's disguise, had a shade of green on their bodies, which blended almost perfectly with that of the plants. If they were not removed, these worms by piercing through the leaves eventually left large perforated areas on them as proof of their voracious appetite for the plants. At auction houses where it was sold to the highest bidders, the quality of the tobacco was judged by the size of the leaves and the amount of perforation on them.

My cousins and I along with hordes of other kids, after removing the worms from the plants' leaves stored them in glass jars, cans or whatever means were available in order to prevent the small animal creatures from escaping. In the evening we took the proof of our labor to Mr. Tomas Vasquez's house where he actually counted the contents in each jar, can or container before giving each one of us one cent for every worm we had brought him. In those times the pennies were considered generous wages, especially when a penny for a young boy had an enormous amount of purchasing power. As an example, for a mere one cent I was able to buy a box of gum drops, or four caramels, or what was most likely to add to the joys of consuming sweets, any kind of candy bar.

Never mind that the candy store, grocery store and virtually everything else within the confines of his lands were owned by Mr. Vasquez, so that the pennies ultimately returned to him, the fact was that tobacco was what made it possible for me to have access to all those delightful sweets.

Two of the crops on the Island during the early 30s, which could be compared with what cotton was to the Southern States before the Civil War were tobacco and sugar cane. Not unlike the Southern States and cotton, the Island's economy was depended primarily on tobacco and sugar cane. Tobacco, unlike sugar cane, can be grown in abundance on a few acres of land. As a result of this fact, farmers, or sharecroppers, were able to grow enormous amounts of the crop, which was later sold for high profits due to the great demand for cigars, pipe tobacco, and especially for cigarettes.

My uncle's brother-in-law, Tomas Vasquez, owned large tracts of land, which he had inherited from his Spanish ancestors. The lands were deliberately divided into small farms primarily for the purpose of growing tobacco. Residing on these lands were the tenant farmers, one of whom was my uncle Cirilo who planted, cultivated and harvest the crop on the land he had previously plowed. Tenant farmers thus exchanged their labors for the privilege of living with their families, growing food crops, and grazing their small livestock on the owner's land.

At harvest time, the tobacco leaves, after being picked from the plants were individually stacked in piles to about five feet in height and a yard in length. Thereafter, one or more of the piles were bundled in burlap cloths, and young men, after heaving the enormously large bales on their heads, carried the precious cargo about two miles down a steep hill to where the warehouse was located. As a strategy for getting the tobacco rapidly to the warehouse to be prepared, or "cure," for marketing, the men were given bonuses after the harvest based on the amount of pounds of leaves they had carried to the warehouse. What may have been another underlying incentive that I can only assume was personal in nature, was the competition among the young men to see who among them was able to carry the largest loads. Most obviously, it may have been their manner of demonstrating their physical prowess and virility as macho men, not to the other men as might have been expected, but to the women who often gazed at them from the porches of their houses when the men were performing their labors. Tobacco, in effect, was the catalyst that made it possible, at least during harvest time for men, women and even children to earn money.

Getting the tobacco ready for marketing involved a process, which by today's standards may seem somewhat primitive; moreover, I doubt it whether the procedure I'm about to describe was ever practiced in this country. Basically, the procedure involved drying the leaves thoroughly until they had turned to a dark brown. The method applied was similar to hanging wet clothes on a line to dry, only instead of clothing, you had tobacco leaves hung on a line. The process, furthermore, was done indoors in the warehouse rather than outdoors. Why not outdoors where the tropical sun could rapidly dry the leaves is still a mystery to me? The reason for this, most likely, may have been that, not only did the tobacco had to be dried of all its moisture content, but also had to be aged for a certain length of time before it was ready to be sold.

What made the process somewhat outdated compared to today's practices, was the method used in the drying and aging cycles, which lasted many weeks. Women sitting on the ground, and usually in circles, the warehouse had no floor, used long needles about a foot long with thick cords to thread each leave through its upper stem. After about 100 feet in length, the cord with its dangling green leaves resembling a long green necklace was strung between two of the numerous poles, which formed a grid throughout the entire warehouse from the ceiling to about two feet above the ground. The women who were exposed to an environment in which they breathed tobacco fumes all day from the leaves that had already been hung and partially dried, was not considered a hazard to their health. The though of developing respiratory health problems, heart disease, or worse yet, lung cancer, was beyond the comprehension of the people. In those times, smoking tobacco, except for the children naturally, was considered everyone's form of pleasure.

CHAPTER 20

The Underlying Forces of Money

The American Tobacco Company, however, did, in fact, know about the ill-effect of their product on humans. In the February 8, 1992 issue of the New York Times appeared an article citing a Federal District judge's statement regarding "publicly quoted secret tobacco industry memorandums." Based on the "memorandums," the judge concluded that the tobacco industry's chief research department had acted for forty years as a "front and a shield" for protecting itself against "harmful congressional hearings, lawsuits or scientific research about the health risks of smoking." Further, the judge cited the tobacco industry as "perhaps the king of concealment and disinformation."

What conclusions can we draw from those findings that, indeed, the tobacco industry had knowingly deceived the public into believing that smoking is pleasurable and a harmless experience? Where have the work ethics gone to? Where has the integrity of those individuals associated with this company gone? It is needless to ask ourselves what the motivating force for these outrageous deception is; nor for that matter, why doesn't the Government put a stop to the abusive powers of the tobacco and liquor industries by simply outlawing the manufacture of these products, which ultimately, with their prolonged usage, will most surely have an adverse affect on people's health.

Money and the desire to acquire it in large sums can corrupt some of us, or perhaps I should have said most of us. A prime example of this malady is the people associated with the American Tobacco Company. Indeed, we seem to be locked into a political and social system that requires the relentless quest for the things that will get us the amenities some of us, or most of us, associate with success. Money is the commodity that will make it possible for us to have access to bigger housing accommodations in the better neighborhoods, good health care, and for our children, the best private schools that money can buy. If we were to combine these parts, and others such as clothing, jewelry and automobiles into a whole, we can say that the whole is the motivating factor for the world wide corruption of political and industrial figure heads, their subordinates, merchant, and in general, some people in the main stream. Namely, these are the masses of people who toil for a living by selling their valuable time and energy to others for wages.

We may now ask ourselves, what about the person who lacks the ethics of greed for acquiring wealth? At this point, I'm referring to the individual who, in a literal sense, has no prize tag. What is meant is the one who refuses to deviate from his beliefs, his ethical values and his overall sense of integrity, no matter what monetary pay-offs are offered to him. Can this possibly be characterized as abnormal behavior in the person who has removed himself from social reality in forsaking the well-being of his family and himself by abandoning the will to gather more riches? To believe this may not be a sound judgment to make, in particular, when we think of those who have the conviction that the means to a better life may not necessarily entail the acquisition of wealth. For instance, there may be other factors involved such as spiritual or religious beliefs influencing the person's behavior. The point to highlight is that there can never be an abnormal behavior in the person who, rather than conform to what society has deemed the true reality of success, instead, elects to function within the bounds of his beliefs, his values and his ethical standards.

Summarizing this discussion, I should add that these have been reactions by an observer and his attempts to make some logical sense in what he perceives to be unethical practices conducted by people; or to reiterate the point, the unethical practices conducted by people who are an integral part of a political system or an industrial organization, and supposedly have a reputable background. Yet, their moral values were corrupted, maybe by what they viewed as the need to protect the source from which their income was derived. Specifically, I'm referring to those employees involved in the American Tobacco Company's research department who for forty years deceived the public into believing that there were no harmful effects from the results of smoking tobacco.

CHAPTER 21

Nature's Forces

Again I have digressed from the main focus of the narrative, nevertheless, the reader has been already alerted that the digressions, principally about philosophical thoughts, will occur from time-to-time during the course of the writing. Now to return to the early 1930s on the Island of Puerto Rico, and the recollections of a fierce hurricane witnessed in the middle of the night from the vantage point of an underground shelter by a very young boy who had absolutely no idea of what was happening at the time. Not unlike that young boy of long ago on a far-away island, some of us may not know what, in fact, is happening that causes the wind to blow. Therefore, a brief introduction to one of the elements, which causes changes in wind flow may not be a bad idea; and it's not another digression, I may add, bearing in mind that winds are very much related to hurricanes.

The wind can be described in various ways. For example, a sea breeze blowing gently on the glowing faces of people strolling along the seashore. Then there are the lyrical stanzas of Christina Rossetti, "When the leaves hang trembling the wind is passing through," or "when the trees bow down their heads the wind is passing by." Seen in this light, the wind may suggests an invigorating or melancholy sense in our feelings. On the contrary, the wind can be described as a ferocious being that, in the process of devastating the land and all that it holds, shows mercy to no living thing.

Viewed in its true perspective, however, wind is simply air in motion. Causes for the movement, whether it's a gentle breeze or the violent winds in a hurricane, are variations in atmospheric temperatures. Air has pressure, and temperature changes acting on this pressure will cause the wind to flow. The higher the temperature changes aloft, and not at the surface, the greater will be the wind's velocity.

The most frightening aspect of a hurricane, at least from a six year old boy's experience, was the sound of the wind resulting from what he didn't know at the time, its high velocity. Winds blowing at about 120 miles an hour with their eerie sounds seem to the boy as though an army of invisible ghosts was marching by howling in the night. The sound produced when one blows over the open mouth of a gallon jug, and multiplying the sound hundreds of times can best describe what I heard the night of the hurricane huddled together with my cousins in la Barraca.

Unlike its Spanish meaning, hut or cabin, the barraca was similar to an underground wooden pillbox, cylindrical in shape with various openings below its roof, which was just above ground level to enable a person a view of the terrain. From one of these openings I saw the terrifying sights of flying objects of all shapes, some of which were small trees that had been literally uprooted from the ground, and corrugated metal sheets used as roof material for the houses flying through the air like missiles heading toward their target. Tall trees once standing upright as though reaching for the heavens above were now seen in the shape of large upside down letter Us relentlessly shaking their limbs like frightening creatures shielding themselves from the forces of the winds and the torrential rains.

Reflecting at this very moment on those early childhood experiences, I'm reminded that, except for the hurricane, and to a lesser degree the sight of the liquor still on the mountains of Cayey, never can I recall experiencing any other fears, or any form of child abuse. Those early years in Puerto Rico most likely instilled in me the inner strength needed for the coming years that were to follow in the City of New York.

PART 11
The City

CHAPTER 22

The Arrival

They said the ship was almost as big as Tomas Vasquez's tobacco warehouse. Thinking about the little sail boat toys my cousins and I made from pieces of flat boards, shaping their front ends like arrow heads and attaching paper sails to the sticks that we used for the masts, I thought it impossible. How was it possible for such a large ship to float in the ocean without sinking? The ship was indeed extremely large, in fact, as big as the cruise ships of today, and accommodating hundreds of people, one of whom was a friend of uncle Cirilo, and my sole guardian during the five day voyage.

As far as I can recall, the voyage was uneventful, and in some ways utterly boring, except for the delicious food served on board the ship. Many of the food dishes seem exotic, to the extent that not only did I enjoy their flavors, but also their colors, in particular, one strange looking vegetable with its vivid orange color. Never before had I seen carrots, perhaps because the Island's soil was unsuitable for their growth. Mashed potatoes was another one of the strange looking food dishes that, however foreign in appearance, nevertheless had a delicious flavor, especially when topped with beef gravy. Potatoes, though small in size do grow in Puerto Rico, however, the custom in those times was to boil and serve them, either saturated in olive oil or mixed with beans in a sauce. They were also diced and fried in lard but never mashed. Sliced bread was also a novel sight, and particularly in the way it was used in preparing sandwiches. The Island's bread, "pan de agua," literally meaning bread with water, and similar in taste and appearance to

French bread, was never sliced, at least in those days. This explains why I never saw slice bread nor had a sandwich until on board that ship bound for the City of New York.

 The initial depressive feeling on arriving was the result of the weather. It was late in November, which was why the closer the ship got to its destination the more I seem to feel the cold weather. On docking at a pier on the Hudson River, I was wearing only a light suit jacket, which uncle Cirilo had purchased expressly for my voyage. The first impression of mother, after not having seen her for over two years, though for me it had seen like an eternity, was that of a person who appeared to be a very tall woman wearing eye glasses. Perched on her head was a round black hat with a distinct feather on top of it. She smelled good with the fragrances of perfume, and wore a seal fur coat, which she later told me had been purchased second hand from one of the numerous pawnshops scattered throughout the City. Hugging and kissing me furiously and crying at the same time with intense feelings, she appeared to be almost out of control with her emotions. At that very moment I became aware in how much my mother loved me. Many years were to past before I realized her love and extreme devotion toward me were the results that I was her first begotten son, and one who was born out of wedlock.

 Mother and I and an unidentified man, the drive of the car, rode toward my uncle Domingo's apartment at 114 street and Morningside Avenue in Manhattan. Viewing the swiftly passing scenery as the car headed north, gradually a melancholy feeling and a sense of mournful sadness came over me because of what I was seeing at the time. The Hudson River's banks were covered with mounds of ugly grayish coal ashes, and trees appeared lifeless with their bare limbs bearing no signs of leaves. There was no grass to be seen anywhere, and the land, which was Riverside Park, looked as though it had been scorched by some unknown evil thing. A cold wind was blowing, and far above there seem to be no end to the dull gray sky. During that ride I had a longing desire to return quickly to where I had come from, to a land where the glowing sun was a daily occurrence, and the earth, with all its plants and trees, was always covered in green.

The ashes along the riverbanks, which had been dumped there by sanitation trucks, were the leftovers from rock coal used to heat some of the City's buildings during the months of winter. Oil was still many years away from making its appearance as the primary fuel for heating. In contrast to this, coldwater flats were generally heated with wood burned on huge black cast iron stoves, which were usually located in the kitchens of these coldwater flats. Rock coal, though providing better heat than wood and with less smoke, was too expensive and too difficult to ignite for the tenants. Not too many years later, I earned spending money by gathering wood from wherever it was to be found, chopping it into small pieces with an ax borrowed from the janitor of the building, storing the wood into bushel baskets procured from produce stores, and selling it for ten cents a bushel to the tenants residing in these apartments. Fortunately for me, as the car sped uptown, I was bound for a steam heated apartment, and not to one of the cold water flats.

CHAPTER 23

Uncle Domingo

A young woman and her two young children, a boy and a girl about the ages of five and four greeted me on my arrival. Her name was Felicita and she was my uncle Domingo's wife. The children's names were Eddy and Dolly whose given name was Catherine, and whom uncle Domingo had named in memory of his sister, Tia Nene, but everyone called his young daughter by her nick name, Dolly. Another young woman having the name Caraciola, and a second cousin of my mother, also lived in the relatively small two-bedroom apartment. The three of us, Mother, Caraciola and I shared one of the bedrooms. About the only relevant aspect I can recall about Caraciola is that I seldom saw her, however, when I did see her, I always noticed her large white teeth, not realizing as a young boy that she had dentures. She kept an 8X10 glossy black and white photo of a young smiling man with black hair and thin mustache. The photo was in a frame, which had been beautifully gilded in gold and kept on a night table next to her bed. The man was the movie star, Clark Cable who was a popular actor at the time, especially with the ladies.

A small two-bedroom apartment is not the ideal setting for accommodating four adults and three children. My joining the family didn't take me long to realize I was somewhat of a disruptive force, particularly to Felicita. In fairness to her, who can condemn the woman for having to tolerate another person, especially another child in an already crowded apartment; she obviously resented my presence in her household. Never did she showed any affection to her husband's nephew. I remember Felicita as the lady who denied me the privilege of playing with her children's toys, in particular, the boy's new tricycle with its bright red colors and shiny chromed handled bars. Always claiming I was too big for it, she never did allow me to ride her son's beautiful tricycle.

Many years later, briefly stopping by her house in Las Vegas where she lived with her second husband, I purposely reminded the now elderly woman of those incidents, and the fact that she had ignored me completely, having time only for her children. The poor woman, on hearing of her behavior toward me as a young boy, broke-down into sobs claiming she had been unaware of her actions, and further, how I could have remembered all those happenings, especially when they had occurred so long ago; but children do remember their past, in particular, unpleasant incidents, and to some extent, able to reason and understand what, in fact, is happening to them.

Psychologists have pointed out that children by the age of six have acquired the ability to reason and make some sense from situations they may find themselves in. This may explain why, at an early age, I had already developed some capacity in detecting ill-considerate and selfish flaws in others. Aside from mother, however, the other flawless person in that household was uncle Domingo, my mother's youngest brother. He was the youngest one among the eight siblings, yet passed away from consumption when only 32 years old.

Remembering him as a handsome man somewhat small of statue and rather thin, with lively bright green eyes and light brown hair, and a man who always parted it in the middle as was the style then, and sleeked back with pomade; At all times, he was a natty dresser who wore double breasted pin stripe suits and shoes with sharply pointed front ends and Cuban heels. Night work as a short-order cook prevented him from being home in the evenings. Hence, he was a late morning riser who on all occasions came out of the bathroom after having taken his shower wearing an elegant burgundy silk bathroom with a pattern of bright yellow flowers, which appeared to have been drawn by hand. Whistling was his method for calling his wife. Whenever he was in another room and desired something from her, he simply whistled with the type of sound heard when someone hails a cab in the City. She obviously adored him, and would rush immediately into the room like a dog responding to her master's commands. Dancing was his only diversion, and on Saturday nights he went to one of the various dance halls in El Barrio, or what is known today as Spanish Harlem.

It was my good fortune that, because of my uncle's night work schedule, I spent many happy afternoon hours with him and his two children in Morningside Park. On those enjoyable outings, he often coerced his children, whose mother's selfish attributes may have rubbed off on them, into sharing their toys with me. As an illustration, many were the times he made his young son remove his roller skates so that I would have the chance to try them; and though I didn't know how to skate, uncle Domingo always had the patience to help me by holding one of my hands until I was able to, more or less, maintain my balance on them. What's more, I can recall my uncle finding a football, and with no one appearing to claim it, gave the ball to me rather than to his son, perhaps realizing that his boy already had an ample amount of toys.

Uncle Domingo, as far as I can remember never scolded or yelled at me in any manner. Rather, everyday on first seeing me, he never failed to greet me with affectionate words, and all the while tousling my hair while he spoke to me. He was an amiable man, and violence and abusive nature were not a part of his character traits. With his pleasing ways, he was caring and unselfish with all those who were fortunate enough to know him during his very brief life on earth. If there is an afterlife and an All Mighty Being, and I'm still ambivalent about this matter, my uncle Domingo does merit someone to look after him. May his soul rest in peace wherever he may be.

CHAPTER 24

Philosophical Thoughts About Life

Doubts about the existence of an afterlife, which have just been mentioned briefly raises some serious questions about man's final end, and his purpose in life before this end. Can the end possibly be death as we know it where all forms of life ceases to exist? Or is there the likelihood that we possess some type of spiritual life after death? Profound questions such as these tend to remove some of us from a social reality, and instead, places us in a mystic frame of mind.

Man's mortal fibers can be said to be made up of a mystic nature that personifies his persistent striving to attain knowledge of mysteries that in some aspects may be beyond his understanding. With this intent he tends to apply the tools of reasoning and rationalizing for dealing with the problematic question of whether there is, in effect, the existence of an afterlife. He explores, weights the evidence and draws conclusions based on his logic and his rationalized considerations. And unless he is a man who has been instilled with religious beliefs of an All Mighty who has created him, and who will ultimately cast him to either a life in heaven or hell, depending on the nature of his moral conduct on earth, man may conclude that all life on earth may be an everlasting recycling process having no beginning nor an end. More precisely, he notices the fact that every living thing has a beginning and does indeed have an end; nonetheless, with the end comes a new beginning. A point to underscore is that the new beginning always conforms to the likeness of the old, or what has ceased to exist, depending on the species of course. This is what is known as common inherited characteristics; it's like a glass of water continually being replenished. The new water can be darker, sweeter or saltier, still, the basic substance of what constitutes the water remains.

All things considered, we can, therefore, conclude that all living matter is in a state of constant and unchanging recycling phase. The species dies and a new species is born having common inherited characteristics, or similar genetic features. Moreover, the species will only breed with members of its group having the same subdivisions. As a result of this fact, we can make the determination that we are born to die, and we die in order to be born again. Thus, this determination may instill in us the concept of reincarnation, or the rebirth of our soul, or what dictionary defines as, "the immortal part in man." To pursue these thoughts a bit further, I have chosen to define this "part in man" as our human entity within our bodies, or in a clearer vain perhaps, the makeup of how we think, reason and reflect on past happenings and future occurrences. And it is this "part" in us that also expires when we die.

At this point, the reader may have the urge to question my judgment, or what has led me to draw this conclusion. A while back I spoke about logic reasoning, analyzing, and how all of us have these inherent abilities, unless we have mental disorders, naturally. We can observe, study, analyze a situation, and then draw some conclusions about it; in other words, the procedure can be associated with our inner powers of logic reasoning. Keeping this line of thinking in perspective, if we were to apply these powers so as to channel our thoughts solely on the question of reincarnation, how many of us can reflect on our lives prior to our birth. In fact, as hard as I have tried, I don't remember any of my life's happenings before the age of four. Further, I suspect not too many of us can recall anything in our lives before the ages of three or four.

The fact is that life for us prior to those years had no meaning, furthermore, we had no recollections, and our ability to remember had yet to develop during the infant phase of our growth process. As a result, our sense of analyzing and reasoning should alert us that, because we do not remember any past life, or life as we know it, before the ages of three or four, there may never be a reincarnation, or the "rebirth of the soul in a new body." Therefore, we should accept the notion that life is an on-going cycle having a beginning, an end and a new beginning, which starts the process all over again. We die to be replaced by other human species having our images in this constant cycle of life. However, with death our bodies fade away into nothing but ashes, and our soul, or what I have defined as our ability to reason, analyze and love ceases to exist once our lives end.

CHAPTER 25

Values and Principles of Behavior

Death is the end of our life's cycle; yet, the other profound question still needs to be answered. What is the purpose of the life cycle for us on this earth? What is the real true meaning of our being? What sense can we make of ourselves in relation to our environment? Do we, in fact, have a personalized mission to accomplish on earth before our lives expire? Questions such as these can best be answered in a somewhat broad perspective, and certainly within the boundaries of this writer's values. Focusing on the last statement, it is learned behavior that applies according to how I view the world, or in a more specific expression, how I deal with all that impacts on my being. More so, these values do indeed have their origin in what has been instilled in me by my parents, family members, the environment, and to some extent, by the knowledge acquired in schools.

First and foremost we must expand our moral vision, in other words, develop a positive sense of worth about ourselves, a sense of harmony with all that surrounds us and develop leadership qualities. This leadership concept refers to the power, tenacity and resiliency with commitments we have to make with ourselves. Our values should conform to those of being honest and having moral principles; and of most significance, we must realize that we have the power and the potential ability within us to make things happen in order to improve ourselves, and to help others who may be in need.

We must take pride in our culture, our background and our family "roots," whatever they may be. In Spanish this is known as orgullos, which means the pride we have in the inherent talents we possess as individuals. We therefore must never strip ourselves of our culture because someone or others desire it. Instead, we must learn to adjust to the foreign culture we're in and mold it to our life style. More emphatically stated, we must come to terms with the system within that culture, and act accordingly so that the system may work for us. We can, furthermore, ask ourselves are our values aligned with those of whom we come in contact with, with the environment and with the organization that employs us? Also, we should take pride in our work ethics, in performing the task, in doing what is expected from us to the best of our abilities, and not necessarily in quantity, but above all else, in quality. To repeat, we have to align our values with those who make up the majority. In effect, our dimensions of behavior should be guided by the fact that we are still a minority group residing in the other man's land. Indeed, we have to recognize and respect his culture, his values and his methods of doing things. The scope of this behavior should underscore a sense of ourselves in relation to what we desire to achieve. We must have the essential self-discipline to commit ourselves to objectives and goals, which will ultimately improve our standard of living. Traveling on this road with all its obstacles and barriers toward our goal, we must never discredit in any form or manner the system, or its people who have built the road we're on. Rather, our primary objective should be that of getting accepted into their social system. Once we get accepted, the obstacle and barriers may disappear, not totally perhaps, but in a way that will ease the traveling conditions for us.

These principles of behavior, which we should apply when in the other man's house, were expressed initially by the Argentine revolutionist, Che Guevara. Despite their implicit analogy with slavery, they can be applied as a frame of reference for us. Guevara said, when in "the master's house," we should humble ourselves totally, and obey all commands, whatever they may be, and we should never fail to listen and observe so that, eventually, we may learn "the master's" methods and how he or she became "master" of the house. In applying this philosophy, though we may never achieve total success in all our objectives, we can, nevertheless, learn the parts that make-up "the master." And ultimately, we can fuse these parts into a whole, which will serve us as a base or guidelines for attaining some success.

To summarize, our primary purpose in life as Puerto Ricans, or as other minorities, should be to build-up our image and establish our credibility; not only as superior workers having self-discipline, but also, as individuals having honorable, generous and responsible behavior toward others. We must never forget that they are observing us constantly, and evaluating and comparing us with others. We therefore must come to grips with ourselves, that is, not unlike actors on a stage, we must perform for them relentlessly by always putting our best foot forward. I can almost guarantee the following: Our skin can be the color of limes, our physical stature no more than four feet tall, and our language too difficult for them to learn, yet, if we know what they know, and are good with all our endeavors, they will finally honor us with the recognition we have earnestly labored to earn.

CHAPTER 26

Remembered Sights

Time relentlessly marches on and waits for no one; indeed, one grows older and perhaps wiser with time. More so, in old age one tends to view life not as goals to achieve, but instead, as a process in which one searches for the meaning and purpose of life. Meanings and purposes, however, have no room in a young boy's mind. Rather, it's the hedonistic principles that are the driving forces during his youth. For many, I may add, these principles never seem to leave them, but to some degree, become an obsession in which they are always seeking all the pleasures that life has to offer them.

In many ways life for a six year old boy, during which he lived with his mother, her second cousin, and her youngest brother, with his wife and their two siblings, was filled with pleasures. There were virtually no unhappy periods to speak of, or what a psychiatrist might label emotional disturbances, except for those experienced in school. Pleasures were keenly felt primarily from the fact that almost all I saw and heard was new to me. Those novel sights and sounds instilled both excitement and pleasures, and at times, a bit of a fear in not understanding what people were saying when they spoke in English.

Glimpses at the odd shape of a football, the huge statue of General George Washington shaking hands with Lafayette, and the hideous 6th Avenue El, with its terrifying sounds as the trains rumbled by, had their way of generating both excitement and fear. The El, in particular, and the trains, which traveled south along 8th Avenue where they made a sharp right turn at 110th Street for about two blocks before continuing south on Columbus Avenue, had the never to be forgotten unique way of intimidating me. With tall black steel girders rising upward from street level to about the heights of a twenty stories building, their purpose was to support what appeared to be a long black bridge having no beginning nor an end. The El epitomized man's penchant, in general, for creating ugliness. The ugliness, moreover, was re-enforced with the horrible loud rumbling and screeching sounds, which accompanied the trains as their wheels rolled along the tracks. And to further add to its unsightly appearance, the ugly structure was covered with grime, soot and dirt that cascaded to the ground below whenever the trains went by.

Many other novel sights held my attention, some for only moments, but others had a lasting effect. Vividly I can still recall my excitement and pleasure on seeing for the first time snow falling to the ground, and wondering sadly why it didn't remain on the ground; instead, the snow quickly melted, never realizing at the time that the ground was not cold enough for it to stick, thus causing the snow to change to water. And still I can remember smelling and eating some of the snow flakes before they fell to the ground in hopes of discovering some hidden aroma, or pleasant tastes in them. Further, there was the initial excitement in seeing tall buildings for the first time. In that long ago era they were known as skyscrapers, and not as what they're known today, high rise buildings. Notably, however, what made a lasting impression, perhaps because of its immense size, was St John's Cathedral, which perched on a high mound overlooking Manhattan park and 114th Street. The cathedral's vast dome had been covered with thin metal sheets made from copper, which with the gradual effects from the weather, had turned to a vivid light green, almost turquoise in color that one could be see miles away from the cathedral. Along the domes' perimeter statues of tall angels stood at attention blowing large long stemmed horns. As a very young impressionable boy, I could almost hear the sounds of those horns reaching out to me.

CHAPTER 27

Remembered Incidents

Memories at times tend to generate puzzling questions. Attempting to analyze them, I find myself questioning the fact that, yes, I do remember the past, the long term memory that's inherent in all of us. Nevertheless, I cannot recall all past happenings, but only certain ones, which are still deeply imbedded in me, though they may not have had any significance at the time of their occurrence. The newspaper incident is a good example of this human attribute in us. Why is it that I have recollections of Felicita giving me two cents, and a note with the words, "The Daily News" written on it? I'm sure there must have been other incidents far more important than that one, yet I have forgotten many of them. That I was able to read the words written on the note, but fearful of pronouncing them to the candy store proprietor, may have had some bearing on my ability to still recall that particular incident.

There were others, of course, some of which I can remember as though they may have happened yesterday. One of those had all the earmarks of a child in need of food, or more to the point, a child suffering from the pangs of hunger. Sunday's ritual was the visit to my uncle's in-laws who by today's standards would be classify as an affluent family of the 30s. Buloy, the head of the household, had a thriving business, which was a bodega, or a Spanish grocery store. They resided in a building having an elevator, and the family had a lived-in-maid and cook whom everyone called "Madrina," or godmother in Spanish.

During those Sunday afternoon meals I noticed my cousins, though younger and physically smaller than I, always received larger portions of food than I did from Madrina who was never discreet about her behavior. What may seem somewhat of a surprise to the reader, was the fact that her inability to exercise sound judgment toward a child was detected by a young boy.

Another incident, also involving food, that had a significant impact on my moral behavior in later years, occurred in Buloy's bodega. It was there that I was caught, "red handed" as the saying goes, stealing an item, which neither my mother or I had paid for. Walking out of the bodega with my mother alongside me, and the luscious ripe banana hidden underneath my shirt, I heard Buloy's harsh words, "where are you going with this," as he grabbed the banana from under my shirt. A profound embarrassment came over me at that moment in realizing, not so much what I had done, but that my mother had been a witness to my act. Speculating on the cause for the behavior, I can only conclude that the purpose at that particular moment may not have been to steal, but in all probability, to satisfy a young boy's longing for a piece of fruit, and who was very much aware that his mother may not have had the money to pay for it. Call it a learning experience, if you will, but never again have I been tempted to take what does not belong to me, nor what I have not paid for.

A young boy can be removed, or better yet, unaware of the social realities in his environment. However, there are situational aspects, which act to produce glaring differences between the boy and his peers. In school, for instance, a noticeable fact were the boys in the classroom, most of whom were Jewish and German refugee kids from middle income homes on West End Avenue and Riverside Drive who always wore long tweed pants and brown shoes. In contrast to this, the few other boys from what was commonly known as the other side of the tracks, or the area east of Broadway, and I was very much a part of these few, wore knickers made from a cheap grade of cotton, and sneakers rather than shoes. Unlike the expensive types worn today, sneakers were the cheapest form of footwear in those times. A pair of sneakers could be purchased for about sixty nine cents. Those boys who were known in the poor neighborhood of Amsterdam and Columbus Avenues as "the rich kids," also wore the popular winter attire, black or brown leather jackets lined with sheepskin wool. I didn't have a jacket or a winter coat that first winter of my arrival. However, my dear mother had bought for me a thick black woolen sweater, which protected me very nicely from those first bitter cold winter months.

How long did mother and I live with uncle Domingo and his family I can't rightfully say I remembered, what I do recall, nonetheless, is that our Sunday outings to my uncle's in-laws gradually came to an end. Thereafter, on weekends we began to visit people whom I had never seen before. They were young people, about my mother's age, and their apartment was seldom lacking in conversation, laughter, or couples dancing to the sounds heard from the recordings of Spanish music. Their sincere appreciation of my presence, perhaps because I was the only child among their social gatherings, made those weekend visits memorable ones. What added to the pleasure were the abundant amounts of delicious food dishes that were served, in particular, rice, red beans mixed with ground beef, plantains and avocado salads. Not until I was a grown man did my mother confide in me that the sole purpose for those weekend visits was "to get some food in our stomachs" without having to depend on her sister in law "to feed us."

CHAPTER 28

Family Values

The true hardships of a child living with a single parent may not be fully realized until the child finds himself in new surroundings; surroundings in which a step-father has absolutely no parental love for him. All of it began when my mother and I relocated to a furnished room. In the apartment, there happened to be another furnished room, which was occupied by my future step-father and his eight years old son, Gerry.

Why the move from a familiar family environment to a strange furnished room setting, I was never to find our at the time. To me, it was quite obvious that Felicita and my mother did not get along well with one another, and that may have been one of the reasons. Another could have been the over-crowded condition in the apartment. From the onset, I was against moving from a family structure that, in general, was a nurturing factor for the development of family values. Notably, I did not want to leave my uncle Domingo, a caring husband and father who had a sincere love for his young nephew. He was the complete opposite of my future step-father whose only perception of me in years to come was what he conceived to be the disturbing fact that I was the off-spring resulting from another man's relation with his wife.

Recently, the Vice President of the country, Dan Quayle, in a speech, which bordered on political overtones, responded to the recent lawlessness that occurred in the predominantly Black population areas of Los Angeles. The intent here is neither to glorify nor to criticize what the Vice President said. Instead, it may serve to highlight some of the issues he cited, which, among others, was the issue dealing with family values. Specifically, Mr. Quayle stated that the primary role of the Government is to maintain law and order, and to protect the property of its citizens. With underlying words he inferred that the duty of the Government is not to instill moral values on the people. Rather, this is the biological family's responsibility. I tend to agree with Mr. Quayle. Our Government's responsibility is to guard against any disorder that may arise, and which can have harmful ramifications on the citizens. Moral values and family values are implanted in the home. What's more, as we grow older, our religious beliefs may have some bearing on these values. As a final note, what should be emphasized is that moral values should be instilled in the home within the family structure.

A child growing up, not in the true biological sense of what constitutes a family structure, but rather, with a devoted mother, a tyrannical step-father, and his son having the tendencies of a kleptomaniac, made not always conform to the values of those "significant others." For instance, many times I have asked myself why I didn't grow-up to be a tyrant emulating my step=father's cruel, domineering and insensitive behavior toward my mother, to me, and to some extent, toward his own son.

CHAPTER 29

The "Fair Lady"

Some values may have developed from closely observing and analyzing my mother's struggles in deciding whether to liberate herself from an oppressive situation, and once again become a single parent. Either she had to confront the many economical hardships as a result of the great depression of the 30s and early 40s, or remain with a man whom she knew would provide some security for her and for her only son. Mother, more or less, came to grips with herself by opting to remain with the man I literally despised. Gradually, this feeling grew from the awareness of the man's firm determination to destroy my mother's self-reliance and self-esteem. Outwardly, the destructive influence he had on her manifested itself almost imperceptibly. Inwardly, however, she appeared to gain strength in realizing his true nature, that of an emotionally weak man; an insecure individual whose sole occupation was molding her as his personal object. As to be expected, the results were to affect the relationship in a negative manner, but more important from my point of view, it destroyed my mother's self-esteem, and her ability to have confidence in herself.

We humans, not unlike plant-life, must be nurtured in order to develop physically and intellectually. Thus, if some individual stumps our growth in some manner, for example, psychologically, our mental framework is weakened. This can be related to "the Pygmalion effect" whereby a man is able to develop a reality from his expectations. Professor Higgins accomplished the effect by altering Eliza Doolittle,s cockney speech and mannerisms in order to pass her off as a princess in Bernard Shaw's play, "Pygmalion."

The very popular Broadway show "My Fair Lady," which was later made into a movie is based on this play.

Unfortunately for mother, "the Pygmalion effect" was instilled in her in reverse order. Still, my mother was, indeed, a "Fair Lady." Her uniqueness was her height. Much taller than the average Puerto Rican woman, she was almost six feet tall. Neither fat nor thin, and by today's standards, she may have been seen as a handsome woman; a woman endowed with striking features, the long black hair, fair of skin and a well proportioned body. The purpose here is not to dwell on her physical attributes, but merely to give some thoughts about the rationale, or what was most likely the cause for my step-father's destructive jealous behavior toward my mother. And rightfully so, I may add, it destroyed not only her self-esteem, but also the self-esteem of a man who saw in all other men, and women as well, a threat to what he considered a human property totally his own. This may sound somewhat harsh, but he appeared to be a primitive thinker having the mentality of a caveman. Indeed, he lost his self-esteem, but of more significance, he lost the esteem others may have had for him.

CHAPTER 30

A Judgment on Self-esteem and Values

In what may be perceived as a moral guidance, or more realistically speaking, some fatherly advice, my attempt now will be to discuss in a more detailed manner the meaning of self-esteem as it applies to you, my son. To further, clarify it, as it may relate to you in the future, and how you conduct yourself with all the many others whom you will come into some personal contact with. What we value, or regard highly in our lives can be one of the ways to define the meaning of self-esteem. Moreover, what we think, consider or have respect for in the attributes of others may be seen as having favorable opinions, high regards, or esteem for others, for example, our approval, or the affections we have for others; In a similar manner, esteem can be defined as the respect and high opinions others have for us; by contrast, self-esteem is the favorable opinions we have in ourselves. At this point the key question that comes to mind is, how do we gain this self-esteem? Or more problematic, once having gain it, how do we know our self-esteem contains all the right ingredients for us? Furthermore, how do we know our self-esteem conforms to that of the norm? In your lifetime my son, this may be judged as the values of your peers. However, as you grow older and wiser with age, gaining wisdom every moment of your life's journey toward its final end, you may become aware that your values may not always conform to the values of others. More disturbing perhaps, the values you march to may not be in step with the ones society or the State deems right or wrong, or good or evil. In a more familiar tone, you may be marching to the wrong beat of the drum.

Our self-esteem and the esteem others have for us are aspects in the form of values that have been instilled in us by our parents, religious beliefs, education, and our environment. These may be said to be factors influencing the formation of our values. In considering whether our values are the right ones or the wrong ones, the question that remains to be answered is, what, in fact, are the right values? Let us suppose we have the wrong values. Yet, we may, nevertheless, still have our self-esteem, and the esteem of others who may also have those wrong values. Again, at the risk of repeating the question, how are we to know whether our values are the right or wrong ones? What may or may not be the correct answer to the question will be dealt with shortly. Suffice to say for now my son that it does require a vast amount of work effort made-up of discipline, perseverance, and self-motivation in order for us to acquire the esteem of others. Further, our self-esteem can be realized by knowing how hard we have worked to achieve our goals.

The supreme goal in our lives can be defined with one word, survival. In essence, we must strive to survive whole, that is, without any injuries, which may harm us, or worse yet, disable us so that we can have the essential mental and physical freedom to enjoy life; to be sure, our freedom can be correlated with our values. Having the wrong values can jeopardize our freedom. Here, I'm speaking about those ones that go against the grain. Specifically, I am referring to the values that in some way or manner violate the laws or mores of society. Consequently, by having and acting-out those values, we are indeed risking our freedom. How can we possibly enjoy life confined in a prison, incarcerated for months, years, or worse yet, for life?

By contrast, conforming to what society, and the State recognize as the right values will preserve our freedom. What this means is that in an overt manner we apply the adage, "when in Rome do as the Romans do." In a covert way, however, we can exercise our own values in whatever manner we choose to. These are the ones deeply imbedded in our mind, and in our inner soul where no but ourselves can have access to them. We are, in fact, masters of them, cherishing and nurturing them along our lives' journey. A few words of cautions are in order here my son. It is imperative that we exercise them purely in our mind, in our inner thoughts, and not act them out outwardly, which can result in doing harm to ourselves, or to others.

Reverting back to how we can define self-esteem, and expressed in simpler terms, self-esteem is that something we earn with hard work. we are not born with it, nor does someone gives it to us. More emphatically, it only becomes a reality, a part of our being, when we realize all we have accomplished with our discipline, perseverance, motivation, but most of all, in how we have sacrifice our most valuable possession, time, for the sole purpose of achieving our goals. The improvement of the self can be one way of describing it. When we improve ourselves, in whatever mode we choose to, we gain the respect and the esteem of others. But of more importance, we acquire the self-esteem within ourselves; in effect, we internalize it.

Finally, to draw some conclusions on the answer to the question, what constitutes the right or wrong values, can be a baffling matter. A way of attempting an answer may be seen in the eyes of the beholder, or more clearly stated, the answer can be based on a value judgment, the individual's perception and his frame of reference. Actually we commit ourselves to a way of life as we grow older; to be sure, our basic values are instilled in us by our parents, religion school and the environment. At some time during the growing process, moreover, we can become aware that our values have the potential for hurting us, as well as others. Conceptualizing this awareness, we should realize this; but to repeat what I have already said, as a way of re-enforcing it my son, to act-out values considered wrong by society and the State is one of the ways of getting hurt, or hurting others. We, therefore, have to be cautious in how to deal with our values, which may not conform to the values of others. They should be exercised solely within the intimacy of our mind. Less we forget, we are held accountable for our conduct and our actions. Let this be our guiding light my son, our frame of reference.

CHAPTER 31

A Bit of Poetry, and Real and Unreal Happiness

As far as I can remember, residing in a furnished room for a brief period, perhaps six months at the most, was uneventful. However, I cannot say the same for mother. The obvious happening was a courtship in progress. The man who was to become my stepfather was courting her. During this time an event that warrants some mentioning was the rapid improvement in English, especially in my speaking skills. Communicating almost constantly, or I should say, trying to with a boy who knew absolutely no Spanish was probably the reason for the improvement.

These improved skills in the English language, as might have been expected, have developed fully to the point where they have become a part of my outspoken attributes. Today I'm very much aware that communicating is basically our means of releasing our thoughts, ideas, or commands to others; in terms of learning, both speech and writing are essential tools. Writing, similar to speech, gives us the ability to communicate, but unlike spoken words, it can be documented so that at a later date we can refer to it as a source of reference. Written words indeed can inculcate us with our inner feelings that may not always have the same effect as when words are spoken. Poetry may be a good example of what I have just said. Poetry can instill in us new inspirations, new insights and new inner feelings within ourselves. It can provide us with various ways of assessing the character complexities, or personalities of others. Furthermore, poetry can teach us about our limits with words, and how these limits may be altered or expanded to meet our needs in a particular situation or setting. Language, whether written or spoken, is a means for communicating, and poetry is part of this language. Poetic language can be associated like a spiritual dimension, beauty, or an imagination we enter into, and which can conceivably create within us thoughtful beings about our lives and our environment. We should have the patience, in particular, during our moments of solitude to reflect, or unfold and dig-out what we believe to be the true meanings of the metaphors and similes in poetry and apply them in our daily lives. A good example, to add some emphasis to my point, is the poet, Robert Frost, who has given us meanings about life and our mortality with the lines, "I have many roads to travel, many promises to keep, before I fall asleep," in his poem, "Stopping by Woods on A Snowy Evening." Before this permanent sleep comes to us, however, we must continue traveling on life's "roads," searching for purposes, for the realities of life, rather, than its many fantasies.

A man's conception of reality is the realization of his mortality. And the ever-constant awareness, especially as he grows older, that time is rapidly coming to an end. On this journey, he, along with all of us, should make attempts to screen-out what appear to be the unreal aspects in his life from what he conceives to be "the real thing." At this point he may raise the valid question, but for what purpose, and what can be wrong living in a somewhat fantasy world where, in the pursuit of happiness reality becomes meaningless. More to the point, isn't seeking happiness the true purpose of one's life?

A philosophy such as this one can appeal to the senses, and does have its merits. Why not seek-out this happiness in whatever manner possible in order to satisfy our longing for it? Doesn't this way of thinking lend itself to what may be for the majority of us the real goal in our lives, in other words achieving happiness by applying whatever means are available to us? To experience happiness is one of the true objectives in life. However, doesn't this reality appear to be a never-ending search for this form of reality? What prompts me to say this is the fact that having attained happiness, we, nevertheless, rest on our laurels in what we have accomplished. Rather, we begin the search all over again in our relentless quest for more happiness. The truth of the matter is that we're never satisfied. What's more, what some of us may not realize is that happiness can be a past experience, or an experience that has already taken place. What this means is that we reflect on this happiness instead of experiencing it at the time of its happening. This can easily be put to a test. Ask yourself this question, "when was the last time I experienced happiness?" At some time in the past is your most likely answer. You're aware that, in fact, you did experience happiness in the past. Contrary to this, can you truthfully say at this very moment you are experiencing happiness? These examples may seem overly simple, nonetheless, they can inculcate in us the conviction that happiness is transitory in nature, and difficult to grasp unless we have already experienced it at some time period in the past.

In the attempts to get a sense of ourselves in dealing with the broad issue of reality, or separating the real from the unreal in our lives, and the awareness of our happiness within the concept of this reality raises serious questions. As an illustration, it can be stated as factual that what may be considered reality for one individual may be unreal, or imaginary for another one. Moreover, what can be a feeling of happiness for one person may be a state of unhappiness for another. Ideally, what should be done at this point before proceeding further, is to define reality and happiness within the context of this discussion. In a broad sense this can be dealt with by citing specific situations as examples. What may be obvious, however, is that these situations will not apply to the person whose failure to distinguish between the real and unreal world is cause by a character disorder, in other words, the person who is out of touch with reality.

CHAPTER 32

Some Types of Reality

One of the realities in our world today is the wide gap that exists between those at the top level of the social/economic order, most of whom remain at this level generations after generations, and those whom I have chosen to label the lower order people; the people who are hopelessly trapped in an order, which is strictly structured by money. G. Golbreth refers to these unfortunate people as, "The Bewildered Herd," in, The Culture of Contentment. Nowadays, the popular term "disenfranchised" is applied to define them. To continue, having wealth in the form of an excess amount of money, a large stock portfolio and a wide range of real estate holdings almost automatically qualifies the individual for membership to the top level order. In effect, part of reality can be said to be these lower order people who are caught-up in an economic gap for failure, not that it's their fault, to acquire a reasonable amount of wealth during their lifetime. Arguably, this gap, in general, also applies to their children.

The reader may now challenge the writer, and rightfully so, I should say, by asking what, in fact, has led me to make this assumption? In answer to the question, less we forget, the discussion is still dealing with reality. Indeed, one type of reality is that the top level people for many generations have been able to maintain and generate new wealth, which evolves into a reality that provides them with the money resources, or purchasing power, as it is know nowadays, to buy quality services at any price; education, for example, is one of the quality services. The wealthy people's children attend the best of the private schools, thus ultimately become professionals, for instance, doctors, lawyers, or men armed with business degrees from reputable Universities. Hence, with their professional credentials these grown-up children are able to acquire the surplus money, or liquid funds, as it is known, that enables them to invest in stocks, bonds or real estate, which will eventually yield more money for them. This on-going process is what has maintained and generated new wealth for the top level people.

By contrast, the lower order people, because of their lack of surplus money, have no options other than to accept low quality services. Specifically, these can be found in the caliber of inferior education doled out in the public schools, poor housing conditions in slum areas, and poor health services in ghetto hospitals. As a result, do children from the lower order people get admitted to colleges with good academic track records, for example, the Ivy League Schools? The answer, of course, is an emphatic no! Academically the majority of these children have not been sufficiently nourished with education in the public schools, and therefore, lack the academic ability to be accepted in Universities where they can acquire a profession; in all likelihood, the wide gap that exists between the top level people and those at the lower level will continue to exists. The lower people, or those who are stuck at the bottom rung of the economic ladder will continue their struggle, most likely to no avail, in order to gain a foothold on the ladder, so as to put them on the same sound footing as the top level people.

Another reality, and one far different than the one just discussed, can be seen by using our powers of observation. These are the inherent powers that give us the ability to observe, in particular, patterns of behavior in nature as well as in humans. With the setting and rising sun, for example, we see the nights and days appear and disappear from our view within a twenty four period. Have we ever had a day that failed to become night? In fact, never is the pattern broken. What I mean by this is the pattern of observing nights and days has always occurred in the past, and most surely will continue to do so in the future. Somewhat similar, observing human behavior will not reveal the cause of the behavior, nevertheless, it can alert us to reality, for instance, the real re-current character traits in a person. To summarize, by observing re-current patterns, we can, indeed, find other forms of reality.

We tend to believe what we see. However, according to one of the early Greek philosophers, he contradicts the concept of seeing is believing. According to Parmenides, what appears to us may not be the real thing. He divided everything into appearance and reality, and claimed that appearance is how we see things, and reality is how they really are. The implication based on his philosophical thoughts is that appearances can be deceiving. This may lead us into realizing that reality and happiness can be correlated. For example, what may be happiness for one person may be unhappiness for another. By the same token, what may appear to be the real thing for one person my not appear to be so for another. Not unlike beauty, we can therefore conclude that reality is in the eyes of the beholder.

CHAPTER 33

Toys, Games, Holiday Rituals, and The Movies

The years come and go, so that eventually old age takes a hold on us, and consequently, some of us may become keenly aware that our mortality, like the receding tide, is persistently drawing us away from life and toward our final resting place, wherever that might be. And with this awareness, there seems to be a need to reflect on ourselves, what we have accomplished, what we have experienced, and perhaps of more significance, how we perceive our world, or our philosophical perspectives from a layman's point of view. Philosophy, unlike experiences, can be dealt with thought processes, or better yet, putting our thoughts on paper. Past experiences, however, have to be remembered before the recollections can be put on paper.

Remembering past happenings can be difficult at times, but there are always those vivid memories that tend to linger on for perhaps a lifetime. Nonetheless, in recalling our accomplishments, we should classify them as inner secrets for others to discover, but never for us to divulge them. Disclosing them is like putting a spotlight on ourselves as a way of telling people how good we are; there is really no need for this, for sooner or later they will, indeed, see what we have accomplished. When recalling the past, most likely, we will screen-out meaningless ones, and instead, focus on those that have some significance for us. This last statement should, more or less, reveal what I propose to do at this point. In addition to observations, reactions, opinions, and other philosophical views on matters that may or may not be of some interest to the reader, the intent at this time will be to inform in a narrative manner. The work will be presented in such a way in which I'm hoping will not be boring, but rather, both informative and interesting. Now, having strayed far too long from the main purpose of the writing project, what follow are the events that occurred during that brief growing-up period.

Relocating to another furnished room at 114th street and 8th Avenue, which was only two blocks north from the previous one, was not exactly a change of scenery. There were the same old tenement buildings, most of which were cold water "railroad flats" not unlike the railroad cars, one room leading directly to the next one, and heating them during the cold winter months was the tenants responsibility. Coal, or wood burned in huge black cast iron stoves, which were usually located in the kitchen provided the heat for the rooms. Augmenting the area's depressive appearance was the 6th Avenue El, which like a long black dragon made its presence felt about every twenty minutes with its horrific rumbling sounds alongside our building. The ugly black dragon of a thing had the evil nature of spewing soot and grime all along its route, which, as to be expected, was not a welcome sight for the areas' residents.

It was at 114th Street where I gradually began to socialize with boys my own age, all of whom were from Irish and Italian households. Black kids were seldom seen in the area. Our block, and the one bordering north of it, 115th Street, were within the boundaries of the "White neighborhood." Harlem began at 116th Street and continued northward to about 145th Street. One of my biggest fears was the thought of having to attend a public school in Harlem, which was only a mere two blocks from our building. My fears were justified seen that on occasions the Black kids invaded our block for the sole purpose of taking from us whatever was of some value to them. For the most part, these were our stickball bats, which were actually old broom handles, our toy wooden pistols made from square pieces of wood that formed the outer edges of orange crates, or our beloved skate scooters.

The wooden toy pistols were our weapons for playing war. Usually, the battleground was the statue of General George

Washington shaking hands with Lafayette at 114th Street and Manhattan Avenue. The game battles were fought with some of us on top of the statue shooting small cut-out squares from old linoleum at our playmates on the ground. Thick rubber bands attached to the pistols provided the sling-shot effect enabling us to shoot the small squares short distances, but with great velocity. From the ground our playmates having the same wooden weapons shot back at us on the statue.

Unlike the wooden pistols, which were relatively simple to make, building a skate scooter was a much more involved task. To begin, finding an old skate was a primary factor in the construction process, and not always an easy one. Of course, if you were fortunate enough to own a pair of skates, using one of them got you started on the project. One skate, at least in those times, actually was made-up of two halves, which were attached with a couple of screws. This allowed for lengthening, shortening, or detaching the two components. Each one of the halves was nailed at both ends of the running board, which was usually a 2X4 about three or four feet in length. Then the front half's mechanism had to be adjusted to allow for the rod on which the wheels revolved (the axle) to slant to one side or the other, thus enabling you to steer the scooter. The adjustment was made by pulling out the steel pin with a pair of pliers, and removing the two rubber bushings encased in what looked like a miniature crankcase located at the rod's mid-point. The pin was then reinserted, and without the rubber bushings, the rod, or axle, tilted to whatever side pressure was applied on it. Thereafter, a wooden crate, the type normally used in markets for storing oranges or pears prior to their delivery to retail stores, was nailed on one of its vertical sides to the front end of the running board, and with the open end of the crate facing you, the rider. Applying pressure to either side of the crate's top allowed you to steer the scooter. As a final touch so as to embellish its appearance, lots of bottle caps of various colors were nailed onto the front, and both sides of the crate. And there you have what may be a fairly accurate description of a skate scooter, and the labor involved in building one.

Ironically, despite their popularity, especially with the poor children residing on Amsterdam and Columbus Avenues, scooters were not sold anywhere, and not even large department stores, for instance, Macy's or Gimbels had them in stock. Possibly, this may have been the reason for their popularity. The self-pride in knowing that you, with your own hands had built the skate scooter reenforced the joys of riding it. You, together with other kids, who at times numbered as many as ten, not unlike the motorcycles brigades that are seen today, rode our home made skate scooters, which with their loud noises caused by many roller skates wheels, added to the thrills of riding them all around our neighborhood. Indeed, in order to be the proud owner of a skate scooter, you had to build one.

We had our toys, and then there were the games, and the special holidays. Marbles played on top of manhole covers, kick the can, ringolevio, and everyone's favorite, stickball, were some of some of the popular games. Hitting your opponent's marble out of the manhole cover with yours entitled you to his marble. Kick the can and ringolevio, the etymology of the word, nor its correct spelling of which I still cannot find, were simply running versions of the game hide-and-seek. Election day, Halloween and Thanksgiving were the special holidays involving, to some extent, particular rituals and customs. The rites on election day were always held in the evenings, during which the custom was to build a large barn fire in the middle of one's block, and just "hang-out" around the flickering bright yellow flames. Adding to our pleasures were the cool brisk autumn winds, which seem to enliven the fire periodically by fanning it. On Halloween, and unlike today, also on Thanksgiving, we did what today is commonly known as "trick-or-treat," only in those times it was called begging. We went begging, not in costumes or painted faces as is the custom today, but simply in our everyday clothes, and not to apartments but to the neighborhood grocery stores and Chinese hand laundries where we were sure of getting delicious lichee nuts from "the chinamen." Macy's Thanksgiving Day Parade, which actually began at 110th street and Columbus Avenue, was another holiday treat for us.

And of course, there were the turkeys and bags of food donated to all the poor families in the neighborhood by the seemingly good Samaritan, Jimmy Hines, head of the Democratic Club, who in years to come would be convicted, and sentenced to a long prison term for running an illegal number's game throughout the City.

The top treat above all others, however, were the all day sessions on Saturdays, which began at eleven o'clock in the mornings, and lasted until about five or six in the evening at the neighborhood movie theater. With a dime, which was always concealed in one of my sneakers as a precautionary measure against the Black kids stealing it from me on the way to the movie house, I saw many wonderful things on a silver screen, and if "lady luck" was with me, also win a toy. It seems almost incredible as I reflect on it this very moment, that a mere ten cents enabled me to see two full-length features, which were known as "a double feature," a serial chapter, numerous animated cartoons, and as a special attraction, toys were given away, by raffling them off to the lucky kids who had winning numbers.

This was my golden age period lasting perhaps one or two years at the most, in which my mother and I were always together; she was indeed my sole keeper. Those were, in fact, the care-free times of a young boy who despite the almost desperate poverty situation of the mid 30s had a mother who loved him dearly. This period gradually came to its unexpected sad end. He always arrived on weekends, and from the very beginning I knew his purpose for coming was only to be with my mother and with no one else. And what seems somewhat strange to me now is how a young boy, despite the man never showing any ill-feelings toward him, can have insights from the early beginning of his mother's courtship about the nature of the beast, the man's true feelings regarding the young boy. I had the intense impression this man did not like me.

CHAPTER 34

The intrusion of Society, and Tradition

They were married, however, much to my surprise, not in a church as I had expected, but in a civil ceremony performed by a clerk at City Hall. What is it that instills in a child a sense of impending disorder in a new setting in which he has no options, other than to live with a man and his son, both of whom were practically strangers to him? One hundred twelve Street at the corner of 8th Avenue was the new setting, or the apartment where every so often the El rumbled by our windows like a black monster in relentless pursuit of its prey. It seem that no matter where mother and I lived, the El was always there as a disruptive force with a will of its own, which no one was able to control. The notion never occurred to me that the lowest rentals were the tenement buildings located close enough to the El where you not only experienced its horrific rumbling noises and vibrations, but also were subjected to the dirt and grime left behind its trail.

Those were the times, particularly in school, when I began to notice differences in the clothing children wore. The majority of the children lived on West End Avenue and on Riverside Drive, and as I have already mentioned, this area was better known as the rich kids' neighborhood. Kids from low income or no income families on home relief, a harsh label, which since then has been replaced with the less offensive one, public assistance, were the minority group. This group resided in the dilapidated tenement buildings East of Broadway. Self-pride was the reason for not wanting the teachers or students to know I was poor, had no father and lived on 8th Avenue. And naturally, I had a pressing need to be like the rich kids, to dress as they did, with their laundered white shirts, tweed trousers, and what had the most appeal for me, to wear brown shoes, rather than my black sneakers. Brown shoes were in vogue, "the in-thing" at the time, and no one but the old folks wore black shoes.

The fact that I was at the threshold of adolescence may have added fuel to the fire, which was the need to be like the majority of my classmates. To conform to them in all aspects, in the manner they dressed, behaved and spoke were my great expectations. Grand delusions were what I was suffering from a belief, contrary to reality, that by dressing acting and speaking as they did, I would succeed in becoming a member of their group. The sensory awareness that this desire was never to be attained had failed to penetrate my senses. This failure occurred despite an incident that, more or less, alerted me to the fact that both the teachers and the students knew of my poor circumstances. Nonetheless, before dealing with the incident, the issue of conforming should be discussed briefly, for perhaps no other reasons, except the somewhat puzzling far-reaching appeal it appears to have for the masses. The discussion, most likely, will act as a catalyst for revealing my concern and attitude about this matter.

For a start, it does appear to this observer that society and tradition mandate their will on us. This can be perceived as a form of tyranny that they, society and tradition, and all those others who conform with the mores, and thereafter, attempt to impose them on us. The final outcome can be defined as people, masses of them, emulating other's conduct by what has been deemed the righteous mode of behavior in a society. These forces can act like a wedge intruding on our being so as to influence and eventually modify our ways of thinking. As a result, the way some, or perhaps the majority relate and act in a particular situation appears to be based on what society or tradition has dictated, or better yet, has conditioned them to do

We should, indeed, cast judgment according to our individual perception. Our human nature should be the guiding light and not society or tradition. It is notable to realize that what is considered traditionally right for the majority may not be suitable for some of us. Human nature is not a model that has been purposely conceived to conform and adhere to the will of others. This, most likely, may be the motivating factor of all those who have the political power to impose on us what they consider to be correct for society. In essence, what their purpose may be is to create a society that can be molded to meet the needs of the political system.

We can, if we dwell on it a bit, correlate human nature with that of a tree. A tree develops on all sides according to its natural inner force. Humans as well have this same force, yet, in many ways fail to grasp it. To expand on this, a significant part of human nature, which is inherent in all of us is made-up in our capacity to discern the underlying circumstances in any situation. Indeed, we have the ability to observe from our own vantage point beyond the façade, which can tend to purposely deceive us in some manner. Emphatically stated in clearer words, the fact is we do have the ability to look beyond the surface of things. Nevertheless, on some occasions we merely look at the surface, the outer cover, and seldom have the patience to take the time and effort to discover what is, in fact, beneath the surface. Rather than accepting traditional beliefs, or experiencing the fears of not conforming, we must, instead, apply our own judgment in drawing conclusions, and not the judgment of others. Fear as defined by Friedrich Nietzsche is composed of shame. Not physical harm mind you, but the shame of suspecting what others think about us may be the dynamic forces that drive us like sheep, to follow the herd.

Arguably, the concept of equating fear and shame as a motivating force in our behavioral make-up may or may not be true. What needs to be underscored, however, is that we should apply our human faculties to judge, and not be tyrannized, or influence by the thoughts and ideas of others, or by what is currently the fashion. In Edith Wharton's novel, The Age of Innocence, one of the characters makes the comment, "Fashion is a serious consideration among people who have nothing more serious to consider." A point well taken, in particular, when we are tempted to take into account what is and what is not in fashion.

CHAPTER 35

The City in The Early 1930's

To digress from the main topic does not disrupt the text's continuity, rather, it may add novelty and a change of pace. Notably, it can add a bit of suspense or excitement for the reader who, in all probability may have become bored with the writer's work. Thus, having made somewhat of a lame excuse for the latest digression, It's now time to get-on with the incident; the one, which alerted me to the fact that they, the teachers, students, and possibly the entire school knew of my poor circumstances.

The incident, as near as I can recall, occurred in the sixth or seventh grade. I was well aware that, unlike most of my classmates who always wore brown shoes, I wore black sneakers. However, what I failed to realize was that wearing sneakers to school was a known give-away sign associated with poverty. The event, which in fact was not a pleasant one, happened during my favorite subject, Egyptian history. Without the slightest premonition as to what was about to happen, the teacher tells me to accompany her to a large closet situated in the hall. She opens the closet, and there I see many pairs of brown shoes placed neatly on shelves. Not that they were new, however, but shoes that had previously been warned, and discarded by the rich kids. Obviously, their parents had donated them for the needy children in the school, one of whom I was soon to realize was I. By her asking me to try on a pair, I knew her intentions were to give me one of those pairs of brown shoes. Perhaps what prompted me to accept her gift was not the customary gratitude I should have had, but instead, in light of the sense of shame that came over me at that precise moment in realizing I was the only poor Puerto Rican kid in a classroom whose students were predominantly Jewish and German refugee children from affluent families. To make matters worse, I was experiencing a learning disability primarily due to the lack of English language skills. The inferiority complex that was to cling to me like a leech for many years to come because I was a Puerto Rican with an English language barrier initially began with this incident. Maybe that's why I never wore those brown shoes to school, or anywhere else for that matter.

The brown shoes incident tends to stimulate many thoughts about what it was like to live in New York City during those times, trying to overcome the obstacles of poverty in the midst of the great depression. It was an era when the Nation was still years away from becoming actively involved in World War II. And it was a time when all that I saw, or came into contact with appeared exotic, exciting, and at times strange. The feeling was like an outsider peering in at the inner part of a cave filled with many wonderful objects that were all new to him. Naturally, toys were his main attraction; not the fashionable Shirley Temple look alike dolls but the ball bearing roller skates made by "the Union Company," and the popular "Flexible Flyer" sleds. Today these sleds are still in demand by children and grown ups. This period was his "age of innocence" that at times resulted in his sense of shame, regrets and helplessness. All the causes for these feelings evolved into an inferiority complex stemming from what he believed he represented to his peers. Aware that he was a short scrawny kid who was not "a bright student," spoke English with a heavy Spanish accent, and known as "Spany" by his classmates, were what in today's vernacular is known as his "hang-ups." "To add insult to injury," I was called "Spic" by the Irish and Italian kids in the neighborhood. In those days the label applied to any foreign or native-born Spanish speaking person.

New York City with its various ethnic neighborhoods of Irish, Italians, Jews, Spanish, and the Blacks residing in Harlem, was in many ways different from what it is today. One of those differences was the noise level. In that era, in particular, the City's blocks, or side streets, were much quieter. Most likely, this was caused by the small amount of vehicular traffic. A factor contributing to this situation were the numerous small commercial trucks, which operated on electric power supplied by batteries. Rather than the loud roar heard from gasoline engine vehicles, the small trucks left trails of pleasant humming sounds as they drove by. This was quite evident in Macy's electric trucks. Painted in bright red colors with a large white star on their sides, they were seen at least once a day making deliveries throughout the neighborhoods.

Another contributive factor lessening the City's noise level were Borden's all white small milk trucks, which made deliveries, not to the retail stores, but to the apartments in the tenement buildings. The trucks, or wagons as they were known, were pulled by one or two horses; However, unlike other horse-drawn wagons with large wheels having many spokes, Borden's wagons had pneumatic rubber tires. Naturally, the rubber tires did not produced any noises, instead, what was heard were the familiar pleasing "klipityclap" sounds from the horses' hoofs. Contributing to the scene, which, to be sure, will never again appear in the City, were the milkmen always wearing their all-white uniforms and garrison caps.

In contrast to the almost noiseless electric powered trucks and horse driven milk wagons, were the "Mack trucks" used primarily to deliver coal, and which seem to date back to World War I. Always they were heard before they made their appearances, mainly on the Avenues rather than on the blocks, which was a relief to the kids whose playgrounds were the City's side streets and not the Avenues. The "Mack truck" had no transmission system, and to compensate for this mechanical deficiency, had a series of gears and large chains that transferred the huge engine's power to the rear wheels, similar to how a bicycle functions. The grinding sounds from the large chains, the roar of the engine and the loud rapid plopping sounds from its tires, which were not pneumatic but solid rubber about five inches thick that covered the steel wheels, all contributed to the din produced by "the Mack" coal truck.

The City also had its icemen. These were the vendors who sold ice, which was a necessity in every household for storing meats and dairy products over-night, or for several days. This was prior to the advent of refrigerators, and all families stored perishable food in iceboxes. Every block had its iceman who sold and delivered ice only to the tenants residing in his territory, or the particular block he serviced. All the icemen, without exceptions, were Italian immigrants who spoke English with a distinct Sicilian accent. Most times they were not by their ice wagons, but somewhere else delivering ice, and as a result, the only recourse for a customer was to leave him a message. The message, which was always the same, the family's last name, address and apartment number, was written on a small white pad that had been placed on top of a stand having a small pencil dangling by a string to one of its sides. The stand was always near the ice wagon, which was usually located in the middle of the block. This method may seem somewhat antiquated by today's standards, nevertheless, unlike the present time where virtually everyone has at least one or more in the house, at that time very few people were able to afford the cost of having a telephone, and therefore calling-in an ice order was impossible. And for those families who may have been fortunate enough to have a phone, it was still an impossibility seeing that the iceman, of course, didn't have one.

The wooden stands were all the same sizes and shapes as though this had been a pre-arranged rule among the icemen, perhaps in order to not compete with one another. They were about five feet in height, two feet square, looking like huge upright shoeboxes standing on their ends, and all painted in bright glossy colors of reds, greens and yellows. This may have been purposely done, since even from a block away the stands were easily visible. The iceman's tools were the common ice pick, large steel pincers for grabbing the large cubes of ice and the black or red rubber mat, which secured around his neck with a heavy cord covered the part of his body used to carry the large cube, his mat, thus protecting him from the dripping water, and the coldness of the ice during the times of deliveries. Selling ice was a highly lucrative business in the 1930s, and as a result, many of these Italian immigrant icemen, after years of selling ice to the tenants, actually became landlords of tenement buildings in the neighborhood.

Along with the ubiquitous icemen, the City had its fashions and styles of dressing. Fashions were very much in vogue despite the widespread unemployment and lack of money people had for non-essentials. A sight you seldom see nowadays, men always wore brown or gray fedoras outdoors. During the hot summer months, some men switched to wearing straw hats, or what were known as Panama hats. Men's suits were double breasted, tight fitting and all had shoulder pads. Neck ties were never the slim type, but very wide and having bright color designs. Knee suspenders held-up the socks, and what may never again re-appear as fashionable, men wore spats covering the upper part of their shoes and ankles.

No discussion in men's fashions prior to World War II can be complete without mentioning the popular zoot suit. The man's garment, which was originally introduced on stage by the Black bandleader, Cab Calloway in the early 30s, was an exaggerated style with baggy trousers narrowing at the cuffs, and a long draped coat ending almost at the knees, and amply padded at the shoulders; it had the appearance of a man's body in a suit that had the shape of an enormous letter V. Almost instantly, it became a popular fashion garment among Black men. Gradually, however, it developed into a widespread fad with all men lasting until the Country's initial military involvement in the war. The large demand for servicemen's uniforms by the Arm Forces created shortages in fabrics, which made it almost impossible to supply the civilian male population, thus the zoot suit era came to its untimely end.

Not to be outdone by the men, women wore hats in a wide variety of styles and colors that seem to reach their high point on Easter Sunday. On that festive religious holiday, women and young girls wore their Easter bonnets, which were always decorated with an array of artificial flowers. Ankle length dresses were the style, and not unlike men's suits, all were fitted with shoulder pads. Wearing new outfits was the traditional custom for both men and women on that Christian holiday. Flowers, real or artificial, were the essential decorating feature, with even the men and boys proudly displaying red or white carnations, most of which were made from crepe paper, pinned to the lapels of their new suits.

CHAPTER 36

More about the City in the 1930's

Poverty's stranglehold on masses of people as a result of the depression of the 30s caused by the catastrophic crash of the stock market on Wall Street in 1929 is a well-known fact. What's more, the poverty situation was experienced not only in this Country, but also throughout the world. My mother and I were very much a part of this experience. Yet, never did I realize, obviously due to the innocence of youth, how widespread it was. However, there were periodic reminders, for example, the times when our evening meals consisted solely of rice boiled in beef's blood. Beef's blood was the cheapest thing to buy at the neighborhood's butcher store, perhaps because of the lack of demand for it. Visions of dining on blood may seem repugnant, but actually, after mother added spices to the blood before boiling it with the rice, the meal was quite tasteful, almost like eating rice with chicken that had been flavored with garlic and chopped onions.

Despite the poverty situation, which resulted in the constant need for money to buy food, the concern for this was his mother's and the man she had married, and not that of the young boy. Indeed, the era was a difficult one still, fond memories exist of a time when the boy was able to buy four pieces of delicious caramels for a mere penny. Needless to say, the boy along with his playmates played games, especially, "kick the can," "ringolevio" and "skelly, all of which were usually played during the cool evening breezes of summer. "Skelly" was a game in which the players progressed through thirteen squared boxes about twelve inches in size, which were drawn with chalk on the streets or sidewalks. Progress was gained with the use of a bottle cap, and snapping the thumb and index finger with the necessary strength to move, or land the bottle cap onto a particular box. The game was always played beneath a street lamp to get the reflection of the lights on the boxes. Augmenting the games were the special events of early autumn, for instance, the roasting of sweet potatoes, or "mickeys" as they were known, in the solid metal trashcans placed on street corners by the Sanitation Department; and then there were the glorious barn fires built in the middle of the blocks on election nights.

Those were the times when the mayor, Fiorello LaGuardia, read the newspapers' comic strips on the radio every Sunday morning for the benefit of the children. Radio was the prime home entertainment, although some families also had phonographs. Actually, they were known as victrolas, most of which were not electric, but mechanically driven so that they had to be wound with a crank in order to get their turntables to revolve. Favorite children' programs on the radio were, among many others, "Jack Armstrong, the all American boy," "The Inner Sanctum," and "The Lone Ranger," "with his faithful companion Tonto," the American Indian. Curious to note that in the 1930s Indians were never referred to as "Native Americans" as they are today. Finally, there were the "comedy hour" programs performed by show business luminaries, for example, the popular comedians, Jack Benny, Eddy Cantor and Edgar Bergen, the ventriloquist, and his highly intelligent dummy, with a tone of sarcasm in his behavior, Charlie McCarthy, who always wore a tuxedo, top hat and a monocle.

Those were also the times when, on various occasions, live entertainment was provided for the tenants by strolling musicians and singers. What is a bit puzzling, now that I think about it, why did they performed only in the backyards of tenement buildings, and not on the streets where they were more likely to have attracted the pedestrians, or customers for an audience? Most likely, a City ordinance established to prohibit musicians from performing on the City's streets may have been the reason. Thus one can assume their audience, to some extent, was limited only to those tenants having windows in their apartments facing the backyards.

Nonetheless, this was not a problem, specifically for tenants who lived in railroad flats with rooms built in tandem, one behind the other. The front rooms of these flats, or apartments, normally the living rooms, faced the streets, and the furthest rooms from the living rooms, faced the backyards. As a result, tenants had some view of their backyards enabling them to see and enjoy the entertainers; and to show some appreciation the customary thing to do was to throw coins at the performers.

Performances were always giving during daylight hours, naturally, and never at night when the absence of light would have prevented the tenants from seeing the performers. Their instruments, accordions, horns, violins, and on some occasions bagpipes, were old and somewhat shabby in appearance, still, they produced pleasant musical sounds. The singers, most of whom were male baritones and female sopranos, sang old ballads of a bygone era from Ireland and Italy. Never can I recall hearing them play and sing Spanish songs. Probably, the reason was that, except for our family, there were no Spanish people living in the neighborhood.

Perhaps not for strolling musicians, but for some of us, poverty predisposes us to circumstances, which are not always conducive to the health and well being of our bodies. Once again, poverty was the sole reason for the family having to move to an area where the inexpensive rental apartments were to be found, alongside the El. Again, when my mother and I, along with her husband and his son Jerry moved to 107th Street and Columbus Avenue, we were to be subjected to the rumbling noises and dirt from the El; and for an added attraction, we also had to contend with the belching smoke from the Lion Brewery's chimney, which periodically contaminated the air in the neighborhood. The Brewery and the El were situated directly across from our fifth floor tenement apartment. To add to the discomfort, the distance between the El and our apartment's living room was no more than twenty feet, so that every so often when a train rumbled by, the living room actually vibrated from the effects of ten or more train cars passing by our windows. The experience of prolonged silence at all hours of the day, and the hushed and stillness of night were not to be had; instead, there were always the relentless noise and vibrations from the El.

The prospect of gaining any joys from this somewhat of a blighted and destitute environment was nil. Still, there were exciting experiences to be had. Namely the one in the Brewery whose huge sign painted in white letters on a black background read, "Established in 1850," and could also be seen above the El's structure from our living room windows. In the Brewery's basement was a large room used to store empty beer bottles. What the attraction for these bottles was for the kids, including this writer, was the fact that they were redeemable in grocery stores; the bearer received two cents for each bottle. Our good fortune was the room's windows where the Brewery stored the bottles were never locked, and as a result, the kids, including yours truly, were able to gain access to the precious small brown bottles that had all the earmarks of candy money. Strange as it may seem now, at the times of those happenings, I never thought of it as a form of stealing, but rather, as finding something of value. Ideally, the plan was always to help our selves to as many of them as we were able to carry, however, there were obstacles, which compelled us against carrying out our plans. Grocery store owners had imposed a three-bottle limit of exchange, moreover, some of them refused outright to accept our bottles. Consequently, many were the times we had to canvass numerous stores around the neighborhood in search of one that would redeem our bottles for the pennies needed to buy candy. Our good fortune eventually came to a sad end. The Brewery, in all probability suspecting the worse, began to store the bottles in places were we were never again able to find them.

CHAPTER 37

Reality, Passion and Reason

Remembrances of happenings that occurred so many years ago and so far removed from the presence is like re-living a twelve years old boy's experiences. The fact is, only the ability to remember has enabled me to reflect on memories from my past; further, barring any mental health problems, all of us have this capability. We, therefore, can conclude that our ability to remember, in particular, significant past experiences of long ago is, indeed, one of life's realities. What may initially appear to be a broad observation, reality does lie deeply imbedded in our senses, and how we perceive our world. In other words, our value judgment can influence us in how we judge reality. More of a point, what may seem to be conceived as real for one person may not necessarily be seen as real for me. Reality, or what makes-up part of its whole, can in some ways be correlated with our capacity to reason and draw conclusions without the influence of other forces, whether they are human or not. In its most simple form, according to the German philosopher, Emanuel Kant, it is "the ability to act free whenever we act, and not free when some other agency acts through you." Again referring to Kant's words as a frame of reference for some thoughts about reality, we have the power to achieve some end, moreover, the action originated by us can only be contributed to us.

This power we posses, however, derives from our reason, which as the British philosopher, David Hume, pointed out, may not always be put into use by our freewill. Reason said Hume is held in bondage by our passions. Furthermore, our reason can persuade us to act, and this only happens when we have been motivated by our passions. Therefore, in understanding Hume's point of view correctly, the ability to guide our actions by reason is not based on total freedom, that is, unless we consider our passions. Accordingly, the final results may yield a part of reality that is not wholly made-up of our choices of freewill, particularly when we realize the freewill is motivated by our passions; but where does this passion originate? Can its origin be the result of An All Mighty God, or from nature? If our answers to these questions are yes, doesn't it strike the reader as overly simple answers in dealing with a complex issue such as causes for our behavior? In other words, in An All Mighty God, or in nature, we have ready-made answers for what mystifies us, for example, where did we come from, what is our true origin, or for what reason or purpose are we on this earth? We can also apply these same answers to questions about the origin of trees, plants, or any other living matter.

An All Mighty God and nature will de-mystify all, therefore, we can relegate all our unanswerable questions to God or nature. This manner of having ready-made answers to these probing questions seems too simple, and arguably, unrealistic; that there is no challenge involved is quite obvious. The process, if we were to apply it tends to foster a passive method of drawing conclusions, without having any need whatsoever to collect the essential data; rather than question, or make an attempt to seek-out factual, or at least reasonable answers, We simply rely on a God or nature to give them to us. Yet, in considering all that I have said thus far relating to this issue, for non-believers of An All Mighty God, these answers may tend to further mystify rather than clarify the mysteries of our lives Reverting to the original premise, reality and human behavior, can we really conclude that passion is what motivates our behavior, and the origin of this passion is not reason? But where does this passion and reason derived from? Aren't these attributes learned behavior instilled in us by our parents, school, religion and the environment? And if we accept an All Mighty God as the creator of all matter, specifically, living matter, where was God before the evolution of life? What was he doing, and what was his purpose in creating us? In the realm of thought, questions such as these can never have what we judge to be the right answers. Nonetheless, some of us can attest to the capacity to reason as part of our reality.

Everything we behold on this earth has a beginning and an end. Can we, in fact, say this is reality, that is, if we were to judge reality as a form of truth? Before proceeding further, I am, indeed, aware that I had previously said reality had many meanings, depending on one's individual judgment. What I had neglected to say, however, was what type of reality I was referring to, the reality of what can be seen and felt, or the one arrived at by inferences. Both methods can be said to be true, though some philosophers have said, and I tend to agree with them, appearance is not always true; what one sees may not always be the true thing.

Conclusive evidence is decisive in nature. It can be the final piece of information that establishes a truth. To be sure, without this conclusive evidence agreed upon by not one individual, but by groups of knowledgeable individuals considered experts in their field, there is no proof or truth for what makes up the real thing. Yet, reality can be an illusive entity that, depending on the individual, can have various meanings. To repeat in somewhat of a variable manner what I have previously cited, what is judge to be the real thing by others may not be the real thing for me. The puzzling question, nevertheless, still remains to be answered, how can we establish a truth? Matter, or the material objects I can see and feel with my hands, and who others perceived and feel the same object as I do can be a form of truth. To re-enforce what I have just said, there are those of us who believe only in what we are able to see. On the other hand, how do we accept a truth, which is perceptible only to the mind rather than the senses? Webster's *New World Dictionary of American Language* defines the word truth as "A material thing," something which is "real," "definite" and "actual." However, these definitions can be applied to abstract thoughts, or what I perceive in my mind to be "real" and "actual" things for me. As an illustration, a dream I have is "real" and "actual" for me; I have experienced it, and if I close my eyes as soon as I have awakened, I can recall parts of the dream. Nonetheless this form of truth can be classified solely as my own and no one else's.

Another case in point, and in some ways different from the one just described, is the person who perhaps in moments of solitude and darkness discerns a vision. The person does not visualizes the vision, but actually sees it. Thereafter, particularly if the vision is of a religious nature, the person proceeds to relate what he has seen to others. To him it is a truth and willing to swear to others that, indeed, he has observed a vision; but is it a truth for others who have failed to see it, nor will they ever see it. Faith does play a significant role in the ability of people to believe in something they have never seen. In contrast to this, how about the people who have no faith, and rely solely on seeing the physical object before believing in it in order to confirm its truth or reality.

In the context of these thoughts, truth and reality can have identical meanings, however, this may be difficult for some people to accept. Reverting to aspects that have previously been discussed, what may be truth as a form of reality for others may not necessarily be the same for me. There is a reality we should agree on, nevertheless, that is, patterns of occurrences, which always replicate themselves. For instance, we always see a full moon about every twenty eight days, and at other times we see it in various forms depending on how much light it reflects from the sun, and the obscuration of clouds. Another example is the cycle of day preceded by night, which is continuously on-going, and we know this to be a truth since we have experienced it. A final illustration is the clapping of the hands; if we clap our hands, we know for a fact, or a truth, that we are going to hear a sound. I have elected to label them patterns of occurrences, which, indeed, can be forms of truth or reality. These given examples of what constitutes reality can appear to be simple ones, and perhaps quite rightly so. Nonetheless, they may serve as practical human applications as to what is real and what is not.

In some ways these thoughts may act to stimulate our senses to judge for ourselves rather to be influenced by others who may want to sell us something, or worse yet, to manipulate our mind.

As a result of seeking out what we conceptualize to be the truth, or the reality of a thing or situation, we become cognizant of how people, in general, are motivated by the desire to satisfy their needs, and quite often whether the needs are essential or not. Suffice to end this discussion by pointing out that the causality for needs that are not necessary for our well-being can be attributed to the capitalistic system we're locked into. A more thorough discussion on the issue of capitalism will be taken-up in another chapter.

CHAPTER 38

The Fair, Stickball, Hockey and The "Silver King"

The Nation was on the brink of becoming actively involved with the war raging in Europe, yet, people, in general, appeared not to be overly concerned in international affairs. Indeed, the depression still had somewhat of a tight grip on the Country, however, all that appeared to be on the City population's mind was the opening of The 1939 New York Worlds Fair at Flushing Meadows in Queens. Ironic as it may seem today, the Fair's theme was the peaceful and prosperous lifestyle for all Americans. This theme was re-enforced for the public with displays of gleaming new automobiles with bright colors of reds, yellows and whites, and an array of electric appliances, most comprised of washing machines, radios and the new marvel of the electronic age, television. Surprising to most people, in particular, the politicians, the fair was a financial disaster for the City losing millions of dollars within a two years span. What made add "insult to injury," the only lasting mementos from the Fair were the shiny new pennies whose surfaces were stamped on a pressing machine to oval shape and made paper thin, which resulted in almost doubling their original size. This was necessary in order to accommodate the small printed words of The Lord's Prayer on them.

The years 1939 through the early part of 1941 was the period when young Japanese men with their expensive cameras hanging over their shoulders were seen everywhere in the City taking pictures of practically everything within their sights. During the summer months, especially when the Navy anchored ships in the Hudson River, hordes of these young men gathered on the River's banks to take pictures of the line of war ships stretching from the Battery to as far north as the Washington Bridge. Also seen all along the River's Eastern banks were the ugly mounds of coal ashes, which the Sanitation Department probably may have used as a preventive measure against floods. They were the residue from the coal burned in the furnaces of commercial and residential buildings to supply heat and hot water. Years later these coal ashes were used as a foundation beneath the asphalt that covered the West Side Highway, which today parallels the eastern side of the River.

Our neighborhood during those hot summer days literally overflowed with kids on vacation from the public schools. Naturally, their recreational areas were the City's streets. Games were numerous, of course, three of which were the very popular stickball games, hockey played on roller skates, and bicycling, which was not actually a game, but a delightful pastime that was made possible only when one had the twenty five cents rental fee for the bike, and the required Con Edison gas and electric bill used by bicycle store proprietors as collateral to ensure the return of their bicycles. Stickball, as everyone from my generation knows is a version of baseball played on the City's streets in which the handle of a broom, more familiar known then as a broomstick, is used to hit a rubber ball almost the size of a baseball. A Pink colored ball with the brand name "Spalding" was considered the ideal one to use in a game because of its high bouncing qualities. Curiously as it may seem, the games were outlawed by the City due to the threat of apartment windows being broken by balls hit into the air with the broomsticks, which seldom happened. More often than not, a strolling policeman, or those cruising the streets in the Police Department's olive green Plymouth coupes confiscated our beloved broomsticks and threw them down manholes where they were never seen again.

Playing roller skate hockey presented somewhat of a challenge for most kids, not because of the intricacies or skills the game demanded, however, but due to footwear. In a clearer sense, this was still the depression period, and children's footwear, at least for the ones who lived in my neighborhood were the inexpensive black high-top sneakers. Similar to the expensive white canvas shoes worn today, the high-top sneakers, unlike shoes, had soles without extended edges. In those days roller skates were equipped with clamps to secure them to the extended edges of shoes. By using a "skate key" to tighten the clamps to the outer edges of the shoes' sole, the front part of the skate was securely fastened onto the front of the shoe. Leather or canvas straps secured the rear part of the skate to the ankle. In order to compensate for not having the proper footwear, (shoes) kids, after tightening the clamps, and aware from past experiences the clamps would eventually slip from the sneakers, rapped strong cord or twine around the front parts of their skates and sneakers. The procedure was used as a precautionary measure against the clamps dislodging from the skates causing a stumble or a fall, especially during a game. Street sewers, which were never known to us as manholes, were used as the goals. As a final note, the puck was usually a squared piece of wood, and never the standard expensive kind made from hard rubber.

Bicycling, even by today's standards, is a popular recreational activity. However, in those days it was a terribly exciting experience, notably because of the amazing "Silver King." "Silver King" was the brand name of an exceptional bicycle that for twenty five cents and the all-important Con Edison gas and electric bill allowed you the privilege of riding the bicycle for two hours. Aptly named the "Silver King," the bike was a marvelous piece of machinery that justifies further description, if only to recall the sheer thrills I experienced whenever I rode one. To be sure, I haven't seen on of those beauties in action since the beginning of World War II. The essence of the beauty was the color, and the unique lightweight features, which required very little energy to pedal, even when going up hill, owing to the all aluminum tubular frame. Its color was silver, including the fenders and the wide extended handlebars, which gave it an appearance similar to that of a motorcycle. Summarizing a mental image of a beautiful thing, two black balloon tires with their outer edges highlighted in bright gleaming white colors, or whitewalls, were mounted on the wire spoke wheels. The era of the "Silver King" is long gone, and like all good things that enter and leave our lives, we're always wondering whether they will ever return to us.

CHAPTER 39

Our Neighborhood

Nowadays ghetto would be the common name used to define our neighborhood. Specifically, rows of dilapidated five stories high tenement buildings adjoining one another on each side of the 6th Avenue El may be a more realistic way of describing it; and as previously mentioned, the buildings' apartments with their small rooms were known as railroad flats, or cold water flats, since heat and hot water were not provided to the tenants by landlords. Beer saloons were on all the corners of Columbus Avenue beginning at 110th Street and ending at 96th Street. In the saloons, more widely known as taverns, bars, or gin mills, men, and seldom women, stood along mahogany colored counters, which extended lengthwise from wall-to-wall, quenching their thirst with the very popular alcoholic beverage, beer. The beverage's popularity, no doubt, stemmed inasmuch from its low price of only ten cents for a large glass. Beer was not only consumed in saloons, but also taken out, (take-out orders), to apartments in aluminum pots equipped with carrying handles. The neighborhood, especially during the hot summer months, reeked with the foul smelling odor of malt, not from the many saloons in the area, as one may have suspected, but from the Lion Brewery.

Despite what may appear to be all negative aspects, our neighborhood did have appealing aspects, with its old world charm and bustling City life activities. Many of the streets and avenues, including Amsterdam and Columbus were paved with light brown cobblestones, which on rainy days gave them somewhat of an appealing glitter, almost like looking at glass on the streets. Peddlers, and they were never known as vendors as they are today, ambled along the cobblestone paved Avenues and Streets selling vegetables and fresh fish on Fridays. Augmenting the peddlers were the junk collectors on their horse drawn wagons offering to buy scrap iron, rags and old newspapers. Adding to these sights were the pleasant sounds of the cowbells attached to the junk collectors' wagons alerting people in the apartments they were in the neighborhood. Pushcarts always appeared on Fridays laden with porgies, an extremely bony fish, and as a result, very cheap, but having the same delicious taste as the highly expensive red snapper. And there were the men, usually dressed all in black with grindstones attached to pulleys and carried on their backs announcing their presence by clanging bells, similar to the ones used by school teachers in school yards to announce to the children the end of recess; these were the men who toiled for a living by sharpening knives and scissors. Also, there were the "sandwich men," no, they didn't make sandwiches, instead, they earned a living by merely walking around the neighborhood with advertising signs, which seem like small mobile billboards, strapped to the front and rear of their bodies. Finally, there was the Italian man who, with his hurdy-gurdy, which had the appearance of a small upright piano with wheels, collected coins by pulling the instrument from one block to another cranking-out Irish and Italian folk songs, and of course, everyone's favorite, "The Sidewalks of New York."

Public transportation, or what today is commonly known as mass transit, was much more than just adequate. This type of service was provided by the City twenty-four hours a day seven days a week, and except for taxicabs and the double deck buses, for a fare of only five cents. A nickel entitled you to ride the subways with their exotic kiosks entrances at the stations, and seats upholstered in rattan; and there were the brightly colored green and yellow trolley cars with their distinct clanging bells on the front and rear of the roofs' trolleys to warn vehicular traffic and pedestrians. Further, one nickel allowed you to ride a bus on one of the few bus routes at the time. Double deck buses, some of which had no roofs on their upper decks, and known as "open-air buses" traveled from "The Cloisters, and then south on Riverside Drive terminating their routes at Houston Street. The buses not only had drivers, but also conductors whose duties were to collect the ten-cent fares from people boarding the buses. Both drivers and conductors wore olive brown colored uniforms similar to ones worn by army soldiers. However, conductors wore brown leather putters, or what are more familiarly known as leggings. Passengers paid in a manner that in some ways is similar to today's method of paying with the exact fare; unlike today, however, passengers were allowed to ask for change before paying. On receiving the change, a passenger, and not the conductor who was not permitted to do so, inserted one dime into a coin slot that accommodated only this size coin. The dime slot was located on the top of a small stainless steel rectangular box whose base tapered to form a thick handle held by the conductor. Soon after the box received the coin, a chime was heard not unlike the sound heard when a bicycle's bell has been rung. This may have been the precursor of the present day method of passengers having to pay with the exact fare before permitted to ride the City's buses.

A custom no longer practiced, except for police officers, was the conspicuous garrison cap worn by bus drivers, trolley conductors, sanitation workers, and even the milkmen who delivered milk to apartments wore them. Police squad cars and sanitation trucks were painted a dull dark-green, likewise, sanitation workers' uniforms were the same color. At various times this color added a note of depressive sadness to a blighted neighborhood of poor people, most of whom lived in shabby housing conditions. An unexpected pleasant event occurred soon after the fair's opening when the sanitation trucks were painted a brilliant white and trimmed in bright orange colors. The workers' uniforms also changed to these same colors. Police squad cars, nevertheless, still maintained their green colors, but with one exception, the cars' roofs were re-painted white, most likely for the purpose of making them more visible.

Though losing a lot of money for the City, the New York Worlds Fair of 1939-40 may have been the harbinger for the gradual improvement trend in socio-economic standards; and of course, the relentless war raging on in Europe played a key role in releasing the people from the grips of the great depression. Many factory jobs requiring skill and unskilled labor became available. Moreover, many of the tenement buildings were rehabilitated with new staircases, fresh coats of paints, and of more importance, new furnaces for heating the coldwater flats were installed. At a later period, the State was to legislate laws outlawing coldwater flats.

For the children in the neighborhood, especially during summer vacations, the City's streets were like huge magnets attracting and beckoning them to what seem to be marvelous playgrounds full of adventure and joys. And for some adults, there was always the beer to quench their thirst. Furthermore, despite the summer's heat, what appeared odd to me at the time, the warm smoke from smoking cigarettes never seem to bother the smokers, not realizing, of course, they were "hooked" on nicotine; and as a result, the weather certainly was not going to deter them from smoking. Cigarettes were extremely cheap, for example, the person lacking the eleven cents to purchase a pack of cigarettes, nonetheless, was able to buy them "loose," at a cost of one cent a cigarette. The tobacco companies in that era can be compared with the oil companies of today, with consumption of their product at an all time high. Soon after the Nation entered the war, the largest tobacco company adopted the advertising slogan, "Lucky Strike green has gone to war resulting in an unexpected windfall in the company's sales. Prior to the change, the American Tobacco Company sold their product, "Lucky Strikes cigarettes in red and green packs. However, the Arm Forces' need for green dye, which was used for military clothing, compelled the company to pack them in the two colors they still use today, red and white.

Nature's onslaught of summer heat failed to discourage children from having their fun on the City's streets. For instance, gushing cool refreshing water from hydrants, which were usually turned-on by thoughtful janitors who perhaps sympathized with the kids' discomforts, were the means for escaping the heat. Contributing to the children's fun were the empty milk crates, which made of sturdy heavy wood with their strong steel wire forming grids, accommodated the milk bottles. When tilted at an angle and placed over open hydrants, the crates produced glorious showers of torrential waters cascading over the heads of masses of children jumping and dancing experiencing sheer delight beneath the sprays of cool water.

CHAPTER 40

"Skippy," and The Model Airplane

On lingering rainy days with overcast clouds that appeared to almost reach the ground, and made their appearances when one least expected them to, the option was to go to the movies, provided one had a nickel or dime for the entrance, or one remained at home and built a model airplane. Going to see a movie at a theatre was a favorite way to while away the afternoon by escaping into a fantasy world as unreal as "Alice in Wonderland." Movie theatres were not air conditioned, yet with their huge fans humming a steady rhythm to maintain the theatres, if not comfortable, at least bearable for the audiences, the movie houses were very popular, even during the hot summer. months.

Entrances to movie theatres in fact were incredibly cheap. Throughout the neighborhood, movie theatres, except for "The Rose," ten cents was your passport to a double feature, and "short subjects," which usually were animated cartoons and "a serial," commonly known as a chapter. My favorite movie house was "The Rose" at 102nd Street between Amsterdam and Columbus Avenues where on weekdays the entrance fee was only a nickel. The purchasing power of a nickel, to put it mildly, was big. For example, you were able to buy anyone of the wide varieties of bottled sodas, or "soda pop," as they were called, candy bars, one of which was the highly popular "Baby Ruth" bar, ice cream cones, and "Eskimo Pies," which today are known as ice cream pops, or a bag of "loose candies." Further, "loose candies" could be purchased for only a penny, for instance, among others, a mere penny enabled you to buy four caramels, or a package containing a slab of bubble gum together with what was highly in demand by the kids in the neighborhood, two "playing cards" with photos of popular professional baseball players on them. A game with these types of cards was played in the following manner. Grasping the bottom edge of one of his card with four fingers and the top edge with the thumb, and with the arm at his side, a player quickly lifted his arm to his mid-section and flipped the card to the ground while standing. Applying the same procedure, the other player's card on landing on the ground had to match whatever side his opponent's card was facing. If he succeeded, he was rightfully entitled to his opponent's card, and if not, he lost his card to the other player.

Referring again to the nickel movie theatre, an incident occurred that brings back fond memories, and some thoughts of how a young boy can be somewhat mesmerized by a movie. The theatre in which the incident took place was "The Rose," and the name of the movie was "Skippy" starring the popular boy movie star of the thirties, Jackie Cooper. I remember entering the theatre at about noontime. After viewing the main feature, "Skippy," I, thereafter, saw the second movie, a western, and "short subjects," patiently waiting for "Skippy" to appear again on the silver screen. All that I can recall was wanting to see "Skippy" again and again. So enthralled was I with the movie that I lost all sense of time, and the capacity to realize it was getting late, and most likely, my mother was at home anxiously waiting for her only son, failed me completely. The movie, by the way, was based on a cartoon character, Skippy," a young boy who was always getting into some mischief. Skippy was published daily in *The New York Journal American*. I must have viewed the movie at least four or five times before a policeman approached my seat, grabbed hold of one of my arms, and escorted me outside of the theatre. There, my poor mother, on seen me burst into tears hugging me, and at the same time crying almost hysterically. Failure to tell her what theatre I was going to resulted in her having to advise the police to search all the theatres, of which there were five in the neighborhood. The policeman must have searched all but the last one before locating me. Later I was to find out I had been in "The Rose" theatre for over eight hours enraptured with the movie, "Skippy."

A lingering rain can at times instill a young boy with urges for activities other than movies, or playing outdoors. These particular activities, unlike movies, allows you to become actively involved both physically and mentally in whatever it is that is undertaken; and along with the process of doing some activity with the hands, or what is referred to nowadays as hands-on experience, you may, and it often does occur, become lost in thoughts about past happenings. Building model airplanes was my indoor's rainy day activities. Enthusiasm for airplanes and flying had such a tight hold on me that it was not until years after the war that I finally managed to release myself from having the interest of flying airplanes. In fact I gradually developed a hate for flying because of their offensive engine noises, but namely, since I had also developed a fear for flying.

Airplane model kits were not expensive. A precious dime made it possible for you to buy either a flying model or the "solid" type, which demanded more skills, especially in carving the body, or fuselage with a single edge razor blade from a solid block of balsa wood. Needless to describe the process of building model airplanes, I believe we're all familiar with it; however, what may not be familiar is how the setting seems to act as a stimulus for the senses while you are involved in this activity. I am not referring to "streams of consciousness," but instead, to deep meditations in which you become lost in reveries. Solitude, indeed, appears to play a key role that predisposes you to idle thoughts. For instance, physically you are actively involved in building the model with your hands, but your mind is the sole occupant of your thoughts. The stillness is broken only by raindrops gently falling past the window on their way to the ground. The streets are bathed in rainwater causing the black asphalt to glow in daylight as it always does at night beneath the street lamps. Yet, you're involved in a silent activity, but with a keen awareness of the quietness that surrounds your being.

Countless critical reflections flash by quickly, and then as though by magic, instantly fade away; I wear glasses, does that mean I will not become a pilot? You need a college degree to become a pilot, and where is my mother going to get the money to send me to college? Why do Jewish kids' parents have money, and why are we so poor? Why do I always have to wear knickers, and when will I ever be able to wear long pants? I want to wear shoes and not sneakers, especially when going to school; when will my mother have the money to buy me a pair of brown shoes with gum rubber soles? Endlessly, thoughts rush by transcending themselves into inquiries about questions without answers. Why are all policemen Irish, and all sanitation workers, produce storeowners and icemen Italians? Why are the hand laundries owned by Chinese? Why do women wear hats and gloves outdoors during the hot weather? Why is bottled milk sold in two grades, grade A and grade B? And why are my stepbrother and I the only Spanish kids in the neighborhood? The model is progressing nicely, but the odor from the Dupont glue is beginning to give me a headache. The sun is peaking out through the cloud layers, and is about to make its appearance. It must be about noontime, and the streets are beckoning me.

Dwelling on the happening at this moment, little did I suspect at the time that the rain's end was to be a bad omen on that rainless afternoon.

CHAPTER 41

A Learning Experience

That fateful afternoon, the rain having stopped and the sun beginning to shine with glaring rays of yellows, I decided to forgo the model project and go outdoors, if only to enjoy the sun's brilliance. At the corner Gerry, with a younger boy about ten years old, unexpectedly asked me if I cared to join them on a journey of fun and adventure. Somewhat surprised by the invitation, I accepted and accompanied them, but only because he had one boy with him rather than his customary band of faithful followers. Of course, neither him or his companion, nor I for that matter, had any idea how and where our journey was to end.

Recalling the incident now, what seems odd then, as it still does today, is that my stepbrother Gerry and I, in all our years together living under one roof, never did form a close relationship with each other. There existed between the two of us a divisive barrier, which can only be ascribed, in essence, to our physical and character differences. We tend to get a sense of ourselves in relation to what we perceive in others; and what I saw in Gerry was a vast difference from what I saw in myself. He was a handsome boy with smooth lustrous black hair, light complexion and blue eyes that blended almost perfectly with those of the Irish kids in the neighborhood. In sports he excelled in all types of games, including stickball and the less physically demanding game of marbles; and he was a fast runner who was able to outrun any kid his age. Moreover, he was as popular with the girls as he was with boys. Never can I recall seeing him outdoors alone. Always, he had an entourage of friends, all of whom followed him everywhere he went, and emulating everything he did. In contrast to all his attributes, I was the complete opposite of my stepbrother Gerry. Having curly brown hair, brown eyes and dark complexion, I didn't consider myself a good looking boy; nor was I popular with the boys and girls in the neighborhood or in school; and as for my running prowess, I must have been the slowest kid on Columbus Avenue.

However, despite our differences, Gerry and I never had physical fights with each other, and seldom did we have verbal arguments. Our distances from one another perhaps stemmed from realizing I was a persona non grata whenever I made any attempts to join him and his friends. Nonetheless, that afternoon I was a welcomed part of a trio of boys who began their quest for adventure by jumping in puddles of water, kicking empty cans and running, with me barely managing to keep-up with my stepbrother and his younger friend. Moments after the journey had begun, Gerry decides we're going to climb stairs to the roof of one building, and jump to the rooftops of other buildings. The activity, or game, was to be somewhat like "follow the leader," and naturally, he designated himself as the leader, and the ten year old boy and I were to be the followers.

Most roofs of tenements buildings are divided by ledges, which are about two or three feet high. As a result, the three of us had no difficulty in jumping or scaling over them. Some of these buildings, however, are detached from one another so that their roofs are separated by nothing more than but open air spaces about three or four feet wide. That I had somewhat of a premonition something dreadful was about to happen as we approached the first of these openings may be true. Yet, I did not, or in a more realistic sense, was unable to prevent what was about to happen. Fate may have interfered with whatever intentions I may have had at that moment. Gerry jumped, and successfully landed on the other roof. The young and smaller boy then attempted to jump, but slipped on the edge of the opening, which was still wet from the recent rain, and plunged to the backyard six stories below. I watched in sheer horror as his small body went tumbling down before striking the side of a fire escape, about the third floor level, before hitting the ground with a loud "plop." Much to my surprise looking down from six floors above, I saw him get-up from the ground crying and limping slowly, calling "Mom," with his face literally covered with blood. Overcome with the frightful sight, Gerry and I rushed downstairs and headed for the building's backyard, however, on arriving there, the boy had mysteriously vanished. We attempted to locate him, but the young boy was nowhere to be found. Finally, after our prolonged attempts to find him had failed, we went directly home, making a solemn vow never to divulge our horrific experience to anyone.

The incident, to some extent, had a happy ending. A few days later I found out the boy had been seen leaving the backyard by a roving police car, and immediately taken to a hospital. Miraculously he had sustained only external injuries, fractured legs, a broken nose and bruises. Most likely the miracle may have resulted from the young boy's body striking the fire escape, thus causing a significant decrease in the speed of his fall prior to hitting the backyard's paved surface. The episode was, indeed, a learning experience; never again did I, alone or with anyone else ventured to play on the roofs of buildings.

CHAPTER 42

The Search for Variables in Our Lives

There can be no doubt that "All our knowledge begins with experience." In quoting the German philosopher, Emanuel Kant, the intent is to re-enforce the fact that we do, indeed, learn from our experiences. A good example to cite is the roof episode. Kant's proposition, though considered by many as true, nevertheless, appears to be too broad in scope. What I mean by this is that, specifically, one does not know exactly how much experience is needed in order to acquire the knowledge. The amount of learning, which in the context of these thoughts can be correlated with the experience needed, depends on the individual's capacity for learning; in fact, some of us learn at a faster pace than others. In other words, because of innate differences, I may need more experience than another person before I attain knowledge for a particular something, whatever that something may be. These thoughts tend to raise the question, why do some people fail to learn from past experiences? Their insufficient amount of past experiences may be the correct answer to this question. The familiar proverb, "Practice makes perfect" implies that time is the underlying factor associated with the practice. That is, the more practice or experience we acquire, the more proficient or knowledgeable we become.

Practice can be related to gaining proficiency in those particular activities that interest us. Often we hear what may sound as the one profound question confounding humanity, what is the meaning of our human existence? The answer may be to live a purposeful life by involving ourselves with, not passive pursuits, but instead, with active activities in which we become participants rather than mere spectators. The penchant for passive activities appears to be the popular "in-thing today. Millions of people involve themselves in viewing television with its abundance of mindless and unrealistic situational comedies known as "sitcoms," where all problems are solved in a matter of thirty minutes, sporting events and the ubiquitous talk shows. These shows, in particular, seem to have the tendency of manipulating, or altering in some manner, our ability to judge for ourselves.

Sporting events appear to lead the field in what can be likened to a popular pastime of indulging in passive activities. These activities, or better yet, in-activities engage hordes of people, especially males, in viewing sporting games on television, at huge stadiums, or at athletic halls. There, their manner of bonding with other males is demonstrated by their ability to describe certain aspects of the game, and identify the players by their names. Realistically speaking, can this method of socializing be a productive activity leading to a purposeful life? At this point, I'll let the reader be the judge of that.

Passivity can, indeed, be a disruptive paralysis for us; it can detract us from our creative abilities. What's more, it may have the effect of demoralizing us into a state of frustration knowing we lack those abilities we have seen in others. The overall effect may be the loss of our self-esteem and our self-confidence; as a result we tend to become unsure of ourselves. That we may have forgotten that those others whom we have seen perform were not born with prowess, is what can help us to become more active and less passive beings. Involving ourselves actively with doing and practicing will give us the opportunity to make mistakes and learn from them, thereby improving our capabilities. In becoming productive rather than non-productive, inactive and submissive beings, we maximize our worth as individuals.

Dwelling on these thoughts from another perspective, virtually at one time or another we tend to seek-out, or better yet, pursue new purposes in life that might perhaps fulfill our longings, desires, or what may possibly bring some pleasures into our lives. These needs can be liken to people who, despite the abundance of drinking water at their disposal, still search for other means to quench their thirst. For these people, this relentless search for fields to explore, other avenues to walk on, or in general, discoveries that can in some manner stimulate their senses, may be seen as a type of psychological or physiological abnormality; others may see it as a character disorder. However, in carefully analyzing this behavior, isn't true that we humans are continuously striving for new experiences, novel situations and new surroundings in which, if only for a short period of time, we are stimulated by the newness of it all?

The stimulus, whether spiritual or from natural causes may, in fact, be what really motivates us into developing new purposes in our lives, for example, concepts, objectives and goals to achieve. This purpose can be seen as a magnet that relentlessly attracts those of us who have the desire to maintain a level of constancy in the manner in which we strive for new goals once our old ones have been attained. In essence, this continuous striving to achieve constitutes a part of our physical and spiritual matters that make up Homosapiens.

But why have a purpose in life? Isn't it better to dwell in our leisure day after day with absolutely no obligations or commitments to anyone, but instead, caring for ourselves focusing only on the essentials, food, shelter and clothing to sustain the cycle of life? Further, how will this purposeless existence affect us, particularly if we were to prolong it for any length of time? Eventually, of course, boredom will be the initial signs of danger. At this point, the reader may ask why is the writer relating danger to boredom? Adding more to the question, how can we correlate danger with boredom?

Before proceeding further with this point of view, danger should be defined as a method of adding more clarity to what may be seen as simply a value judgment, or perhaps, the philosophy of a layman. Clearly brought into focus, danger can be comparable with anything that may cause physical or psychological harm on our being. To be sure, this harm can produce additional stress on our love ones who may be witnessing our gradual submergence into depths of danger. Indulgences with drug abuse, excessive alcohol consumption, or worse, coming into physical contact with a person who has the aids virus, will result in harmful effects on our bodies.

Referring further to the original thought, boredom, indeed, stems from too much leisure, and boredom can be the devil's advocate for getting us into danger. In our lives' cycle, it may be a fact that too much of anything tends to create in us a sense of restlessness to the point where we seek other outlets, if not to amuse us, at least to occupy our mind in our relentless search for what I have chosen to label the variables in our lives; the danger may in fact originate from the abundance of too much leisure. In making this statement, I may sound somewhat of a doomsday quack to the reader. Nevertheless, isn't it a fact that leisure, rather, than motivate us with constructive concepts, instead, generates in us thoughts in how we can amuse ourselves solely for the purpose of enjoyment? It is this search for joys that perhaps may be beyond our reach that is apt to make us vulnerable to unforeseen dangers.

Activities as the means for involving ourselves with efforts so as to attain some purpose in our lives can be the solution, not to boredom, but rather to the leisure that in whatever manner it chooses to approach us, ultimately can cause adverse results, or needless pain and hardships. The leisure in our lives appears to be the demon in disguise that lurks around us waiting patiently for the moment it can pounce and assault us with all its might. But what exactly are these activities, which may serve us as the weapons to defend ourselves from the evils of leisure?

CHAPTER 43

Activities, and Fear of the Unknown

Of course, at this point I'm not prepared to cite all the activities accessible to the reader. What I propose to do, however, is highlight a few of them in order to perhaps generate some enthusiasm in how we can best utilize our times of leisure. Lets begin with music; not the passive act of listening to it, but actually producing pleasing sounds with a musical instrument. Some of us may not be aware there is a distinct difference between a musical sound, or tone, and the common noises we hear every day. A musical sound has a specific frequency according to its low and high tones. For example, when we pluck a string on a guitar, it will vibrate a particular number of times; likewise, the sound waves produced by the vibrations will also have the same identical number of waves. In effect, this number is the frequency of the sound wave, or its equivalent, the musical tone. Musicians, in order to produce high or low tones on a string instrument, vary the length of the strings. For instance, the strings on a guitar are lengthened and shorten by simply pressing down between two frets on the instrument's neck. On a classical guitar, the frets on the neck of the instrument divide the strings that lie along the neck into twelve sections. On a violin, varying the length of the strings is done by pressing down on the strings that are along the neck's instrument. To conclude, it can be said that the shorter and thinner a string on a musical instrument is, the higher will be its tone and frequency. In contrast to musical tones, however, the common sounds heard in our everyday lives have no distinct frequencies, only their irregular vibrations.

Now lets return to the proposal of music as a way for expending our moments of leisure. Learning to play a musical instrument can not only be a way for entertaining others as well as ourselves, but of more importance, it can be a method for developing our capacity to acquire the discipline, patience and perseverance that are the prerequisites for achieving any success in whatever we are striving for. Discipline is developed as a result of the hours devoted to practice sessions during which we attempt to gain proficiency in playing the instrument. Thus, we become aware that the more we apply ourselves to a task, the better we're able to perform it. Undoubtedly, it is valuable to note that the ability to devote ourselves persistently to any particular task is what increases the potential for improving our skills in whatever endeavor we undertake.

Another activity in which we can involve ourselves is learning to speak and understand a foreign language; granted, it is not something that is learned quickly. Nevertheless, if one acquires the patience and the realization that, most likely, it will be a lengthy process, which for best results should be related as a hobby, one can, indeed, achieve some success in the ability to speak and understand a foreign language. Associating the process with that of a hobby rather than an arduous task resulting in learning anxieties should instill the learner with some amounts of pleasure. Maximum learning, in fact, can be achieved when the task becomes a pleasurable experience, rather than an ordeal requiring an immense amount of time, work and effort. Learning a foreign language can also reward a person with knowledge of another country's culture, customs, beliefs and values.

The process of learning another language, moreover, can be made less demanding and more enjoyable by selecting a language, which, in all probability, will not be too difficult to learn; ideally, this can be a foreign language that is heard and spoken in the community. Some languages are extremely hard to learn, for example, Chinese, Japanese, and believe it or not, English, and one of the problems is the letters do not always represent the sounds of the words. From experience with learners, I have discovered that most foreigners encounter this problem when learning English; a phonetic language such as Spanish can be easier to learn. As an illustration, each of the twenty seven letters in the Spanish language's alphabet has its distinct individual sound, and the sounds of the letters do not vary from one word to another as they do in English. Once a person memorizes the sounds of the letters, he or she is able to pronounce any word in the Spanish language. A notable aspect to point out is that, in order to accelerate the process, learners should make the effort to hear the language being learned as frequently as possible. Languages are like music, the more we hear tunes, the sooner we're able to learn their melodies. Similarly, the more we hear foreign words, the sooner we're able to learn their sounds and meanings.

A third activity that may be of interest is painting, not house painting of course, but painting with oils on canvas. In effect, it can be the therapeutic relief we need for the ordinary stresses that at times get a hold of us. Indeed, the "peace of mind," and the elusive tranquility we often yearn for can be difficult to grasp. Attaining them may allow us to escape into a world in which the latent creativity that's inherent in our being can be released for others a well as ourselves to admire. The hobby can also be the remedy for calming jangled nerves, thus soothing the body of its uneasiness, and in all probability, arousing the senses. This arousal allows us to slip away to a world of glorious colors and creativity. What's more, unlike learning to play a musical instrument or a foreign language, painting does not require any previous training. Eventually however, the novice should acquire some formal instructions in order to further develop the skills. For the beginner painting may be like the non-swimmer who plunges into the deep water, moves the arms in stroke fashion, and is able to remain above water. Likewise, the neophyte painter by simply mixing various colors can obtain some good results on canvas. The activity may not only arouse the senses, but can also be the precursor for your first abstract painting. In short, there you have but a mere three of the countless ways in which to cope against boredom during our times of leisure.

Actively becoming involved with activities may not only nurture the soul, but can also be an outlet against the fear of the unknown. Isn't it a fact that at some point in our lives we experience some anxiety from not knowing the outcome of a situation? Knowledge, whether acquired from reading, observing or experiencing, that is, the actual experience of doing something, can be a remedial source for our mental distress arising from the fear of the unknown. In answer to the question of how we process knowledge, some philosophers have provided us with the traditional answer that that knowledge is gathered "entirely from sense experience." On the other hand, other philosophers have argued that knowledge is attained by our inherent reasoning abilities. It's not the purpose at this time to cast judgment on the merits of these answers. Rather, what may be of significance, at least from my point of view is what, in fact, is the meaning of knowledge?

The question of how we acquire knowledge can be a philosophical issue that's beyond the scope of this writer. In a practical mode, nonetheless, three ways of acquiring knowledge have already been stated. Keeping this perspective on a practical level, knowledge may simply mean having answers to unknown questions. Once we know the answers to specific questions relating to particular settings or situations, the knowledge, to some extent at least, relieves us of the anxiety directly related to not knowing. One of the country's past Presidents, Franklin Delano Roosevelt, in a far reaching statement and often quoted said, "The only thing we have to fear is fear itself." Whether intentionally or nor, what he failed to do was to specify the fear, for example, the fear of what?

Generally speaking, fear can be said to be the expectations of physical or emotional harm from unknown sources, or unfamiliar situations. In order to cope with these types of fears, we should obtain some knowledge, and a "sense of experience" of the unknown. By reading, studying and receiving guidance from others, preferably in a formal setting, we can, indeed, gain some knowledge; the experience, of course, is attained with practice, in effect, by actively doing whatever we're going to be tested on, or required to perform in a specific task. We humans, in general, have an inborn capacity for learning on our own. Nevertheless, there are times, in particular, when confronted with the unknown that we must prepare ourselves by seeking other sources for the information, which will most likely relieve us from the fear of the unknown.

The reader may now draw our attention to what may be the biggest fear of all, the fear of dying. How can we ever prepare ourselves against this fear? Further, if there is an after-life after death, how can we also prepare ourselves for this afterlife? We can classify these as two profound philosophical questions, which I have neither the expertise nor the background experience to answer them; nor will I ever attain these prerequisites. I can, nonetheless, speculate about answers to the two questions. However, in dealing with the former one, the thought that readily comes to mind is religion. For some people religion may serve to not only regulate their conduct, but also to prepare them for death. Fear of mortality may have led most of the humans on this earth to seek some type of religious following in which an All Mighty God is worshiped most likely for the sole purpose of providing them with an everlasting life after death; and the Savior, as long as they behave themselves on earth, will provide them with a blissful life in heaven after their death. These words may have a tone of mockery, however, the intent here is not to offend or ridicule anyone's religious beliefs, but merely to cast an opinion on how the writer feels about religions. In many respects, all religions, barring none, are beneficial to man, for example, they provide him with rules of conduct which will serve as guidelines for conforming to the standards of behavior in a society.

Religion may, indeed, help some of us to deal with the fear of dying, and its aftermath, which still remains unknown to all mankind. But what about the agnostic individuals, the non-believers of a God, nor about "the final nature of things?"

At the risk of repeating myself, assuming there doe exists the emotional fear of dying, how can we protect ourselves against this fear? The realization that nothing on this earth lives forever may be of some comfort. Everyone and everything has a final end; this is nature's basic law. Moreover, this leads me to question whether we have a spirit or soul, and if so, does this spirit and soul also have their end. The answer is far beyond this writer's knowledge; I simply don't know. What I'm aware of, nevertheless, is that we are, indeed, part of nature, and a nature that recycles itself over and over again. This on-going cycle never ends, and the awareness of this fact may relieve us from the emotional fear of our inevitable end. The human animal is a species having common inherited characteristics who will breed with other members having these same common characteristics. Analyzing this evolution of life pattern, we should realize that we just don't vanish into thin air once our lives end. Rather, we leave an imprint of ourselves on those who have inherited some features of our physical self. Similarly to what our ancestors have handed down to us, we leave a legacy of our physical being on our off springs.

Nature, to some extent perhaps, may prepare us for coping with our mortality. Unless the occurrence of instant death in wars, or by catastrophic accidents in which we are oblivious of their happenings, nature does alert us with warning signs. Our bodies' energy gradually diminishes to the point were we become immobile and confined to bed. This tends to happen when we are seriously or terminally ill, and imminent death is near. All physical, and at times spiritual drive fade from the body. There is no motivation whatsoever, and all purposes for living become questionable. We lose all sense of time, and perhaps this is when we no longer have the will to go on living, and have reconciled ourselves for the moment of death to arrive. Indeed, perhaps nature does prepare us for our inevitable end, and the awareness of it may further help us to deal with the fear of death.

CHAPTER 44

Afterlife

There will be no attempts to answer the question, how does one prepare for an afterlife? In doing so might imply that I'm a believer in an afterlife, which I am not. Instead, before returning to recollections from my past, opinions and reaction will be offered briefly regarding this issue. For a beginning, what in fact is afterlife? Is it made-up of a heaven or a hell? and can this heaven or hell be our afterlife after death? Death is the mortal nature of man that awaits us all, and there can be absolutely no doubt in any one's mind that we are, indeed, mortal beings. But realistically speaking, can there ever be an everlasting life in a blissful heaven where all is good and free from evil? And in contrast to this, can there also be an everlasting living hell underground in which the burning fury of fires and heat offer no mercy to any of its occupants? The good people, because of their virtuous, righteous and honorable behavior on earth are granted admittance to heaven; whereas, the wicked, dishonest, vicious and immoral ones are condemned to a hell that offers them no amnesty, no possibilities for redeeming themselves in any way or manner with their good behavior. Before proceeding further with this issue, we should accept the fact that there are many people who are firm believers in a heaven and a hell, and this must be honored as their exclusive rights to choose whatever faith suits them.

There are, moreover, people who believe the body has a soul that has a re-birth in a new body, after having expired. This reincarnation belief has the meaning of an afterlife for those people; furthermore, there are those of us who are non- believers in an afterlife. For some, including this writer, there is the conviction that heaven and hell are right here on earth. Related to this opinion is the though that the level of dedication and perseverance of individuals in whatever endeavor they may choose to participate in can be the determining factor in considering the ones who most likely will experience on earth all that personifies the good life in heaven. Clearly defining this point of view, it is those individuals who realize that they have the capability to make things happen by means of their will power, tenacity and resiliency who will, ultimately, reap the rewards of success. We can correlate this with persons who undertake personalized missions by placing demands on themselves to succeed at any cost in order to accomplish whatever task is undertaken. Their attempt may not always be achieved, nevertheless, one of the rewarding aspects is that they begin to feel a sense of worth in becoming aware they have indeed made the effort, and will of course continue to do so.

A clear line of distinction can be drawn by those who attain success, and the unfortunate ones who are destined to become failures. In our political, social and economic structure, success, in effect, can mean unlimited access to dollars, which will buy whatever needs we desire, including the basic ones, good housing, good health care, and a good education for our children. When we have the power, that is, the money resources to satisfy all our needs, we may have arrived at our heaven on earth. Lacking this form of success, and granted, there are many types too numerous to cite in the context of this work, many hardships can be the reality we can expect to encounter in our daily lives.

At the opposite end of the spectrum there is a group of pitiful people who, because of unforeseen circumstances beyond their control, have failed to climb the ladder of success.

Further, another group who has failed to succeed are the social dropouts or misfits, the drug abusers, alcoholics and those who practice some types of deviant behaviors. Finally, there is a group who may not merit any pity whatsoever in their failure to achieve. These are the people who lack the motivational drive to get ahead, or worse, are the lazy individuals with absolutely no purpose in life other than to exist from day-to-day on the charity of others. These groups of failures, with some exceptions of course, are destined to experience the hardships directly associated with a poverty level, which can be compared to a hell right here on earth.

CHAPTER 45

Amusements and Fashions

A poverty existence beyond a boy's comprehension appeared to be ebbing away with the passing of time. The country was rapidly preparing for war, not with Japan, but to come to England's aid in that Nation's efforts to defeat Nazi Germany. Factories, better known as defense plants that manufactured war materials were opening-up everywhere, notably in the northeastern part of New Jersey creating jobs for both men and women. Mother and my stepfather were busy working for the Nation's "war effort," she toiling away as a seamstress sewing garments for the Arm Forces, and he had managed to obtain a job painting war ships at the Brooklyn Navy Yard. The Nation's economy was growing, and though I was not aware of it at the time, the depression was rapidly coming to an end.

The war in Europe, from the Allies point of view, was at its grimmest level. Germany's armies had succeeded in the objective they had failed to achieve in World War I, and that was to occupy Paris. With the fall of its beautiful city, France's military resistance totally collapsed. France had relied primarily on its vulnerable Maginot Line for protection against a feared enemy, and as a result, paid a heavy price for it. Germany's armies eluded the line, which was a system of heavily fortified pillboxes and tank traps along France's eastern border, by merely outflanking it; and they succeeded in invading the country from the borders of Belgium, which they had already added to their collections of defeated countries.

Aside from improving the economy, the war in Europe appeared to have no effect on the people in this country. However, no one realized it at the time, perhaps not even the government, that in less than a year's time, the Nation would be at war with Japan. Ironic though it may seem, during an earlier period the Sixth Avenue El had been torn down, and its enormous amount of scrap iron was sold to the Country's future war enemy, Japan. The El's departure to Japan brought a wealth of sun light, clear air and the quietness the neighborhood never realized had ever existed. The environmental improvement for people long accustomed to a situation of rumbling noises and daylight darkness seem to invigorate them with a new found energy and vitality. Moreover, with the rapid growth of the economy, they finally had access to surplus dollars enabling them to amuse themselves in their hours of leisure.

"Swing" music had become the Nation's passion. The bands of Glen Miller, Tommy Dorsey and Benny Goodman, among others, were at their peak in popularity. Playing, or "spinning" records as it was known, on radio station WNEW, Martin Block and Art Ford were the icons of the airwaves with their programs, "The Make Believe Ballroom," and "The Milkman's Matinee." Art Ford's program, in particular, was aptly titled since the latter part of its "air time" occurred during the time milkmen were making their deliveries. "The Milkman's Matinee" was broadcast between the hours of midnight and 6AM in the morning. The radio and the phonograph were the home entertainment mediums in that pre-World War II era. In dance halls, better known as ballrooms, church recreational halls and at school auditoriums, young people danced the "foxtrot," and "the jitterbug" to the sounds and rhythms of "swing" music. Indeed, this type of music was the Nation's prime choice in popularity, and dancing had become the national pastime.

Other types of entertainments, for example, the comedy hours and melodramas on radio, sporting events, and notably, the movies provided escapism for masses of people, most of whom spent their time, not in the luxury activities of traveling, dining in expensive restaurants, or attending the theatre, the opera, or concert halls, but instead, in a dreary existence in which their days were consumed in tedious monotonous factory work. Radio's comedy hour programs with Jack Benny, Fred Allen, Fiber McGee and Molly, and the exciting and often frightening melodramas, especially, "The Shadow," "Inner Sanctum," and "The Lone Ranger, which had a vast appeal for both young and old alike, was one of the reasons why radio had become the most popular medium for home entertainment in its day. Another reason may have been the extreme low cost of owning this appliance. A mere ten dollars, which was the average price for a good table model, made it possible for a person to own one of these small gem appliances that furnished its owner with an array of entertainment fare for only a few pennies a month, the cost paid to a utility company for the use of electricity.

In contrast to the low cost paid for the entertainment heard on the radio, one had to pay, though very little in comparison to today's prices, to see a movie, or a sporting event at a stadium or arena. The movie, "Gone With The Wind" was in its cinematic glory, and the movie stars, Mickey Rooney and Judy Garland reigned as "king and queen" in popularity, both of whom were under contract to the biggest producers of fantasy entertainment in Hollywood, Metro Goldwyn Meyer Studios, widely known as M.G.M.. "The New York Yankees," with their roster of star players, one of whom was the graceful center fielder and power hitter, "Jolting" Joe Dimaggio, dominated professional baseball. Later in his career "Jolting Joe" would establish a baseball record, which has yet to be broken, by getting one or more hits in fifty six consecutive games.

Crew cuts were the prevailing fashion with boys. The widespread style most likely originated in Germany by army soldiers who were always seen in Hollywood movies with these types of haircuts. Teen aged girls known as "Bobby Sockers," wore their hair in bangs that covered half their foreheads, and the length of the hair never exceeded beyond the back of the neck. A distinct feature noticeable to all were the bright colored rayon ribbons worn on their hair; and how was this done may be asked? A long ribbon about an inch or more in width was pinned at its middle to the top of the head, with both ends of the ribbon dangling, and reaching the back of the girl's hairline to form what appeared to look like a large upside down letter U. To the keen observer, crew cuts and bright rayon ribbons symbolized the rites of passage for these adolescents in their impressionable years.

Clothing styles of the young adolescent generation were significantly more conservative than what they are today. In those days there were no "T" undershirts, at least I don't recall ever seen them on men or boys who, as was the custom, wore undershirts that were sleeveless. Not until I was issued clothing "gear" in the Navy did I see a "T" undershirt, or what was to become after the war the highly popular Navy "Skivvy" shirt, or the white undershirt with sleeves extending from the shoulder to just above the elbows. Usually, the custom for boys was to wear flannel shirts in various bright colors over their white shirts and neckties to school. By contrast, sweaters were the popular garments with the girls. In fact, the garment became so popular that a pretty eighteen year old blond movie star named Lana Turner was given the title "The Sweater Girl" by her movie studio bosses. To a Spanish speaking person, the name Lana, which in Spanish means wool, may have personified a girl who had a penchant for wearing sweaters. Realistically however, I suspect the title may have been given to highlight the girl's ample bosom.

Trousers, or long pants, were, of course, worn by men, however, young adolescent boys wore both trousers and knickers. On the other hand, girls were never seen in slacks or jeans, which in that era were known as dungarees, and worn only by carpenters, electricians and janitors. Instead, the popular fashion for girls were the knee length pleated skirts, and their ever-present sweaters. Notably different from nowadays among the adolescent boys, was the manner in which they wore their long pants. Pants were rolled-up to at least four inches above the upper part of the shoes. This was the accepted fashion at a time when to be a non-conformist automatically categorized you as an outcast. Furthermore, the style was ideally suited for displaying the extremely popular "saddle backs," which were white shoes with bands of brown or black leather across their insteps and at the back of the shoes. On occasions, these types of shoes can still be seen worn by both men and women, but particularly by men who often wear them at golf courses.

CHAPTER 46

The Young Teenage Years

These were the initial teenage years when the sufferings from the fears of not belonging were fading away rapidly. No longer was I called Spani, a nickname that I loathed then, and which I still do to this day. To better submerge myself in a neighborhood made-up of predominantly Irish and Italian families, I Italianized my middle name to Angelo. And finally, I had acquired friends who only knew me as Angelo, a name that appealed to me, most likely perhaps because of its Italian origin. In those years when all teenagers, with some exceptions of course, were held in constraints by the innocence of their youth, I had delusions of someday in the future passing myself off as an Italian. As near as I can recall, there were times, though I must admit not too many of them when, in fact, I did identify myself to newly acquired friends as being Italian. Shameful as it may seem to me at this moment, I was under the impression at the time that there was indeed some sort of a stigma attached to being Spanish, and therefore, I had to rid myself of my Spanish heritage.

During the course of a life time, and there may be a whole lot of truth in what I'm about to say, the self-esteem of a person is most vulnerable in the formative years of physical growth when all that matters to the innocent youthful mind is to be like all the others. Granted, it's a broad observation, and one which should be perceived solely as the writer's point of view; nevertheless, it can be the innocence of youth that undermines our capacity to cherish our uniqueness, to realize that we are, indeed, human entities endowed with individual physical attributes, traits and values. Yet, during our youth, or more precisely, during the teenage years, we tend to suppress our individuality in order to conform to our peers' mainstream values, their styles, and all that relates to popular trends. We mimic all that we observe, ever fearful that to be different from the others will alienate us from the herd. The formative years, in terms of associating them with a sense of ourselves, can be a period when our self-doubts are at their highest level, and as a result, we become emotionally insecure. Coming to terms with ourselves, in effect, with critical reflections of external realities, and how they apply to us, and to our inner being, come much later in our lives. It is then that we become keenly aware of our antecedents, who we really are and where we came from. This, however, is not the wisdom that's imbedded in a teenager's mind in today's world, nor for that matter, during the world of my youth. Many years were to pass before I acquired the wisdom and sensibilities to apply these observations I have just discussed.

The growth process during the teenage years can, to some extent, be like the budding years of human nature. Not unlike all animal beginnings, the process has a gradual start before accelerating rapidly into the peak of manhood years. Midway through this growth process, we become cognizant of psychological and physiological changes in both our minds and our bodies. Further, it is during this period that we lose our childhood innocence, an attribute that can never again be re-lived in our lifetime. Actively participating in athletic and social activities, I had arrived at the threshold of these budding years. As for the progress in school, it was more or less on an even keel, that is, the ship never sinking, but always moving ahead, though rather slowly on occasions, and to a destination unknown to me at the time. This was a period when I earned a bit of spending money by delivering bags of groceries and dry cleaned garments to apartment dwellers. Tips were the sole means of earning what in today's times is referred to as "loose change." Wages were earned only if one were lucky enough to find an all-day delivery boy's job on Saturdays or Sundays in a grocery store, and I was never that fortunate.

Selling The Saturday Evening Post magazines was another way of enabling a young teenage boy to earn gifts rather than money. The magazines sold for five cents a copy, and were picked-up at a stationary store, or what was known in that era as a candy store. Once the magazines were sold, the money was mailed to the company, and in about four or five weeks you received whatever gift you had selected in the gift catalog, depending of course on the amount of magazines sold. One of my gifts was a beautiful small jackknife with a red plastic handle and stainless steel blades, similar to the super expensive Swiss army jackknifes that are sold today. Another one of my favorite gifts was the "candid camera." The camera, though much cheaper by today's standards, had a fast shutter speed, which allowed you to take a clear picture of a moving subject, and its unique feature of having to hold the camera against the eye to see the subject and then snap the shutter was a new concept in hand-held cameras. By contrast, a "box camera," such as the popular "Brownie" had to be held against the stomach to take the picture, and the subject had to be perfectly still, otherwise the image on the print appeared blurred, or out of focus.

A precious possession obtained, not by selling magazines, but bought with the scanty savings from tips earned delivering groceries and dry cleaned garments, was my first dictionary. Huge is the right word to describe the dark green book containing over two thousand pages of English words, most of which I still didn't know their meanings. The reader may question the feasibility of purchasing such a large dictionary when a small paperback would have been less expensive and more practical. This is quite true, however, I had no other recourse since there were no paperbacks in those times. I can only assume the technology for binding books with hard paper covers had yet to be developed. The first time that I can remember seeing and reading paperbacks was on board a naval troop transport bound for Guadalcanal Island in the South Pacific. Reminiscing about this experience, what arouses some feelings of regret about the early teenage years is that I had to wait until the eighth grade in school before I was able to own a dictionary.

Those were the years of athletic clubs, primarily made-up of teenage boys, though there were one or two girls clubs in the neighborhood. All the boys wore jackets with their clubs' names and colors. Individual members' names were printed on the front of the jackets; Celtics, Pirates and Shamrocks were some of the clubs' names. I was a member of "The Raiders," and our club's colors were red and white. That I was already a member of one club didn't prevent me from being a member of another. In the "Longhorn" club we not only had jackets, but also jerseys with the gray colored letters of the club's name on a maroon colored background, and the emblem of a longhorn steer on the front of the pull-over jerseys. Members of the two clubs were actively involved in athletic activities, and to some extent, in social functions. Stickball played on City streets, basketball on Riverside Park and football in Van Cortland Park were the games in which we competed with other clubs. In addition to the sporting games, there were, on numerous occasions, the house parties; More enjoyable, however, were the church dances held on Friday nights. At these dances where the customary boys' attire were flannel shirts, corduroy pants and the always present saddleback shoes, we jitterbugged to the recorded sounds of "swing" music. The favorite record we danced to was Benny Goodman's rendition of "The Jersey Bounce."

Basketball was the popular spectator sport in the neighborhood. A weekly ritual, usually on Saturday evenings, were the games held at "The Police Athletic League," which was a newly formed community center sponsored and supervised by the New York City Police Department. Widely known by its acronym, "P.A.L.," the center had acquired an old church at 108th Street off Manhattan Avenue, which was no longer used as a house of worship, and had converted the small building into a small sports complex. In the basement was what today may be referred to as a professional size boxing ring surrounded by paraphernalia associated with this physically violent sport, namely, punching bags, large canvas bags dangling by chains from the ceiling and thick rubber mats on the floor. The oval shaped gym with its basketball court was on the main floor, and on the second floor directly above the gym was a balcony that enabled spectators to get an overhead view of the basketball court. It was on this balcony that on many Saturday evenings I watched, with carefully disguised pleasure, ever mindful not to offend my friends, the hated "Aztecs" basketball team beat the much taller players from our neighborhood. The smaller players on the Aztecs team were all Spanish teenagers from upper Manhattan.

Reflecting on these happenings, what strikes me at this moment as somewhat of an anomaly is remembering the lengthy training sessions that were devoted by instructors in teaching kids how to become good boxers. Mindful of the fact that all the instructors were police officers, one is inclined to seriously question what appeared to be a flawed philosophy of the P.A.L.. Why sanction a brutal sport that essentially involved two boys pommeling each other's bodies with fists covered with leather until one of them was declared the winner, for what purpose, perhaps to influence violent and destructive behavior among young teenagers? Critically remembering this, one becomes aware in how a City's Police Department legitimized a program, which realistically speaking, could benefit only a few unfortunate boys who, most likely, eventually would become prize fighters.

CHAPTER 47

The Unexpected Factor

The sport of boxing, unlike basketball, had no appeal for me whatsoever, either as a participant or as a spectator. What did in fact held my interest was swimming. Despite their limitations, there were only two inexpensive outdoor park pools in the City, and naturally, opened only during the summer, swimming still had a special attraction for me. Of course, there were indoor pools in hotels opened to the public all year. However, all of them, including the highly popular one at the St. George Hotel in Brooklyn, were too expensive for the average teenager from my neighborhood to patronize, and as a result, the swimming sessions were confined to the months of summer.

Interest in swimming most likely may have begun at an early age in a river near the small farm in Puerto Rico where I lived with my uncle, his wife and his siblings. It was there that, barely six years old, I acquired the rudiments of swimming, for example, how to float in deep water without any fear, and swim from one side of the river to the other by "dog paddling." Many years later these basic skills were to be further developed during the annual two weeks of summer camp for "underprivileged children" from the City funded by the New York Herald Tribune's "Fresh Air Fund." The point to underscore is that as a young teenager I was indeed a good swimmer; so good in fact that one memorable scorching hot day in August, I decided to join two of my friends from the "Longhorn" club in what no boy as far as we knew, had ever attempted, swim the Hudson River from one side to the other.

Unfamiliarity in a strange environmental setting, or in any situation, can be a breeding ground for unforeseen problems, or worse yet, for a life-threatening crisis to occur. Without any prior pre-planning, any endeavor, whether it's taking an examination, making a presentation to a large body of people, or for instance, the following incident in which three teenage boys attempt a dangerous task, is doomed to fail in one way or another. Not one among the three of us was familiar with the movement of tides, nor the treacherous current of the river. We boarded the 125th Street ferry after each of us payed the five cents fare, and crossed the Hudson River so as to begin our adventure from an old dock at the River's western shoreline in Fort Lee, New Jersey. Unfortunately, we chose to start our swim from the New Jersey side, thus preventing us from realizing the tide's movement was from west to east, or from the Jersey side to the river's New York shoreline.

Removing our clothing and hiding them underneath some logs on the old dock, we swiftly swam in our bathing suits to about the middle of the river with the strong tide aiding us all the way. That we stopped at the mid-point to admire a small schooner anchored there, may have been the deterrent factor that caused us to realize the river was too wide, and requiring stamina, which we may not have had for swimming to the New York shore. As if to restrain ourselves from an unknown fear, we decided to turn back and head for the Jersey shore. No sooner had we reversed our course that we felt the strength of the tide acting like a hidden force impeding our forward progress in the river's murky waters. Compounding our misfortunes was the fear of impending distress in noticing the swift current was literally dragging us southward, and away from where we had begun our adventure. Despite all efforts to compensate for the strong current, we were still moving at a much faster rate downstream than toward our intended objective, the old dock. Oblivious of time, with minutes turning into hours, and with both the tide and current gradually draining our stamina, the likelihood of not having the endurance to swim to the Jersey shore became a matter of great concern for us. Swimming side-by-side struggling to reach the shore, and almost at the point of total exhaustion, we kept encouraging one another not to give-up, but to keep swimming toward the shore. Finally, we did succeed in reaching the shoreline, and immediately collapsed on tierra firma for about an hour. The scene was one of three youthful bodies clad only in bathing suits lying on the river's Jersey shore thoroughly drained of all energy. The long hours consumed in what initially was to be a great adventure had evolved into a frightening ordeal in which three boys found themselves struggling desperately with the forces of the Hudson River.

The area where we had reached the shore must have been somewhere in the sixties or seventies, so that it took us over two hours to walk back to the old dock where we had left our clothes. The hot August day had cool significantly with gentle summer breezes by the time I arrived home late that night. While my stepfather and his son slept soundly, my poor mother had kept a vigil watch for her only son, always worrying about his welfare and safety. On seeing me she burst into tears hugging me tightly as if I had been away from her for a year. Graciously I accepted my mother's love for me, and a sincere and caring love it was that I was never to doubt in all the years of her long life. She was a young woman then, in her early thirties, though at the time I considered her to be much older, perhaps because she was my mother, or more likely due to the fact I was at a young sprouting age when what seem to matter the most was how "the significant others" perceived me. Naturally these were dimensions of behavior that applied, in general, to all teenagers in those days, and in all probability, may also apply to present day teenagers.

A keen sense of how these "significant others" perceived me may have reached its utmost point on graduation day, after completing the ninth grade in mid-level school, or what was known then as junior high school. Ninth grade in the City's public schools was actually the first year of high school. On graduation day the proper attire, or what is now commonly known as "the dress code," for young men on the threshold of beginning their second year of high school was the suit with jacket, vest and matching pants. I was not to own a suit until discharged from the Navy after World

War II, and there was the problem. Predictably, the need to wear a suit for that special occasion almost overwhelmed my dear mother. Ultimately, she made arrangements to borrow a suit from one of my cousins that she promised would fit me as if it were my own. Needless to say, the suit never did fit me; yet, I had no other options except to wear the suit. And despite the major alterations made by a mother's skills as seamstress, she was unable to adjust the large jacket to fit my small frame. Lingering memories persisted for months from the shame I endured on that horrible day in knowing my teachers and classmates were aware that the suit I wore to my graduation was not my own.

Unlike the shame caused by humiliation, disappointments in life, though less penetrating to the soul than shame, can be directly related to depression. This state of mind may be a permanent nature in some people, particularly in those individuals with mental health problems. Nevertheless, in the majority of us, as we grow older and wiser with age, we tend to become cognizant of the fact that depression in humans is an ailment which sooner or later occurs in all of us. Usually it can be caused by the failure of our expectations, or failures to achieve a goal. Knowing the depression is transitory in nature and not an everlasting illness, but rather, a brief adverse interlude lasting but a short period of time, or perhaps no more than a day, and which time will gradually heal the wound, we learn to cope with this state of mind.

Learning to deal with depression unfortunately for most of us may seldom happen during our teenage years. This observation may serve to highlight an incident that happened at the very beginning of the high school years. I should, however, preface what I'm about to say with what has previously been mentioned, my interest in learning to play a musical instrument. Hence, on finding out the music department was recruiting student freshmen to enroll in musical instructions for the purpose of eventually joining the school band, I immediately applied. Great expectations were envisioned at that very moment without realizing a particular criterion had to be met before one qualified to receive musical instructions.

The day of that fateful meeting with the music teacher finally arrived. Without any premonitions as to what was about to happen, and terribly excited over the prospects of someday playing in the school band, I entered a room, which at first glance, and later confirmed, appeared to be a small auditorium. A tall muscular black boy was standing with the teacher who was holding a beautiful silver trombone in his hand. Never before had I been so close to a brass instrument with such large dimensions. The horn was almost the length of my body. Handing me the instrument, which was heavier than I had realized, the teacher advised me to blow into the instrument's mouthpiece. It was my misfortune that as hard as I tried, I was not able to produce any sound or tone from that big horn. Finally, after my numerous attempts, the teacher asks for the instrument, and hands it to the tall muscular youth who instantly blows a blaring tone that almost pierces my eardrums. The teacher then takes back the horn and says to me that since there is only one trombone available for practice, and doesn't think I have the required strong lungs to play the instrument, he is therefore selecting the tall youth to receive the musical instructions.

Initially, disappointment in my failure was the immediate reaction. As the hours passed by, I began to feel despondent, discouraged and depressed at my inability to perform for the music teacher. Searching for the right metaphor to describe the feeling for the reader at this moment, the only thing that comes to mind is how dark clouds can quickly dim the glow of sunlight from our being. Activity, which can be the effective remedy for curing some forms of depression, and which I indulged in by playing basketball in the gym after school hours, was what removed the dark clouds of despondency hovering above me for many hours after the incident.

Critically reflecting on the incident the following day, I came to the conclusion that I deserved the outcome from that meeting with the music teacher. Walking into what can be referred to as untried waters without any prior preparation, not unlike the river adventure, predisposed me to failure. A self-analysis of the situation in which sooner or later I would be interviewed by a music teacher, and perhaps demonstrate to him or her some potential musical ability may have led me to, somehow, find a horn, any type and practice on it before walking into that small auditorium. Nonetheless, it was a learning experience, and one that served me well in years to come. Never again was I to walk into untried or unknown situations without first preparing myself. Indeed, preparing ourselves can be correlated with the blocks we must use to build a framework of prudence to deal with, among other things, people whom we have never met before in a business setting, tests we are compelled to take in order to qualify, or be accepted to a position, speaking to a large audience, or the all important job interview.

To prepare ourselves for the unexpected is a guideline we should adhere to every moment of our lives. The truth is that sooner or later the unexpected does happen, though it may not always have an immediate impact on us. A good example of this is what occurred on a particular Sunday evening many years ago. As I have previously mentioned, the radio was the primary source of widespread home entertainment for virtually every family in the Nation; in fact, the custom at some time during the day or evening was for one or more members of the household to listen to the radio. Sunday evenings, in particular, was a special time for radio audiences when millions of people listened to favorite shows such as, "The Jack Benny Show," and "The Shadow." I was one of those millions who on Sunday evening at about 7:15 on December 7, 1941, heard the interruption of "The Jack Benny show" with the announcement that the Japanese Navy that early Sunday morning had bombed Pearl Harbor in the Hawaiian Islands. The following day Congress declared war on the Japanese Nation, and two days later Germany and Italy declared war on the United States. Consequently, within a period of three days, the Country became directly involved in the wars in Europe, Africa and Asia.

PART III
The War Years

CHAPTER 48

The Home Front

The rapid development of the war seem to swiftly engulf the Nation in a state of frenzy. Without any hesitation, legislators passed conscription laws requiring all males between the ages of eighteen and thirty five to register for the draft. Factories and shipyards went into full production, which quickly created manpower shortages resulting in women becoming the primary source of labor in factories or war plants. Not surprisingly, the songs "Rosie the Riveter" and "Let' Remember Pearl Harbor" became instant hits. Production of all aspects of war materials were accelerated to such a high level that the Henry J. Kaiser's shipyards were building one merchant ship a day. This was the same man who after the war manufactured the first, and extremely popular compact car in this Country, "The Henry J."

A sense of patriotism and "proud to be an American" took hold of the Nation's population. The large masses of Japanese residing on the west coast, most of whom were American citizens by birth were exiled to concentration camps in Nevada and Arizona. Everyone was instilled with an instant hatred for "the yellow skin enemy," perhaps stemming from their "sneak attack" on the Country's naval base in Hawaii. No longer were they referred to as Japanese, but instead, as the slant eyes Japs who had to be vanquished at whatever cost it took to defeat them. Overnight President Franklyn Roosevelt became the Savior who was going to lead his people to the promise land of victory. In similar fashion, General Douglas MacArthur was declared the Nation's war hero whose forces would quickly overrun the hated Japs. Indeed, besides the atomic bomb, the General did play a leading role in defeating the Japanese, but certainly not soon enough as expected by the American people. When the loss of the Philippine Islands was imminent, President Roosevelt ordered MacArthur to Australia to built-up new forces for the eventual invasion of these Islands. It took the Japanese forces only two months to defeat the General's army and take sole possession of America's largest colony.

The home front, as it was to be known for the remainder of the war years, had changed dramatically. New York City became bathed in almost total darkness during the night. A "blackout" had been imposed from sunset to sunrise as a precautionary measure against enemy air attacks. Illumination of all outdoor signs, including the huge neon lit billboards in Times Square was prohibited. Even the upper halves of automobile headlights had to be painted black in order to shield the glare of headlights from penetrating the night's darkness. As a result, the front of cars with a headlight at each side of their radiators had the odd appearances of human faces having enormous eyes whose eyelids appeared to be partially closed as though the face was dozing off; and no matter where one ventured at night and looked-up, all that was to be seen were the many light beams emanating from the large searchlights crossing one another constantly scanning the night sky for enemy aircraft.

Underground areas throughout the City were designated air raid shelters, and air raid wardens easily identifiable by their white steel helmets patrolled the streets at night. Air raid drills were a weekly ritual for City dwellers. Amidst these activities were also the endless sights of young servicemen on leave in their brown army uniforms and garrison hats, and sailors in "dress blues" during the winter months, and spotless white uniforms in the summer. Most of them were from the nearby Fort Dix Army Base in New Jersey, the Naval Air Base at Floyd Bennet Field in Brooklyn and the Navy ships that regularly arrived at the Hudson River's piers. As to be expected, the servicemen had a preference for Times Square where most of them flocked in groups to be met by droves of teenaged girls who congregated there specifically to meet them.

The United States Treasury, because of the deficiency of copper, minted the cent coins in a dull bluish gray metal, which were lighter in weight than the copper pennies. Of more important to the war plants, however, were the shortest of human resources. Most of the young men were either drafted or enlisted thus acute shortest of young civilian males soon developed creating a great demand for women labor. And what first became an inconvenience but soon evolved into a hardship for civilians were the shortest of some consumer goods, some of which were sugar, coffee, clothing, shoes, gasoline and name brand cigarettes. To compensate for this, ration stamps were issued to all who were eligible (the City dwellers) with imposed quotas for obtaining these goods. The aftermath of the rationing system, as to be expected, resulted in some individuals acquiring the penchant for hording. Even my dear mother, though with good intentions, became involved in this practice. About two years later, after having arrived home on leave from three months of basic training at the Naval Base in Sampson, New York, much to my surprise, I found many five pound bags of sugar under my bed. Confronting my mother about the discovery, she explained that to honor her request, her brother Juanito who had a bodega (grocery store) in Puerto Rico had been sending her bags of sugar; and because she had no need for all the sugar being sent to her, willingly, she had become the supplier for the much in demand commodity for all her friends and neighbors.

Despite the inconveniences and hardships of shortages, air raid drills and the depressing sight of darkness, which took hold of the City once the sun disappeared beyond the horizon, surprisingly, no anti-war sentiments existed; the people's morale seem to be at its highest level imagined. Confidence and a firm determination toward defeating the Germans in Europe and the Japanese in Asia permeated throughout the land; all human efforts were mobilized to achieve this objective. Production of war materials went into high gear both day and night. Tin cans and all other forms of scrap metal were saved, collected by the Sanitation Department, and eventually recycled into war products. Buying war bonds was declared by the Federal Government as everyone's patriotic duty to help "the war effort." And to continually replenish the arm forces with men, all young males who had not become seniors in high school by the age of seventeen were permitted to drop-out from school, but only on conditions they would enlist in one of the arm forces' branches. In about two years time, I was to become part of this group, though rather than enlist, I was drafted by the Navy.

Almost the entire Nation's population set its sights on developing the means for the ultimate destruction of other nations. Notable to bear in mind is the fact that these nations, then, as they are today, were inhabited by human beings. We can, therefore, conclude that this all-out effort was meant for the destruction of human life. How do we, as people endowed with the ability to reason, deal with what may be seen by many of us as the senseless reasoning that has always been prevalent in world societies? Does retaliating for what they did give us the moral right to destroy them? At this point, these questions prompts me to digress from the main topic, the home front, so as to expound briefly on one of the attributes of war, destructive behavior.

A bird's eye view of this destructive behavior, as if someone from above were looking and judging it, may aid us to get a clearer sense of what indeed is happening. To begin with, we should accept the fact that, in effect, man is an aggressive being. This innate attribute may have been instilled in him by an All Mighty God, by nature, or perhaps by both forces. However, isn't it also a fact that the aggressive behavior in man can be controlled? A controlled environment, whether in a group setting, a classroom or in Nations, is one in which the leaders have the power and the ability to, in some way or manner limit aggressive behavior. Before proceeding further with this line of thinking, it may help to define the type of behavior I'm referring to. Clearly, it is not the rowdy or disorderly conduct, which can be restrained with discipline, rather, it is the type of behavior that when acted-out inflicts severe bodily harm, even to the point of killing other human beings. How do we judge this destructive behavior? Or better yet, whom can we hold accountable for the carnage of wars?

Applying our power of reasoning, we can conclude that it is, in fact, the Nations' leaders and their subordinates who should be held responsible. We certainly cannot blame the followers, who unlike a bewildered herd, will follow commands without first questioning the moral logic in them. A good analogy that can be applied to this thought is a film a very young boy once saw many years ago; a young boy who had yet to mature to an age where he had acquired the capacity to better comprehend the film's underlying theme. Fortunately for him, he had the opportunity to view the film again at a much later time as a young man who fully understood the movie's message, and the impact it would have on him in years to come. The film, which was based on Erich Maria Remarque's classic novel, had the same title as the book, "All Quiet On The Western Front." Toward the very end of the movie, a "tight" close-up of the expression on the young German soldier's face visually and vividly defines for the viewer the absurdity of war. With his body crouched by the edge of the trench amid the explosions of bursting artillery shells, all that the young soldier sees and hears are the cries of wounded men whose bodies litter the trenches. At the moment he realizes he is destined to die soon, perhaps within a matter of minutes; and then, there is the "flashback" scene.

The young man who is not yet a soldier, but a college student listening to a lecture given by a supposedly knowledgeable and wise professor. What follows is a prime example of how innocent youthful minds can be easily manipulated. The professor instilled with intense patriotic fervor is expounding the Country's past military successes, and ends the lecture by advising them that rather than being in a classroom learning mostly "nonsense," they should be in the army fighting for the glory of their "Fatherland." The scene ends with all the students standing, their right arms held high with clenched fists singing Germany's national anthem; then, led by the old professor, they march off to enlist. Interesting to note that the American actor, Lew Ayers who played the role of the young German soldier in the film would become a conscientious objector in World War II.

Leaders such as the fictitious old German professor in the film, "All Quiet On The Western Front," or in the real world the heads of States are the political villains who by means of their rhetoric expertise, and under the guise of patriotism, inseminate the passions of war on the masses; in particular, they target young men who ultimately will be the ones engaged in combat. If we were to seek-out the common enemy in our world, we may well find it to be the leaders of State who lacking any empathy for mankind are motivated by the grandeurs of self-power, and the ethics of greed. These are the individuals who have the know how to influence and persuade large masses of people to mount hostile activities on other Nations. In similar fashion, religious leaders with their moral vision prey on the poor, the uneducated, and on innocent youth in order to achieve what they believe to be justifiable goals. Like animals, that if given the opportunity, will overpower smaller and weaker ones, these political and religious leaders with their political skills and psychological training are able to "brainwash" their followers.

CHAPTER 49

An Alternative to Capitalism

This may sound like an idealistic point of view and far fetched, but can't we develop the technology and skills not for the purpose of destroying human lives in world wars, but instead, to help others who may be less fortunate than we are. True, we're locked into an economic system that may not always allow us to be good Samaritans; to be sure, we must be able to fend for ourselves. In fact, we should have the discipline to sacrifice many hours of our lives devoted to studies, which will eventually reward us with the success of attaining the skills we can sell to others. However, having reach this pinnacle of success, or what may be defined as the ability to earn wages that far surpass our needs, and the needs of our love ones, what do we do with the surplus left over. In most cases, whether involved as merchants of our business establishments, employed in positions that yield for us a great deal of wealth, or with the ugly business of politics, greed seems to take hold of us; not unlike caught in the firm grips of a vice, which refuses to let us go, and we can only be release by coming to terms with ourselves. And what can these terms be?

Overly simplistic as they may seem, these terms can be made-up in the realization that, indeed, we are all mortal beings. Our lives on this planet are limited; there is no other truer fact than this one. When the greed to accumulate wealth and materialistic possessions that we don't really need finally subsides, most likely, it may be directly related to the awareness that we cannot take anything with us, whether it is wealth, material objects or love ones on the final journey to whatever destination may lie ahead for us. However, this awareness only occurs, and I may be over generalizing the point, when we become seriously or terminally ill. It is at this juncture in our journey that the vicious vise begins to loosen its grip on us. Thereafter, we, in effect, are overcome with the desire to help others with acts of charity. We, in fact, become philanthropic individuals at the moment when we realize we cannot take all that we have accumulated in our lifetime with us.

Why not stop the needless hoarding of surplus wealth before we're on our deathbed? Wealth, surplus wealth that is, should be shared with those who are in need. This concept may sound utopian, and rightfully, it can well be, nevertheless, it can become a reality. Political leaders do have the power to legislate laws that can, to some extent, equalize people's wealth. Why should one individual have more money than he can spend in a lifetime when there are others in dire need of some economic assistance? We should be aware that as individuals, we blend equitably with all others because of our mortality, therefore, why not expand this blend to include the human needs of others?

Death follows us all, wherever we may be, and at whatever moment of hour of day or night of our existence. Ultimately, death does embrace us. Thoughtful of this fact, we thus develop the instincts for exercising self-preservation, realizing that we are in the grips of an unknown force beyond our control. Moreover, we become cognizant of the fact that we're not eternal beings, and that our lives are not everlasting ones, but only temporary cycles on earth. Still, we should also be aware that we have the power to practice our free will; with this free will we can, among other things, create, or at least attempt by any means possible, to prolong our lives. Rather than destroy our most valuable possession, for example, by the mass destruction of human lives in political wars, we should, instead, seek altruistic methods to aid others who are in need. This ideology may seem unrealistic, and one perhaps tinged with images of a fantasy world where there is no evil to be found in man. But what in deed influences me into drawing this conclusion?

As I have previously said, man is born an aggressive being. Acting out his aggression, he will eventually commit some wrong doing. He will in indeed violate some principle of moral conduct. Some religions legitimate this fact by claiming man is born a "sinner," and therefore will not always obey the divine laws of an All Mighty God. Nonetheless, if he performs some penances in the form of prayers imposed on him by a priest, he will receive absolution from the church and God for his committed sins. The purpose here is not to expound on a religion's doctrine, but to underscore a significant point. Knowing that man's aggressiveness is an inherent behavior, and in general, the likelihood of him sharing his accumulated surplus wealth with others is wishful thinking, why not allow the Government to channel these traits for man's benefit and the benefit of the State.

A socialist political system may be the way of bridging the huge gap that now exists in our society between those who have it all, and those unfortunate ones who have little or nothing. In broad terms, the system can be one in which all members of the State own, operate and share the means of production, rather than limited to one, or some individuals. In whatever field or setting we're involved in, if something is not working for us, our logic dictates that we attempt to find other ways until the desired result is achieved. Obviously, our capitalistic system is not working for us, and there seems to be a pressing need for a change; therefore, why not try something else? Probing the issue with another question, on what premise do I base what appears to be sweeping generalities about capitalism?

For a start, divisiveness and polarization between the rich and the poor are two products of capitalism. Naturally, the by-product of this cleavage is poverty, which results in poor housing conditions, poor health care and inferior or little or no education for the masses of impoverished people who inhabit the earth. Yet, the rich with their purchasing power have access to luxurious housing, the best doctors and hospitals that money can buy; and as to be expected, their children attend prestigious private schools that prepare them for positions of wealth and power when they enter the business world. Hence, the result is a system that propagates itself in which the rich continue to accumulate wealth generation after generation, and the poor most always remain in bondage, permanently shackled to their poverty. Do we need to have this inequality among people? A system that allows for equitable standards of living, with economic, social and political rights can eliminate the hardships associated with poverty. Furthermore, a system that allows for adequate housing, health care and education can enhance man's situation on earth.

A socialist type of government will make provisions for a man to be compensated for his labor according to his skills, and in how much he produces. Viewing the individual parts rather than the whole, which make-up a socialistic system, we can envision man as part of a network of human resources who will produce at the utmost level goods that the Country will sell to domestic and foreign markets. The whole part of the system may be seen as the peaceful co-existence of Nations trading, or selling and buying from one another what has been produced by their people. Thus, in the final outcome, the more a Nation is able to produce the more it will have to provide for its people and sell to other Nations. To be sure, man's natural aggressiveness will be directed toward the production of goods. Undeniably, the concept of producing and trading with each other is a common method for Nations to bolster up their economy; but do all members own and share equally the results, the profits from what the Nation produces? Eternal peaceful ways of co-existing among Nations is indeed a fantasy. Nations in the past, and as long as history has been recorded have waged war on one another, and most likely will continue to do so in the future. Nevertheless, a socialistic type of government is not an unrealistic new concept, but one that is very much a reality in this present age.

A good example is Sweden today. The Country has a socialistic type of government, which provides housing, health care benefits and educational needs for its citizens. Much to my surprise, during a visit to the Nation's capital, Stockholm, I saw no slums, no visible poverty and no panhandlers or homeless people. What I did see, however, was an immaculate clean City with modern residential buildings, and modern public school facilities for both lower and upper levels of education. Nonetheless, what I didn't expect to see, but was very much in evidence, was the specter of the Nation's past military glories hovering over the City. A late 15th century warship that had sunk in the City's harbor on its maiden voyage had been salvaged and restored to its original splendor. The warship, which is named "The Wasa," is still on display in an elliptically shaped building, not unlike the shape of a huge egg. Its location is by the shores of the harbor almost at the exact point where it sank over three hundred years ago. Somewhat disappointing at the time, was the fact that in this beautiful cold City, in the most northern part of Europe, a weapon of war, of human destruction, had become a popular attraction for both the native population and for foreign tourists

CHAPTER 50

How An Alternative to Capitalism Can Work

The capitalistic system is made-up of a class society in which those having the wealth are on top, and in a glaring contrast, the unfortunate ones who with little or no wealth are at the bottom of the system. Realistically thinking about this inequitable political structure, the system does classify you according to the amount of wealth you posses; and this wealth provides you with the purchasing power to obtain whatever is needed, desired or craved for, including the services and endorsements from others. Indeed, wealth can represent a powerful weapon, and one which can be lethal if placed in the wrong hands of unscrupulous people who lack any ethical standards.

Lethal ideally lends itself to the words of the English philosopher, Thomas Hobbes. Hobbes declared that as long as "men have the same motivation," and can acquire "similar power, conflicts and wars will always exist." This "same motivation" is the spark that seems to ignite the cause for man's greed. Further, the "similar power" the philosopher refers to can be our realization that there is always the possibility for acquiring wealth in order to have the power as an individual, in a group setting or as a Nation. The capitalistic system's creed, the relentless attempt to accumulate wealth as the source for attaining power, namely, purchasing power, or power over others, can eventually result in "conflicts and wars."

Aren't there any alternatives for a political system such as capitalism, which tends to create a divisiveness among people into those who have a surplus amount of wealth, and the vast majority who do not? We should take note that these people, most of whom have the wealth which can never be depleted in their lifetime, in general, are the ones who wield the power. This power most always is in the hands of political figures, lawyers, and those who control the production of goods, the executives of large corporations. One of the underlying evils of capitalism, to be sure, is that the rich remain wealthy from generation to generation. We may now ask, how is this possible? What does indeed make it possible is that lack of monetary funds prevents the majority of poor people from sending their children to the elite private schools where the wealthy kids develop the skills, which ultimately yield surplus wealth for them when they become adults. By contrast, children from poor families are relegated to the public schools, which are free. The maxim, free services are usually poor services can apply to the public schools. Not intentionally perhaps, but one of the causes for the poor services is the average ratio of about thirty five students to one teacher in a public school classroom. These large amounts of students who are taught by only one teacher can be counter-productive both in the teaching and learning process.

Rather than have a capitalistic system with its built-in unjust inequalities, why not have a society based on an economic structure that has equality for all. The concept may sound communistic, and perhaps it may be, but it can serve to satisfy the basic economic needs of a Nation's population. This form of political system is not a novel idea by any means, but one whose innovator was the Greek philosopher, Plato, who also provided the guidelines for implementing it. In applying his guidelines, leaders who have been selected by the people will carry-out the functions of governing; and what might these functions be? The Government can furnish the people with the basic needs of food, shelter, clothing, and of course, health care benefits. Further, people will not be permitted to own property to generate income, instead, will work solely for the State, and not for other individuals, nor for any private enterprise. In other words, the State will be similar to a private corporation supplying goods for its inhabitants and for global markets. Moreover, people will be compensated with wages according to the size of their families, their household needs, and how much work they perform. Work duties will be based on the principles of division of labor, and contingent on the person's skills and aptitude.

To complete the concept for establishing a political system, education, which can serve as the structure's foundation, will be the sole responsibility of the State. However, unlike the education system, which exists today with its public schools and private schools, there will be no private schools; instead, all educational functions will be conducted in public schools administered by government workers trained in the skills of teaching children and adult learners. The mandatory process of educating children will begin at ages of four to five years old. Periodically thereafter, children will be tested for natural abilities in respective learning areas. At the mid-level cycle, candidates will be selected for either advanced academic studies or technical training. In the final analysis, education's primary function will be to determine a child's natural or inherent abilities, and develop them into professional skills, which will ultimately be applied in a work setting owned and operated by the State.

This totalitarian type of government may not sound very appealing to some of us but let's come to grips with ourselves and deal with the metaphysics of the situation, or the real world. What will future generations be like with the form of government and environment we now have? Our cities and parts of the suburban areas now appear to be almost uncontrollable with rampant lawlessness, in particular, with the extreme violence of young people. Killings, robberies and drugs are common occurrences in a Country where it's almost as easy to have access to a hand gun as it is to buy a quart of milk at the corner deli. The Country, to be sure, is at the mercy of the insidious National Rifle Association, (NRA), whose vested interest and huge profits enable it to make large contributions, the euphemism for pay-offs, to politicians not to legislate laws against fire arms. There is indeed an element to gun violence that must be blamed on political figures who are the only ones having the power to ban the use of guns. No one, except the military and law enforcement officers should have the legal right to have fire arms. True, "the right to bear arms" is in the Constitution, nonetheless, these fundamental laws can be amended.

Continuing with what may read like a horror tale about a society, the high crime rate, drug abuse, homelessness, teenage pregnancies, and the widespread of the dreaded Aids virus does merit labeling it a society of horrors. Another part of this horror may be the fact that over fifty percent of our Black and Hispanic youth population are now in prison. The destructive influence of drugs and the large scale of violence seen on television and in movie houses that appeal to young people, particularly those residing in blighted ghettos, have created an almost out of control youth culture. Kids from the culture, for the most part, appear to have no self-discipline, no respect for private property, for adults, and no ethical values. The intellectual person, moreover, is perceived as offensive, and as some sort of an "odd ball" who is not in-step with the times. Finally, adding to the horror is the public education system. A system that with its enormous bureaucratic structure produces almost a fifty percent rate of drop-outs, namely those kids who leave school before earning the required credits to graduate from high school. Obviously, the system is not meeting the needs of these kids, or in a clearer vain, educating them so that in the future they can become productive law abiding citizens.

To underscore the point, and what is one of the on-going themes in this work, what in fact is the reality of the situation? Indeed, we should admit to ourselves that the future is in the hands of our youth. Knowing this to be true, we may have to begin thinking about re-structuring our present form of government in order to build a society that is equitable. With this thought in mind, we should strive to achieve the long termed goal of educating our youth, not only with the skills they will need in their adult lives, but also in a manner in which they will learn to obey the laws, and be an asset to the Country. These reforms perhaps can be attainable by adopting Plato's concept for a system of governing a "Republic." People tend to be like herds of cattle or sheep, if not fully controlled, will run wild, and as the saying goes, disobeying the laws, which in all probability, will ultimately result in anarchy. Therefore, what may be required is an authoritarian type of government with a strong and skillful leader. This leader will have subordinates who have the essential skills in all aspects, and are experts in their respective fields. Furthermore, the Government will have full control in enforcing the laws, the means for acquiring wealth, which will be distributed equitably, provide health care benefits, and responsible for the effective education of children. The Nation today, and I think we can all agree on this, is not ready to adopt this form of government; however, in future generations it may well prove to be the salvation of the Country.

CHAPTER 51

Boot Camp and School

In March, 1943, the initial exposure to what can be referred to as a minor supporting role in a drama of human destruction, and arguably, one of the two greatest tragedies of the 20th Century, the other, which should come as no surprise to anyone, was the First World War. A mere three months after registering for the draft, I was drafted. Unexpectedly, primarily due to my weight, (119lbs), I passed the routine physical examination, and still clad in my shorts, I was told to proceed to the end of a long line of young men who were also in their underwear shorts, and inching their way forward toward the front of the line. There, at the front of the line stood an Army sergeant, a Marine and a Navy Chief Petty Officer, all of whom were involved in visually inspecting each one of the draftees. Reflecting on this event, it occurs to me at this moment, and certainly not when it was happening, the scene was reminiscing of three male butchers whose task was to select prime specimens of young bulls for their respective slaughter houses. Confronting them after what seem to be endless hours on the line, but, in fact, was no more than about an hour, the Petty Officer inspected my hair. had me turned a complete circle for him, and asked me if I liked boys. On hearing my reply of an emphatic "no," he said to his other two colleagues, "I'll take this one." And that, in effect, was the beginning of the naval experience in World War II, or how I became a human product owned, and at the full disposal of the U.S. Navy.

The initial experience was not an enjoyable one by any means. At the very beginning, after realizing the Navy was, in fact, segregating the Black inductees from the Whites, the worst fear was to be placed with the Blacks. This fear of course was the result of my stepfather, who no doubt because of his hatred toward me, often made comments about his son's skin being lighter than mine, thus implying I had some Negro blood. My fear, naturally, never materialized, and I was ordered to the back of a truck with about twenty other White inductees and driven to the Sampson Naval Base by the shores of a large lake in a small town that, despite the time of the year, was the coldest and windiest place I had ever been exposed to; the town was Geneva in Northwestern New York.

On our arrival at the Naval Base, we were ushered to a warehouse and issued naval clothing, or what was referred to in Navy jargon, as "navy gear." Among the items of clothing given to me were a winter coat, which was actually a mid-length wool jacket called a "pea coat," and a black turtle neck sweater, both of which I was later to discover were inadequate for the frigid cold and windy weather that was common then, as it is today in Northwestern, New York. Thereafter, we were escorted to the barbershop, where, according to military tradition, but probably copied from the Germans, we were given crew cuts. After the haircuts, we went to a large dining room known as "the chow hall," and there we had dinner that, to say the least, was different. Accustomed to my mother's rice and beans, my taste buds were not prepared for mashed potatoes, various other vegetables, chopped meat, and a salad named, "waldorf salad" consisting of lettuce, carrots and slices of apples. Adding to the difference, the meal was not served in a customary plate I was used to, but instead, on a stainless steel tray having individual small indented compartments to accommodate the vegetables, meat and the salad.

Marching instructions in a large open field surrounded by cabins, which were to be our housing units, or "sleeping quarters," was the next activity; there we were given the first basic instructions in how to march. This activity conducted on the open field, known as "the drill field," was to become a daily ritual lasting an hour or more after every meal, until an unforeseen occurrence, I came down with bronchial pneumonia. Prior to the happening, or shortly after the arrival at the base, I began to experience constant chills day and night, body aches, and always a tired feeling, even when waking up in the mornings. During these three weeks of "basic training," we went on all day hikes, rowed the large "whale boats," and worst of all, exposed to tear gas, which had the adverse effect of causing burning sensations on our faces, this occurred despite wearing gas masks. The chills and tired feelings, nonetheless, never subsided. Finally, in the midst of a sleepless night, during which my body felt like it was on fire, I got-up out of bed, went to the night guard stationed at the outer hall of the cabin and told him I was very sick. He must have realized at that moment that, indeed, I was ill, and rushed me to the naval hospital.

The following afternoon, on waking up and finding myself under an oxygen tent, but feeling better, the nurse advised me that I had had a temperature of 104 degrees the previous night when I arrived at the hospital. For the following three weeks, I was subjected to what must have been dozens of penicillin injections to the point were my buttocks were extremely sensitive with light pains from all the injections I had endured. As a result of the penicillin, I had fully recovered in about a month's time and sent back to my cabin; much to my surprise, however, all the fellows I had been with were gone, and I found myself among unfamiliar trainees whom I had never before seen.

Once again, among other less arduous activities, the marching drills, rowing the monster whale boats on the windy lake and the hikes through the vast cold wooded lands of upper New York State resumed. Nevertheless, feeling my normal self, and in good spirits despite the lack of enthusiasm for these activities, time passed by quickly. A week before completing the twelve weeks of "basic training," actually it was known as "boot camp" since all trainees had to wear leggings, we were given placement tests dealing with reading comprehension, vocabulary and computation. Returning from thirty days leave, I was somewhat puzzled on finding I had been scheduled to attend a naval radio school at the University of Wisconsin, rather than assigned to a war ship. How odd I thought, that the Navy was sending me to school to learn how to repair radios.

A week later I started the first phase of a ten month's course in cryptography, and how to communicate by radio utilizing the International Morse code. Cryptography, as the reader must already know deals with devising ways in which to encode and decipher coded messages into English, or as it was known, plain language. Known as "crypto" in school, the method appeared to be somewhat primitive, and perhaps an antiquated way of converting plain language messages into coded forms. Both procedures of encoding and decoding were accomplished with strips of thin cardboard having their surfaces lined vertically and horizontally with small holes similar to the old International Business machines' "punched cards" used with the Company's first commercial computers. When overlaid onto a coded text, the strips of cardboard enabled you to see a series of groups of letters made-up of five letters in each one of the groups. After jotting down the series of letters on paper, you looked-up their meaning in an enormously large black book, like the dictionary you see on a stand in a college library. The "science" of cryptography in the time frame I'm referring to was a tedious and time consuming task, and to be sure, not a very exciting one.

Communication, in contrast to cryptography, was a much more exciting field in the military, and certainly not a dull vocation for a sailor. This may have been attributed to the ease with which you were able to communicate by receiving and sending messages long distances all over the world using transmitters and receivers. The medium, furthermore, was ideally suited for transmitting and receiving the Morse code, which in fact is an International language of sounds representing no barriers in understanding it to a no-English speaking person.

Understanding the code is a skill that one acquires by literally memorizing the sounds, rather than the amount of dots and dashes contained in each of the letters and number characters. Each letter in the alphabet, because of its specific amount of dots, dashes, or both dots and dashes, has a unique sound unlike any of the other letters. As a result, once the letters are memorized, one is able, with lots of practice of course, to copy the code at generally thirty words a minute with a pencil, or preferably on a typewriter. Not all trainees succeeded in memorizing the sounds; consequently, those who demonstrated little or no progress after three months failed the course, or in Navy jargon, "washed-out, and re-assigned to "sea duty" aboard a ship. To this day, I still don't know how, or what method or strategy I used to memorize the sounds of the letters and numbers, but I did. This may have been an inherent attribute, and one I was to apply many years later to memorize the correct sounds of each string on a classical guitar in order to tune the instrument correctly. There were many trainees who were not as fortunate as I was to be given the opportunity for "upward mobility," and were relegated to "seamen," which was, and still is today, the bottom rung of the ladder of success in the Navy.

The fortunes of a sailor training to become a "radioman" at the University of Wisconsin were not all good ones. Almost at the completion of the ten months course, there occurred a bitter incident that still tends to leave a foul taste in my mouth. The "superintendent" of the naval school was an ex-submarine captain, who by way of rumors was said to be a strict disciplinarian to those who disobeyed the training school's rules of conduct. These rumors were soon to become an unpleasant reality for me. I met the captain, not by chance however, but only after summoned to a "captain's mass" for arriving thirty minutes late from a weekend of leave. The weekend's leave, or "liberty as it was officially known, had ended at midnight on Sunday; and the following Monday I was to find-out how insensitive, and lacking any remorse whatsoever a human being can be who has the power and authority to impose harsh punishments on others, specifically, on a seventeen year old boy. I still can almost visualize the scowl on the man's wrinkled face as he sentenced me to be confined to "the brig" for one day for each of the ten minutes I had been late from leave for a total of three days on 'piss and punk." In naval language this was the equivalence of three days in jail without any food, except for bread and water.

My only concern at the time of the happening was missing classes. And no thoughts about the fact I was going to be deprived from having food for three days. Thinking about this incident now reminds me of how Melville's hero "Billy Budd" must have felt to be unjustly punished for a crime he didn't commit. A guard escorted me to "the brig," which ironically happened to be located in the basement directly below the dormitory building. The jail was a large room that appeared to have been converted to a cell by adding iron bars to the room's entrance. In the room were the bare necessities, a small bed and a toilet, but no sink to wash one's hands or face; and as was to be expected, there was the always-present guard who sat on a chair directly across from the room where, no matter what part of the room I moved to, he always had me in his sight. The first day of my confinement, at about noontime, he gave me three slices of white bread and a large glass of water, both of which I took, and though the bread was not very appetizing, ate two of the slices and drank some of the water.

    I was lying on the small bed, which was not very comfortable because of the mattress's thinness causing my back to feel the bedsprings, when the first hunger pangs struck. Quickly I got-up from the bed and ate the last of the three slices of bread. Nonetheless, the hungry feeling persisted, and grew progressively worse all afternoon. By early evening, prior to the guard's entrance with my ration of bread and water, I was famished to the point where all that occupied my mind were cravings for food, and visions of how I would gorge myself on ham and eggs when released from "the brig." When the guard arrived with what was to be my last meal that evening, I ate the bread rapidly, however, this was no relief from the hunger, which had grasped on to me and was not about to let me go.

    The unpleasant aspects about the hunger was that, no matter how hard I tried not to think about it, the urge for food had become so sharp that I literally thought of nothing else but food that night. Before finally falling asleep, I had recollections of similar feelings experienced as a young boy who had recently arrived from a small farm on a tropical Island where the lush fields from its rich earth produced an abundance amount of what I was in desperate need off that night, food. Still, I was no longer a young boy, but a young man lying on an uncomfortable bed thinking only about food, and not prepared for the experience of going to sleep for the night having acute hunger pains.

Awaken by the guard the following morning to offer me a breakfast of three slices of bread and a glass of water, a strange thing happened, I was no longer hungry. I have heard it said that if humans go without food for a certain period of time, they tend to lose their desire for it. Apparently, this was what must have happened in that depressive cell on the second morning of my sentence. I ate half a slice of bread and drank some of the water, with the guard urging me on to eat more. Politely I refused, telling him I would save the bread for later, and he left to sit on his chair outside the cell. There are moments in our lives when we get a sense of our feelings in relation to others; and it was at that moment that I felt some pity for the man sitting on that chair who in some realistic way, to some extent at least, was as much of a prisoner as I was, condemned to guard me for three days. That afternoon and evening I had another two slices of bread, however, not to satisfy my hunger, actually there was none, but merely to have something of substance in my stomach. Unlike the previous evening, I had no feelings of hunger, though much to my surprise, the guard kept offering me bread, but I only drank some water before going to sleep.

The third and final day of confinement was uneventful. No longer was I experiencing any hunger, nor did I have any cravings for food, despite the guard earnestly urging me to have some bread. That the evening meal consisted of three slices of rye bread rather than the customary white ones I had been getting, may have been the reason why I had two of the slices. Curiously, I detected a sight of relief on the guard's face on observing me eat, and thinking at that moment that perhaps he did feel sorry for my predicament. The fact that I was unable to eat very much the first morning after my release didn't surprise me. What in fact did, however, was the manner in which my "chief supervisor," instructors and all the other sailors' behavior towards me changed significantly. From the time of my release until graduation, all the people whom I encountered in the school appeared to be friendlier and supportive, more so than at any other time before my three days of confinement in a Navy "brig" on bread and water

CHAPTER 52

The Mexicans

The reward for having successfully completed the required courses was graduation, and with it a new rating classification. No longer was I a "seaman second class," but instead, a "radioman striker" certified to begin the internship phase in the training program at a Naval Base. A radioman striker was not unlike the student of today who matriculates at a college, and becomes a candidate for a degree. Of course, the Navy didn't issue degrees, nevertheless, at the completion of a training program, specifically, one in which you acquired special skills, you were issued a "petty officers rating," or as it applied to me, the rating of radioman third class. My internship was to begin on the West Coast, considered "choice duty" by the training school, therefore, I was quite amazed on finding out I had been one of the few fortunate ones selected for this duty, not realizing that perhaps this had been the Navy's way of making amends for their harsh punishment inflicted on a very young sailor for arriving at a Naval School thirty minutes late from his weekend leave.

The Naval Training Base was indeed on the West Coast, more precisely, in Oceanside, California, about ten miles south of San Diego, and very close to the Mexican border. Internship dealt primarily with field activities transmitting and receiving voice messages with small battery operated transmitters/receivers strapped to our backs. Encased in dark green canvas bags, they were not a pretty sight, nor where they light in weight. Each one of the transmitters/receivers weighted fifty pounds, and their effective range was limited to a mere four-to-five miles. What was somewhat interesting about the equipment was you had the ability to calibrate the small transmitters, or tuned them to any frequency you desired to transmit on. Moreover, with simple calculations on a grid graph, you were able to determine whether your transmitted signals were drifting to another frequency; and if this was happening, you simply made the appropriate adjustments to compensate for the drifting. Field training with the heavy transmitters/receivers on our backs, and classroom sessions practicing receiving and sending messages in morse code lasted six weeks prior to our transfer to a port of embarkation in Seattle, Washington. However, throughout this brief period I had the opportunity to spend "liberty weekends" in the City of Los Angeles, which was a three hours journey by bus from Oceanside.

For reasons that will be explained at a later time, I always traveled alone and never with a companion; and during those times while gazing from the greyhound's window scenes passing me by rapidly; in silent pensive reflections, I viewed the sunny landscape literally covered with orange groves and oil well rigs, two of the sights I had never seen before in the States nor in Puerto Rico. Unlike the large orange trees on the Island, these were smaller, appearing like shrubs with their branches covered with the brightly colored fruit. Adding to the idyllic scene were the familiar palm trees. One particular sight that caught my attention were the small pots with flames shooting upward, and situated alongside the shrubs. How strange I thought, on seeing these small fires, never realizing the fires were there to protect the small fruit trees from the near freezing temperatures that were a common occurrence in Southern California during the months of spring. The numerous oil well derricks viewed in the distant were no match for the pretty orange groves. Indeed, they added very little beauty to the landscape, looking like giant black caterpillars standing on their hind legs as though trying to reach the white clouds above them. In contrast to the oil rigs, the palm trees, which I had not seen since leaving the Island, offered an enchanting scene instilling somewhat of a longing to be back in Puerto Rico. One surprising aspect about the palm trees were the absences of coconuts beneath their lovely green branches swaying gently with the breezes of a sunny morning. Traveling rapidly on the Greyhound bus taking me to my destination, the City of Los Angeles, I was not aware that only date palms grew in California.

Los Angeles, which in Spanish means the angels, was not what may have been considered a City of angels, at least not from this writer's point of view. The City, excluding its large suburban areas, was relatively small, particularly the section known as downtown. Its southern boundary began at the Union Railroad Station, and the section ended about twenty blocks northwest of the Station in the business and financial district. Prior to my first visit, the City had become involved in sporadic hostilities that, in reality, were race riots between the American sailors and the Mexican youths; we were therefore warned by the base commander to exercise extreme caution in the City, in particular, when walking along the downtown area's side streets. However, despite all the weekend excursions to the City, never did I have any problematic encounters with the many Mexicans residing in an area that appeared to be designated specifically for them.

The Los Angeles race riots merit some discussion, not in defense of the U.S. Navy, and the sailors, as the reader may have surmised, but as a way of venting my moral outrage for the unfair way in which these people were treated by the City's residents during the war, and not surprising, a situation, which is very much in existence today. Perhaps, knowing that both Mexicans and Puerto Ricans share a common language, and in some aspects similar cultural traits, has fueled an anger that began in the City of the angels in World War II, and has been simmering ever since.

Ghetto is the word used in today's vernacular to describe the blighted slums where masses of Mexican families lived in deplorably overcrowded conditions. Clearly drawn were lines of social, economic and physical distinctions between the extremely poor Mexicans and the mainstream Los Angeles population who, realistically speaking, were not the native population they rightfully imagined themselves to be. Instead, they were people, or descendants from those who had migrated to a City that had been populated for hundreds of years by Mexican and Spanish families. For the Americans who had come predominantly from the Central and Southern States, the Mexican inhabitants with their black hair, dark skin and oriental features were personified as exotic people who spoke a foreign language, and in many ways reminded them of the American Indian savages. Most likely these differences laid the foundation for the polarization that so obviously existed between these two groups whose culture, language and skin color differed significantly.

From an overall perspective one can indeed make inferences and draw conclusions about situations. Thus, critically reflecting on this particular situation, what, in essence, now sticks in my mind was the underlying hatred that Americans appeared to have had for the Mexicans living in Los Angeles in World War II. Not only were they hated, but exploited in every conceivable manner imaginable, in particular, as farm laborers earning meager wages picking fruits and vegetables in the State's vast farmlands. In the over crowded slums with their dilapidated houses, or shacks might be a better word to describe them, men were picked up in the early morning hours, driven to the outlying farms to work in the fields, and taken back to their shacks in the twilight hours of evening. In general, the youths had the option of either working as farms hands or attending the public district schools in their slum area. Typical of the mindlessness political mentality associated with the way public educational systems function today in many large cities. The Los Angeles public schools were divided into districts. As a result, Mexican children were restricted from attending any of the better schools outside their district. Confined to schools that were in dire need of, among other things, sufficient State funding, adequate building facilities to accommodate the children, and trained bilingual teachers, many restless Mexican youths opted to roam the City streets rather than attend the ill-equipped schools.

I have no answers now, nor to be sure, did I have any answers then to the question what, in fact, caused the riots between the American sailors and the Mexican youths in Los Angeles. Nonetheless, based on what I saw in that particular setting during a war time period. I can, however, draw conclusions about some of the underlying factors that may have contributed to the riots. Mexican youths, in particular, were hated, or at least appeared to be by the dominant City population. To the average City dweller, they represented an inferior group of people. Furthermore, it didn't help matters any that these youths had adopted the black zoot suits as their dress code of honor. And as to be expected, they seem to become a threat, especially to American families with teenage daughters, who perhaps perceived these young men as wild primitive savages who were liable to contaminate their female off springs. Others saw them as hoodlums, tough and aggressive youths who had nothing better to do than to be on the streets in search of mischief. With the failure of the schools to instill in these youths any incentives for learning, and lacking skills, so that manual labor was their only option, they chose the streets. What may be of more significance, however, was that the youths were well aware they were hated, and seen as foreigners, despite the fact they had been born in the State, and rightfully and legally, were American citizens. Adding fuel to the fire was the Navy's policy of segregating its personnel; and not unlike the Blacks and Philippines, Mexican young men's only entrance to this branch of the Arm Forces was as stewards working as valets and waiters for the American naval officers. Deprived from serving their Country in a war against a common enemy may have predisposed these Mexican youths to rebel against what they knew they could never be, American sailors.

Critical reflections sometimes sharply define for us aspects about situations from our past. For example, like the Mexican youth who might have been allowed to be a sailor only to realize he would always be cast in the role of the outsider, I was, indeed, the outsider in the Navy. Peering at the inner dynamics occurring inside the circle of happenings, but at all times aware I could never penetrate the inner part of the circle, or to be specific, be a part of the group, or "one of the boys." Never can I recall nurturing a close friendship with any of the others, or for that matter, having sailors seek me out to be their friends. There was really no self-esteem to speak of, hence, I had misgivings about my ability to socialize with my peers. I was physically, and otherwise, unlike the others, as an illustration, a small scrawny 119 pounds Puerto Rican youth having a foreign name and with a slight Spanish accent. Many, including some of my superiors, (officers) called me by a name I hated from the very first moment I heard it. Naturally, there were times when I was curious in knowing why they had adopted that particular name for me, never realizing that Humbriago rhymed with my surname of Santiago, and perhaps it was easier for them to pronounce. Call it human nature, if you will, in the way in which we get a sense of ourselves in relation to a group of people, an environment, or from another culture. Rather than resist, or challenge them in any manner, I accepted the hated nickname, and the role of the outsider I was destined to play in the Navy during World War II.

CHAPTER 53

The Ship

The six weeks training period in Southern California, somewhat to my regret, ended sooner than I had expected it, and our communication "outfit," "Acorn 27" was transferred to Seattle, Washington. Why the Navy selected that odd name for a group of radiomen sailors numbering fifty men I was never to find out. The concept for the origin of the name may have derived from the small size of oak nuts, which in effect, are the fruits of the oak trees. Similar in fashion, we were a small "outfit," along with a small naval air squadron and a construction battalion attached to a much larger body of military personnel, or the oak tree. On our arrival we were issued combat "gear," which resembled, not the customary dungarees and blue cotton shirts we were used to wearing, but field clothing worn by Army soldiers. The combat "gear" consisted of clothing whose colors were a mixture of dark greens and browns, including the camouflage "jump suits" which were similar to overalls, brown ankle high boots, sun and steel helmets and carbines. The carbine, a popular firearm among military men, was a lightweight semi-automatic thirty caliber rifle with a short barrel, moderate fire power, but with limited range. In contrast to the carbine, officers were issued the highly prized powerful forty five caliber automatic pistols.

Equipped with combat clothing and firearms, we boarded a troop transport bound for what was to be the first stop on the long sea voyage, though we didn't know it at the time, the Island of Guadacanal in the South Pacific. The horrible voyage, and there is really no other word I can think of at this moment to describe it, in an ancient and dirty cargo ship that appeared to have been built for World War I usage, was indeed an ordeal of the worst kind from its very beginning to the final end. We were literally "packed like sardines" having little or no room to walk below decks, or above on the main deck without bumping into other sailors. Thus, your only option was to either lie in your bunk in almost unbearable heat, or if you were lucky enough to find an unoccupied spot on the main iron deck, you sat beneath a blazing hot sun using your life jacket, (life preserver), as a cushion. The bunks below the main deck were situated in a large room, or cabin that, because of its cavernous appearance, was known as the hole. Bunks were vertically stacked one above the other from the floor, or deck, to just below the cabin's ceiling. There were eight bunks to each stack with about three feet separating each bunk. To say the least, obviously these were cramp "sleeping quarters." Adding to our discomfort, if we had no other choice but to stand on the main deck, we had to wear our life jackets as a precautionary measure against an enemy air attack, or what was our worse fear, for the ship to be struck by a torpedo fired from a Japanese submarine.

The long sea voyage from its initial beginning to its final end had the aspects of a continuous nightmare, briefly subsiding only during the night hours of restless sleep. One of the many ordeals experienced on the overly crowded ship, especially the first few days of the voyage, was the intense stench of vomit from hundreds of seasick sailors who never before had been on board a ship on "the high seas." Once our bodies adjusted to the ship's constant motion, we had to contend with our bodies' odors from the relentless perspiration, and not too successful I may add, due to the lack of fresh water. The only means of cleansing our bodies were the showers, that much to our frustration, spouted only salt water, and no matter how much we tried, the soap used refused to give us any lather. For those who have been to beach outings, they should be familiar with the aftermath of swimming in the ocean, or the uncomfortable sticky feeling experienced until they rid themselves of the salt water in their bodies with soap and fresh water. As a result of this discomfort, we took very few showers, gradually becoming accustomed to a part of our human nature, body odors.

Confining masses of people on a ship with minimal space for movement can be thought as, not physically painful, but nevertheless, a rather distressful, and to put it mildly, uncomfortable experience; further, the lack of adequate sanitary facilities can add to the discomfort. However, nothing can add more to the discomfort than the hardships of having only two meals a day, in effect, one in the early morning hours and the other during the twilight hours after sunset. What's more, the meals were served in a huge room with long ugly tables that extended from one side of the ship to the other, and with their tops level to one's mid-section. Why, because there were no chairs or benches to sit on, and yes, we had to eat our meals standing up. Can the reader ever envision what it must have been like, to eat meals in this manner for over thirty days on a ship that was constantly swaying from side to side, much as a cork top floating in turbulent waters?

Indeed, the days were long and might have been dull and monotonous except for the fact that we had what was our only salvation from boredom, books, notably, lots of them. Every few days a fresh supply of large cardboard boxes filled with brand new paperbacks were brought-up to the main deck, (topside), where we ransacked through them searching for what ever reading matter appealed to us. In those times the word paperback was unheard of, and the books, all of which had been donated by the American Red Cross, were know as "Pocket Books." They varied in thickness, but unlike most of today's paperbacks, the pages' horizontal lengths were twice as long their vertical dimensions. Most novels were the quick reading type with lots of dialogue, and the easily forgotten variety; though I read many of them, the only one I can still remember was Joseph Conrad's, The Outcast of The Islands. They did, nonetheless, served the purpose of relieving the weariness of that long sea voyage.

Almost at the end of the voyage, there occurred an incident that brings to light at this moment what may be an unanswerable question, how much hardship can a human being endure before the onset of a mental breakdown? Readily, one may be tempted to conclude that it depends solely on the person's inner strength for withstanding the sufferings, whether large or small, which sooner or later will be experienced during a lifetime. Why is it that some of us have acquired the mental stamina for dealing with stressful situations while others lacking in what perhaps can best be defined as their inner strength resort to chemical substances, for example, drugs and alcohol for coping with anxieties associated with difficult conditions? Distress imposed by circumstances such as mental or physical torment, or on a more complex level, poverty, can ultimately drive a person to choose what he believes to be the only permanent solution. But how do persons acquire this inner strength, or mental stamina to deal with hardships that may arise?

Growing up in an environment in which people are subjected to the hardships of extreme poverty can instill in them the resistance to withstand almost unbearable situations. A long training process geared solely toward developing the discipline to endure mental or physical stress may be another way of building up this resistance. Nonetheless, there is the individual who is beyond help when dealing with stress; and "on the spurt of the moment," he or she can have a mental breakdown. Recently I confronted an acquaintance, Doctor William Teabull, a psychiatrist, with over thirty years experience in the field, with the question, why does a person commit suicide? Bill's response was that often, but not always, the person with schizophrenic tendencies is more prone to committing the act than the person with normal behavior. In layman's term he added, schizophrenia is a character disorder in which the individual "withdraws from reality, has hallucinations and delusions of persecution."

The incident, as the reader may have already guessed, was a suicide, however, not aboard the ship, but in the vast waters of the Pacific Ocean. It was past mid-day when I heard the three blasts from the ship's foghorn, and thereafter a voice yelling "man overboard." The initial reaction was to rush to the ship's railing to get a better view, but on approaching the railing, I saw nothing but water and the swirl of waves about twenty feet high. The ship slowed its speed significantly, almost to a crawl, and slowly began turning making a sweeping circular path along the restless waters. Then, at a distance, which may have been one hundred yards from the ship, I spotted him in the water bobbing like a bottle on the crest of a huge wave, with his life jacket keeping him afloat. The ship came to a complete stop, and men began lowering one of the lifeboats into the water. The last thing I remember seeing was the bright gleaming sun shining on his blond hair, just before he removed his lifejacket and quickly disappeared from my sight.

CHAPTER 54

The Island

What at first sight appeared to be a dark cloud extending as far as the eye could see along the distant horizon, gradually, within a span or two or three hours, revealed itself as what I had not seen in thirty three days, land. Word rapidly spread throughout the ship that we were approaching Guadacanal. The sight was somewhat familiar, as though I were again viewing the film "King Kong," and my first glimpses of the dark mysterious Island with its towering mountain peak. Guadacanal, viewed from where the ship had been anchored indeed seem to be dark, mysterious and in some ways forbidden, but unlike Kong's Island, it was much larger, with a mountain range that stretched from one end of the Island to the other. Soon, a small fleet of amphibious boats, or LCIs, the acronym for "Landing Craft Infantry," came alongside and many sailors boarded them by lowering themselves on rope nets, which had been placed alongside the ship from its upper deck to the waters' surface, and had the appearance of gigantic brown spider webs. This was the closest point I came to the Island, and in a matter of hours, we were on our way heading for what I rightfully guessed must be another Island.

Early the following morning, still lying half asleep in my "bunk," I realized the ship was no longer moving. After breakfast, we were ordered to the LCIs, and once on board headed for a tiny flat Island that must have been no more than four miles long. As the small boats approached closer to land, I noticed that most of the Island was literally covered with palm trees. Later I was to find out the Island had been a coconut plantation owned by the

American firm, The Colgate Palmolive and Peet Company. Closer to shore, I was able to see that the palm trees in the middle of the Island were being knocked down by bulldozers clearing a path, or "landing strip" for planes to land on.

Finally, after thirty four days confined in an old troop transport on the high seas, I found myself on solid ground, on a small Island's beach, however, the enemy was nowhere to be seen. Instead, we were greeted by a large group of relatively small black men wearing, not the lovely bright colors and prints on the sarong worn by the lovely Dorothy Lamour in the movie "The Hurricane," but rather, drab dull sarongs with faded brown colors worn like skirts around the lower parts of their bodies. Notably, what was startling about their appearance were their smiles displaying teeth that looked as though they had been coated with red paint. To the unaccustomed observer, this may have presented somewhat of a hideous sight, nevertheless, as I was to discover in the fifteen months on the small Island, these were extremely friendly natives. Of course, all were bare footed, but what added to the anomaly were the peculiar shapes of their feet. Virtually all had flat feet with unique features; a rather large gap separated the large toe from the other digits on their feet. This deformity, as I was to find out, was the result of years of climbing the tall palm trees for coconuts, which were a primary source of food for them. The process of climbing the tall palm trees, so I heard, began in early childhood when the children, barely able to walk, started climbing them by gripping their small toes unto the limbless trunks of the tall palm trees to get at what was inside the fruit, the sweet coconut milk. Moreover, I was to find out the reddish stain on the natives' teeth was caused by their habit of chewing red fibered nuts for their mild stimulant effect.

Not greeting us as the natives had, were the CBs who were erecting tents clustered together to form what appeared to be a camp sight. No buildings were to be seen anywhere except for the tents. However, about a half mile or more from the camp sight, and at each side of the path the bulldozers were clearing, I saw many red steel arcs lying on the ground. These were to be the foundation for the Quonset huts, the prefabricated structures whose surfaces were covered entirely with gray corrugated metal, and were to be, in about two weeks time our permanent housing facilities. Prior to re-locating to the Quonset huts, which to this observer had no visible attractive features, other than the palm trees surrounding them, our temporary living quarters were the tents in which four sailors occupied a tent having an area the size of a 9X12 room.

In general, the CBs seem to be much older than the sailors in "Acorn 27." Most of them must have been in their late thirties or mid-forties. All, without exceptions, wore green sun helmets, olive colored short sleeve shirts and trousers. What sharply contrasted the CBs from us, however, was the shade of their skin. Nothing similar to a tan from prolonged sun exposure, rather, their skin color resembled the dull yellows seen on chrysanthemums in the fall season. This was the same shade of skin color I was to acquire in about a month's time as a result of having to take atabrine tablets before each meal as a precautionary measure against contacting malaria. Within a period of a few months these resourceful men, all of whom were admired, and at times envied by us because of their constructing prowess, built not only the "landing strip" paved with crushed coral, the control tower, but also the radio station, the dining hall and a road for vehicles to travel around the small Island's perimeter. With the abundance amount of plywood which was the primary building material, the CBs were also able to built small sailboats from the surplus plywood. Because of the surrounding reef, the Islands calm waters made it ideally suitable for sailing.

Torrential rains, which were a common occurrence didn't help matters any in relieving the discomfort and lack of privacy in having to share a small tent with three other sailors. We slept on cots with upright poles on each of their four corners to support the nets draped over them as a protection against the ubiquitous mosquitoes. When the rains arrived, especially at night, and driven by strong gusty winds, adding to the discomfort of getting drenched were the small land crabs that always managed to crawl under the nets, and inside your pajamas as though seeking your body's warmth, and some refuge from nature's onslaught. Two weeks later, when we moved to the Quonset huts, everyone's morale seem to improve after the ordeal of having to live in crowded tents during the Island's rainy season.

 We moved ourselves, and our belongings into a spacious and well-ventilated Quonset hut, which though ugly in appearance, protected us from the rains, the land crabs and the heat of the sun. The hut's interior was insulated with fiberglass material, thus providing us with a cool environment, and a sharp contrast from the sweltering heat aboard the ship, and later in the tents. Located inside the hut were rows of bunks with lower and upper beds, all of which had been built by the CBs with 2X4 inch boards. They had no steel springs in them, instead, the ingenious CBs had drilled small holes alongside the bed frames, and inserted clothed line ropes through the holes, both vertically and horizontally, to form grids which supported the mattresses on our beds.

 A much larger Quonset hut was the radio station where we worked sending and receiving coded messages from the mainland and other outlying Islands. Deciphering one of these coded messages on one of my first "radio watches," I found out the small Island was to be used primarily to train Navy pilots in simulated aircraft landings. A week after moving to the huts squadrons of fighter planes began arriving on the Island. To a young man who till then had seen only small model airplanes, it was indeed a thrilling experience to see all those aircraft, and all brand new, as though they had just come off Grumman's assembly line on Long Island. There were the "the Hellcats," (F6Fs), the "Corsairs," (F4Us), the new dive bombers, also named "Hellcats," (SB2Cs), and the older and slower torpedo bombers, "Avengers," (TBMs). Their aluminum bodies and wings glowed brightly with the sun's reflection bathing them with rays of sunlight, and for a now eighteen year old boy, it was a beautiful sight. But like William Blake's poem, "The Tyger," which symbolized how danger can disguise itself in the form of beauty that appeals to the eyes of the beholder's senses, these beautiful machines were, in fact, lethal weapons of war made by man solely for the purpose of destroying other men.

CHAPTER 55

Critical Thinking

What is it that influences men into taking a path that will ultimately lead them to acts of destroying other men? Some men, whether persuaded easily, by force, or driven by their emotions stemming from fears, hate or grief stricken, will kill other beings; and there are those who by some form of urging or reasoning can be induced into causing the deaths of others. Likewise, there are people who can be led or persuaded by the doctrines, opinions, or ways of thinking of other groups, into committing the act of killing other human beings. A prime example is in wars when it is permissible to kill people who have been declared by the State as the enemy who must be destroyed by whatever means possible; even resorting to a weapon that has the lethal power to destroy all mankind, the atomic bomb. Finally, there is the puzzling fact to consider, and this is, man is the only mammal on earth who for the sheer pleasure of it, practices the sport of killing animals.

Reverting to the question what influences or leads men to kill, the answer that comes readily to mind, and one which may seem overly simplistic, is that it's inherent in all of us; or in other words, our distinct genes dictate our behavior. The answer may add credence in justifying the violent act of killing, however, I cannot see myself agreeing to this line of thinking. Isn't it a fact that one's behavior is learned? Further, our behavior, whether moral, immoral, violent, or non-violent, are not behavioral traits we're born with. Rather, they can be like a learning process whereby in gradual stages, we are conditioned to believe, particularly during the formative years, the same values as our parents, our peers, and certainly the values of our cultural environment. As a result, if our parents and peers believe and practice some form of violence, and of course, if our environment is violent, most likely we're going to develop violent traits in our behavior. This exposition may sound all too familiar, but bear with me, I'm leading toward some personal thoughts, and not about killings, I think I have said enough about that. Instead, in light of what I have said thus far, how can we thwart efforts by other individuals, or groups, to manipulate us in any manner, and impart on us ideas and beliefs that can be harmful to others, especially when we act them out as members of a group attempting to achieve some goal. The most difficult aspect in discussing this issue is this: How do we know or suspect when we are being used, taken advantage of, or manipulated in some way for the benefits of others?

What I'm about to say may be debatable, but whether or not we have acquired violent traits in the home, associating with our peers, or in our cultural environment, the behavior may not be completely altered, nevertheless, it can be modified. The change may be made possible by a person's true sense of reality, common sense reasoning and critical thinking. Reality, as the German philosopher, Emanuel Kant argued convincingly, is derived from our experience. For instance, unless I am dead, if I strike one small stone against another, I know for a fact I will here a sound, whether I perform the act once or many times; the effect will always be the same. More precisely, however, what in fact is critical thinking? In essence, it can be playing the role of the non-believer, a skeptic who doubts, questions and suspends judgment in order to satisfy his sense of reality. For a start, we can begin by functioning on a selfish level. In effect, this means thinking about the ways in which the unknown something, a belief or whatever, will benefit us rather than harm us. Simply stated, it's thinking about what's in it for the ones who are attempting to manipulate us in some manner so that we will conform to their ways of thinking. We become analytical beings, analyzing all situations, and seeking out the benefits and discarding all others, which may tend to harm us. Remembering always that our most valuable possession is our lives, and without life we fail to exist. To briefly summarize these thoughts, critical thinking can be the barriers that guard or warn us against those who practice the ethics of greed.

William Blake's symbol for how beauty and danger can be mutually related, and in some ways correlated with the opinions I have just cited, reminds me of an event that may also have some bearings to the poet's poem, "The Tyger." The only vehicular road on the Island, though narrow, still had two lanes enabling trucks and jeeps to pass one another, and officers and enlisted men to walk along its outer edges; the event happened while I was walking on this road. Ahead of me, a short distance away, the animal emerged from the woods, not running, but instead, ambling along cautiously in its attempt to cross the road, as though aware of the fast moving vehicles. The animal was enormous, a hog, which must have weighted at least four hundred pounds. Suddenly from behind me, the lieutenant appeared, running with his right arm extended, and gripping his 45 automatic gun ran past me; and at close range, emptied the gun's seven shells into the animal's body. The impact from the velocity of the shells literally lifted the hog about four feet off the ground and held it momentarily suspended in mid-air before the animal came crashing to the ground snorting loudly and gasping for air; it died almost instantly.

Despite the fact of witnessing the horrible scene, especially the agony of the animal dying, the sight was not frightening. What was frightening, however, was the expression on the lieutenant's face while in the act of shooting the animal. He had the sadistic look of a man who seemingly had gone completely mad, with his eyes bulging, and his face crazed with a raging fury. What made it all the more puzzling was I had previously known the officer as a likeable person, extremely friendly, always smiling and telling jokes. Never before the incident had I ever observed this expression on his face. How a small firearm, the prized possession of all the naval officers, and the "black beauty" all the sailors admired was able to destroy a four hundred pound hog in a matter of seconds was one of the perplexing aspects that amazed me about the event. The other was how the small gun had converted, almost instantly, the behavior of a person from one of friendliness to that of an ugly individual who appeared to have lost all sense of control with himself while shooting a defenseless animal.

The gun's "beauty," and the silver colored flying machines rapidly faded away. And the roar of the planes' engines during take-offs and simulated aircraft landings on the small "landing strip" became an every day annoying occurrence. Our assignments as radiomen, or "sparks" as we were commonly known evolved into an endless monotonous routine of "standing" eight hours "radio watches" each day or night sending, receiving and deciphering coded messages. For those curious about the origin of the nickname "sparks," the name derived from the rating logo on Navy radiomen's uniforms, which depicted a series of three small jagged lines in the shape of a saw-tooth on a carpenter's saw that symbolized a band of sparks or arc lights between two closely spaced terminals from an electrical source, for example, an automobile's storage battery.

Radiomen with special training in gunnery were assigned to flight crews on TBFs, the torpedo bomber fighters "Avengers," and the new SB2Cs "Helldivers," both of which had three men crews, the pilot, navigator, and the "airdale sparks" who was also the gunner; "airdale" was the name given to enlisted men assigned to flight crews. I had had neither the training to fire guns on aircraft, nor for that matter, the desire to be on a flight crew despite the fact that, not unlike submarine personnel, "airdales" received extra pay known as "flight skins." More appropriately, it should have been called hazardous pay. Even in those times as somewhat of an innocent youth, I had misgivings about flying, especially in fighter aircraft. An incident, which in a way relieved the monotonous routine day, re-enforced the fear I had for flying. Though it may tend to sound like an inconsistency, many years later, perhaps only to satisfy my curiosity, I learned to fly aircraft.

The likelihood of better understanding the cause of the accident may be made possible with a basic explanation of the procedures a pilot must strictly adhere to in landing on an aircraft carrier. When a plane approaches the carrier, its air speed indicator instrument must be at the lowest possible speed for the aircraft to remain airborne, or maintain its lift. Any lower speed than the one specified by the plane's flight manual Will result in the aircraft stalling, or literally plunging to the ground. Understandably, this is the most critical phase in the landing, and the purpose for the speed limitations is to enable the plane's tail hook to engage the cable that lies across the carrier's flight deck and bring the plane to a sudden stop without ripping the aircraft apart. This is most likely to happen if the aircraft approaches the carrier at fast speeds.

The incident, or more realistically speaking, the accident occurred when I was near the edge of the "landing strip" in full view of the plane, a "wildcat" fighter, as it was making its approach for a simulated carrier landing. It must have been about a quarter of a mile from the "landing strip's threshold, and at an altitude of about fifty feet. Suddenly, the aircraft dropped vertically from the sky and plunged straight down into the water. It floated momentarily, and I saw the pilot slide the cockpit canopy backward and dived over the side before the plane submerged. A powerboat was dispatched, and within minutes he was removed from the calm turquoise blue waters of the lagoon. I ran toward the small dock to see the pilot when he came ashore, however, on his arrival I noticed he was not smiling, but rather a glum young man about my age. What surprised me more than his youthful appearance, or the lack of a smile on his face, was the order given for him to immediately take off in another aircraft and attempt the landing again. Thinking about the incident at this moment, I can only speculate that the order to take off and land again must have been given to dispel any notions of fear the pilot may have had as a result of his accident. Two other similar accidents occurred during the many months on the Island, but odd as it may seem, never did I witnessed any attempts made to salvage any of the super-expensive aircraft from the lagoon's shallow waters. Most likely because of their probable extensive damage, the Navy had decided there was no longer any need for the obsolete aircraft.

CHAPTER 56

More On Logic Reasoning

The lagoon's magnificence, especially highlighted during sunset hours, was the remedy for the long days of boredom when the blazing sun acted as the catalyst for the inactivity of the soul. By contrast, sunsets accompanied by cool sea breezes were the stimulating source for exciting one's senses with thoughts of the splendors of being alive, healthy, able to perceive some of the wonders of nature, and indulge the soul with reveries full of imaginations. These were the daydreams and musings incited by the glorious powers of viewing in total silence a sunset casting its golden images of gleaming light on the turquoise colored waters of the lagoon. Far off in the distance one was able to see the white foam from the ocean's waters as it splashed against the reef. Beyond the reef, and toward the Island's shore, the calm shallow waters provided the ideal setting for the CB's small sailboats gliding swiftly and silently along the glowing waters. The lifelong enthusiasm for the joys of sailing, for moving effortlessly without the aid of power engines and their irritable roar, had its origin on this Island. A tiny Island encircled by the natural beauty of a white reef, which was the sole barrier protecting it from the violent waters of the Pacific Ocean.

Purposely, I have attempted to paint with words an idyllic picture of the lagoon at sunset in order to contrast it with the ugly effects that only man can impose on nature with his destructive forces. For reasons that are still not clear today, one morning the CBs began to, what I was only able to guess, deepen a particular area in the lagoon. Perhaps lacking a dredge, the essential tool for performing this type of work, they proceeded instead to embed sticks of dynamite in the lagoon's shallow bottom. Thereafter, when the dynamite was set-off, the waters gushed upward almost ten feet into the air. The thunderous sounds from the explosives must have been heard miles away from the Island. Soon after, the waters were literally covered with dying fish flapping their bodies helplessly before death put them to rest, floating but never to move again. Indeed, it was not a pretty sight, but nonetheless, one, which had some redeeming values. About an hour after the explosion, many natives from nearby Islands surmising what had happened, arrived in large outrigger canoes, gathered the enormous quantities of fish, and sailed away, happily chanting strange sounding melodies; after which, and in days ahead they would be consuming delicacies from the sea.

I was not as fortunate as those Islands natives; never, in a span of almost two years in the South Pacific, can I recall having fresh fish, or in fact, any other fresh meats or vegetables. Everything associated with food came from cans, was dehydrated, or converted into powder, for instance, the milk, mashed potatoes, and powder eggs, which naturally were always served scrambled. Canned corn beef and spam were the staple meats, and there were times when even at breakfast spam and baked beans were served to us. On Sundays we had what was considered the treat of the week, and what we thought was roast beef. The meat, however, was always abnormally dark, and exceptionally tough to chew. Surprisingly, one day I found out from one of the cooks that the supposedly roast beef we had been eating was actually canned horsemeat from Australia. Nevertheless, our special delights really happened on Tuesdays when all enlisted personnel received their weekly ration of two cans of beer and four Hershey bars. As to be expected, beer was very much in demand, and therefore, I never had any problems exchanging my cans of beer for bars of chocolates. Of course, the bars always melted in their wrappers from the heat of the relentless tropical sun; still, who can dispute that eight bars of delicious melted chocolate once a week were better than not having any chocolate at all.

The Sunday struggles with horsemeat, Tuesday's delights and our military duties on the small Island came to an unexpected end. After what seem almost like an eternity, but actually were fifteen months, all personnel were ordered to other Islands, however, some weeks before the move, we were treated to a special visitor whom everyone knew, not from any personal contacts, however, but from his movies and radio shows. Bob Hope arrived one morning with a small troupe of musicians, Francis Langford, and the hilariously funny man with the walrus mustache and rolling eyes, Jerry Colonna. That evening on an open-air makeshift stage, and in a steady downpour of torrential rains, we sat on palm tree logs roaring with laughter at the antics of both comedians; and especially at Bob Hope's opening monologue in which he referred to the Island as "Alcatraz with palm trees." Ms. Langford's radiance and lively singing added luster to the fact that she was the first white female we had seen since leaving the States.

Our unit, "Acorn 27" was dispersed, and we were assigned to various other Islands. A radio technician and I were the only enlisted men ordered to report to "Fleet Air Wing Ten," a Naval air squadron based on another Island unknown to us at the time. So, as a result, the "tour of duty" on Ponam Island came to an unexpected end. Yes, the small Island did have a name, and what's more, it was part, a very small part to be more precise, of the Admiralty Islands. Yet, on second thoughts, I may have been mistaken in describing a particular period in time as coming to an unexpected end. What prompts me to say this is the well-known fact that sooner or later everything comes to its final end; it's what makes-up a part of reality. This should explain why I was wrong in stating the words, unexpected end. Even stones have their end, moreover, with the passing of time, they will erode to sand, eventually to drift upward into the atmosphere as dust.

In coming to terms with ourselves in relation to the element of time, we realize that time is indeed an artifact invented by man, and therefore can be on-going as long as there is human life on earth. Nonetheless, we cannot say the same for the conceptual meaning of the word end. End is distinguishable from time in that it can never be ongoing. More precisely, nothing in our world is endless, nor is it forever, without any exceptions whatsoever, and all material things, or what is known as matter, whether living or not have their ultimate end. This is the independent variable man can never hope to manipulate. If we were to base it on our human capacity to reason, or perhaps of more relevance on our past experience, we can conclude that, in fact, there is a definite end to everything. Further, this end repeats itself in all things, not in a laboratory of course, but in the real world. This may be the enigma that tends to haunt us throughout our lifetime, which is that, indeed, we are mortal beings, and some day our permanent end will arrive.

It may be the innate nature in some of us who are inclined to always search for answers that most likely will never be found; but why is this so? In our quest for answers, or for reasons for our temporary existence, answers to our inquiries are nowhere to be located except in religious dogma, or physicists' theories. The religious dogma is based on the belief that the universe and all living matter are the sole creation of an All Mighty God. Furthermore, God's purpose in creating mankind was for us to worship him with rites of references, to love him, and for us to be virtuous; yet, he made us sinners. And as the English philosopher, David Hume, critically pointed out, "if God is all powerful and all loving, the question is why is there evil and suffering, and why doesn't God eliminate this evil and suffering as a way of showing his love for us?" Before proceeding further with these thoughts, I should declare my purpose to the reader, however. The intent is not blasphemous by any means, nor is it displaying in words contempt or mockery toward a God. Rather, it can be related to an exercise in logic reasoning about religion's answers to questions regarding our origin, and causes for what I have already stated, our temporary existence on earth.

Continuing further with this line of reasoning, why the need for God to have our love when he has the power to implant this love for him on us? And for added measures, what was God's purpose for creating the universe and Adam, and from Adam's rib Eve, and then proceeded to punish them and their off springs, and all mankind by making them mortal beings because Adam had disobeyed his order? These mortal beings, moreover, if they are not vegetarians, and it can be said the majority of them are not, kill animals to satisfy their urges to consume meat, and some even kill animals for the sheer sporting pleasure it brings them. What's more, mortal beings psychologically and physiologically torture and violently kill one another, not only in times of wars, but also in times of peace when there are no wars. And to make matters worse, mortal beings are subjected to anguished sufferings from mental and physical pain, and from the distress of knowing that, ultimately, they will die from wars, old age, an incurable illness, or from an accident in the early or late years of their lives.

Intellectual man is constantly seeking answers to the unknown, and searching for causes. This may be a factor to consider in analyzing the following thoughts. If there is a God, a righteous God, why is he so harsh with us? Isn't our mortality enough of a punishment? Why has he also inseminated us with traits of cruelty behavior, and imposed on us the sufferings of pain and sickness? Applying logic reasoning to these thoughts, we begin to wonder, and become somewhat puzzled in realizing that it happened only because Adam disobeyed God's order. Why wasn't Adam given a second chance to redeem himself? Why was he not entitled to a second chance, specifically, when it concerned his compulsive behavior toward Eve? To go on with the questions, and the search for causes and answers, where was God, and what exactly was he involved in before creating the universe and man? Logic reasoning keeps reminding me something must have existed before God. I keep telling myself, isn't there always a beginning for everything, or a cause and effect for all that confronts us on earth? At the risk of repeating myself, what cause, purpose or reason did God have for all his creations?

Religion, so it seems to this observer, is not to question, but rather to accept and believe in an All Mighty God Who is to be obeyed and worshipped. Questions about the evolution of the universe and man are simply answered by believing in the powers of a God. As a result, one becomes aware there are no profound mysteries to solve about the origin of the universe and one's existence, since God created both the universe and us. At this point the reader may detect a subtle tone of skepticism in the writer's mind, and rightfully, this may be the case. In a clearer sense, however, religion can mold one into a passive individual who accepts the religious doctrine, rather than question it. Moreover, religion can be seen as a concept of believing in something without perceiving it or understanding it. Thus, in some manner, religion can instill fears in one, for instance, fear of the unknown, fear of not going to heaven and an everlasting joyous life, or worse, the fear of going to hell if one fails to love God or to do good deeds on earth. A critical analysis of this may influence us to conclude that there may be an ulterior motive underlying religious beliefs. And that is, religious people, in general, may be motivated, not unlike many of us, by their selfish needs. Their beliefs may not be associated with the joys of believing in an All Mighty God, but conforming to the religion's doctrine so that God will grant them an everlasting life in the heavens after death. Nevertheless, in the final analysis, religion, in fact all religions can harm no one, specifically, with their code of ethics and guidance in moral behavior.

Religion can indeed provide answers to questions relating to one's existence; but what about the atheist person, the non-believer in a God? Will the "big bang" theory possibly furnish him with answers about his existence on earth? Reflecting on the theory that claims the universe originated approximately twenty billion years ago as a result of a violent spontaneous explosion of gases, I have my doubts about this. A skeptic's doubts no less, debating whether to accept the "big bang" as the source of origin for all living matter; however, what if we were to accept the theory? If so, doesn't it seem odd that since its origin, all forms of nature have replicated themselves in all their forms. Without any exceptions whatsoever, all the complex structures of nature, whether man, animal or mineral have replicated their unique physical arrangements in symmetrical cycles, which correspond to their original forms. Therefore, is it probable, we may now ask, that the results from a spontaneous explosion have been repeating themselves for billions of years? Logic and our sense of reasoning should cast some doubts on this. Nonetheless, not being a scientist nor a physicist, the two professions that lend themselves to making inferences in these matters, my assumption can be regarded only as perhaps nothing more than mere speculative guesswork.

CHAPTER 57

Manus and Leyte Islands

Fleet Air Wind 10 was not based on Manus Island; and why was I to spend a week's time there without much to do, except for one memorable "guard duty" experience, I was never to find out. The Island of Manus, which is the largest one of the Gilbert Islands, was to become well known after the war for the research work about the native population carried-out by the anthropologist, Margaret Mead. Moving along its shoreline's relatively calm waters in the slow moving flat bottom "landing craft infantry boat," (LCI,) the initial reaction was the Island's immense size. Manus, in comparison to Ponam Island, was enormous, with a high mountain range extending along its center as far as the eye could see. What appeared to be the main road, or highway, because of the congestion of vehicular traffic on it, had been paved with a mixture of sand and gravel, and located along the Island's coastal area. Army trucks of various sizes, "command cars," used exclusively by Army officers, and jeeps rumbled along the highway generating engine noises and dust in what appeared to be an endless chain of vehicles. Shifting my gaze from the shoreline to the distant horizon ahead, I saw what looked like a long rocky jetty extending from shore to about a half mile out on the ocean. However, as the LCI approached closer to it, I realized the jetty was actually a long wooden pier that was almost level with the ocean's surface waters, and anchored alongside the pier was a large cargo ship. The landing boat pulled-up near the ship, where, on the pier, a "personnel carrier" truck waited to take us, not to a Quonset hut or a tent as I had expected, but to a wooden barrack about an hour's drive from the pier.

Prior to boarding the truck, a scene confirmed what had previously been only rumors. Bags of Portland cement, each weighing ninety four pounds, were piled up six feet high along the entire pier. Young men, all of whom were blacks dressed in olive colored trousers and shirts, and wearing the familiar sailor hats, were busily involved in lifting the heavy bags of cement from the pile and loading them on to trucks; also, many of them were unloading the ship's cargo. At the time, it never occurred to me to question why those men whose customary work was usually that of cooks and servants for naval officers had also been relegated the duties of stevedores. Nor was I aware until then that the United States Navy was, in fact, influenced by race distinctions in their selection of personnel to perform heavy manual labor assignments.

We left the pier in a truck that resembled an Army troop carrier with benches on both sides to accommodate us, and wooden bars arching from one side of the truck to the other to support the canvas roof; however, no canvas was draped over the bars so that we had full view of the landscape. Traveling along the bumpy graveled highway toward our destination, I suddenly began to detect a slight odor of rotting flesh. And the further we traveled the stronger the offensive odor seem to get, until it became almost unbearable to breath. Then, at that particular moment, I discovered where the source of the stench was coming from. About a half mile ahead of us, and perhaps no more than two hundred yards from the highway I sighted what appeared to be a large burial ground used to temporary inter servicemen who had been killed in combat. No doubt, the lack of a morgue facility on the Island to store the bodies until a ship with refrigerated compartments was available to take them to the States, was the reason for the makeshift cemetery; apparently, the ship docked at the pier was the one that was to take the dead servicemen's remains to the mainland. That must have been the reason for the numerous groups of Black native men with bandanas rapped around their faces just below their eyes, which most likely served to ward-off the offensive odors, who arduously labored with picks and shovels around the graves. Purposely I presumed, the truck slowed down almost to a complete stop for the driver and his companion to get a better view. What the natives were involved in was the ghastly task of excavating the dirty pine coffins from the shallow graves and transferring the bodies into new pine coffins. Thereafter, the coffins were placed alongside the opened graves ready to be taken to the pier. Adding to the gruesome sight were the yells and screams heard from the natives every time they unearthed a coffin. These screams, I assumed, were caused by the natives' initial encounter with the strong and almost suffocating odors rising from a pine coffin that perhaps had only been buried for a week. As the truck began to increase its speed, I thought never will I forget this scene, in particular, the odors that emanated from decaying human flesh.

The event that I'm about to describe cannot be defined as the somewhat morbid one witnessed on the highway, but rather as a memorable experience that happened a few days after my arrival on Manus Island. Along with other sailors, most of whom detested the assignment once they heard about it, I was selected for "guard duty." The fact that I had never received training for this type of work, nor had I had any previous experience in it, did not deter the lieutenant from assigning me to this "line of duty;" and to make matters worse, I was scheduled for what was commonly known in the military as "the dog watch," or the time period from midnight until 6AM in the morning. Naturally, I was not happy with the assignment, especially on finding out I was to guard an ammunition depot.

Contrary to the building I had envisioned, the ammunition depot was nothing more than a huge outdoor mound rising to a height of a two story building. Wooden cases and crates of every conceivable size were piled-up one on top of another giving the mound somewhat of a pyramid appearance. Olive colored tarpaulins covered the top portion of the mound to protect it from the periodic rains. About one hundred yards from the mound, the terrain suddenly sloped upward to meet the wilderness of the mountainous jungle. The ammunition depot, according to widespread rumors, was suspected of presenting an inviting target for the known remnants of Japanese forces whose soldiers had opted for the mountain's jungle as their only means of escaping from the Americans.

On the night of my "guard duty," I was driven to the base's outer perimeter, which was where the depot was located, and where I was to relieve the sailor who had been on duty the previous six hours. There, I was handed a fully loaded carbine with a "magazine clip" containing seven shells, an extra "magazine clip," and orders to fire the rifle at any one approaching from the jungle, or at any unusual noises I may hear coming from the surrounding area. The technology for long range wireless field telephones was still decades away from being developed, therefore, at that instant I knew the weapon was my only practicable way of alerting others far away from the depot. Soon after the truck drove away with its two occupants, I found myself alone, in total darkness, and somewhat fear stricken guarding the portion of the mound facing the jungle.

Imagination can play strange tricks on one's psyche, especially in darkness of night. Reflecting on this experience, a passing thought comes to mind, the memories of a popular song's lyrics from that era, "Imagination is funny, it makes a cloudy day sunny." During those long hours of constant dread, I heard, not what they actually were, the sounds of birds chattering, but what I had imagined to be Japanese soldiers imitating the wild life sounds of nature; or worse yet, what I had conceived to be human voices speaking a foreign language. Often, there were times when I was tempted to fire the carbine but the fact my eyes had become accustomed to the darkness, thus enabling me to see neither mental nor actual images of men or animals approaching from the nearby jungle, discouraged me from firing the rifle. Dawn with its gradual appearance of daylight, and what was more important to me, the sounds of an oncoming truck was a welcomed relief from those anxious hours I had endured guarding an ammunition depot on Manus Island in the South Pacific.

Four weeks after the successful invasion of Leyte, we landed on the Island. The voyage from Manus Island to Leyte, which lasted three days aboard an amphibian ship, specifically, a landing ship tank, (LST,) was not a smooth one despite the calm waters we encountered. Its flat bottom hull made it almost impossible for the craft to navigate smoothly, even with the absence of rough waters. Similar to a small transport, the ship had two huge swinging doors on its bow enabling it to unload a cargo of tanks on a beach. On this particular voyage, however, the cargo consisted solely of military personnel, and tanks were nowhere to be seen. The landing on Tacloban Beach whose shores were cluttered with many wooden crates housing all kinds of supplies was relatively peaceful. Shredded leaves on swaying palm trees along the Island's shoreline were the only visible signs of past battles. Not unlike the arrival on Manus, we were put on a convoy truck and driven five miles inland to a rather small sloping area with tents scattered along both side of the main road.

Leyte's native population was oriental, and with its constant heat periodic rains and the ubiquitous palm trees that by now had become a common sight, appeared to be no different from any of the other Islands in the South Pacific. Nonetheless, an uncommon sight were the Philippine women walking along the side road usually carrying bundles on their heads, and always a few steps behind their men who, grasping their customary canes made from short branches of trees, appeared to serve only as guides for their women. Dating from cultural attitudes perhaps, women obviously were the subservient commodities of men. Whether toiling in the fields or tending to the life stock, women always seem to be occupied with some form of manual labor. An everyday ritual for some of them was their appearance at the tents volunteering their services as laundry women for a small fee. Their quality service of picking-up our dirty clothes and returning them the following day cleaned pressed and neatly folded was a welcomed luxury for us, who unlike the officers, were not accustomed to the amenities of having others do our dirty laundry.

Not until leaving Leyte two weeks after my arrival did I realized the Island was just another stopping point on the journey to join my "outfit," Fleet Air Wing 10. One bright sunny morning the radio technician and I were put on a small motorboat that took us about a mile offshore to a waiting PBY destined to fly us to our final destination in the Philippines. The PBY, a twin engine sea plane, or Catalina as it was popularly known, was a majestic sight in blue and white colors with its fuselage looking like a large boat's hull, and having a huge graceful wingspan. That this was my first experience in an aircraft surely contributed to the excitement of the moment. Nevertheless, once inside, and seeing the drab interior with visible exposed ribs that provided the foundation for the fuselage's "skin," or covering, and with its dull olive colored sides, soon diminished the initial impression. Adding more to the disappointment, was the intense roar from the plane's overhead engines, and as a result, everyone on board had to wear earphones attached with microphones in order to communicate with one another.

CHAPTER 58

Palawan Island

Approximately two hours after the departure from Leyte, the aircraft landed on a bay in Puerto Princesa, Palawan Island. The City of Puerto Princesa was the Island's capital, though during the many months there, I cannot recall ever seeing anything resembling a city. However, what I do remember was the bumpy jeep ride on a dirt road, which sliced through the jungle, and abruptly ended before a large wide opened area that on first glance appeared to have been enclosed by the surrounding jungle. Almost in the area's center was a long runway with the smell of gasoline fumes permeating its entire length, and the outer areas of the runway were literally covered with parked B-24 "Liberator" bombers. Beyond the aircraft, many Quonset huts were scattered throughout the landscape, and all with their familiar depressing gray corrugated steel shells. One of these huts, the radiomen's residence, or in the Navy's jargon, "sleeping quarters," was to be my home shared with nineteen other radiomen who were also attached to Fleet Air Wing 10.

Fleet Air Wing 10 was a group of air squadrons assigned to fly bombing missions, or "strikes" as they were known, to Borneo, which was still occupied by Japanese forces. Assigned to the squadrons were the "airdale" radiomen who were part of the B-24s' flight crews, and twenty "land based" radiomen, one of whom was this writer. Using Morse code to transmit and receive messages, "land based" radiomen maintained radio communications "around the clock," or twenty four hours a day seven days a week with airborne B-24 "Liberators" patrolling South China Sea, and B-24s on bombing missions to Borneo. Similarly, the "airdales" had the responsibility of "guarding," or listening continuously on the frequencies for any pertinent messages for them, and transmitting to the base navigational "check points" both on the "outbound," and "inbound legs." Further, they reported attacks on enemy targets, and any emergencies during the flights. For example, any mechanical malfunctions, or what was considered worse, they reported enemy attacks, either from anti-aircraft guns on the ground, or from airborne Japanese fighter planes.

A brief description of the squadrons' destructive weapon may be a way of underscoring man's corruptive capacity for devising ways in which to destroy other human beings. The B-24 was a monstrous four engines aircraft that enabled its ten men crew to fly great distances of thousands of miles for the sole purpose of dropping a load of bombs each weighing 12,800 pounds on what had been declared by the U.S Navy as enemy territory. These powerful bombs were, to quote an often used phrase, only "the tip of the iceberg,' or a preview of bigger destructions to come. The atomic bomb was about a year away from making its appearance. A B-24's crew consisted of the commissioned officers, the command pilot, co-pilot, and the bombardier. Completing the ten men crew were the enlisted men, two of whom were "beam gunners," one "vental ball gunner," one "turret gunner," and one "tail gunner." The radioman was also a gunner who had his own compartment, which was like a mini-radio shack, with a gun turret on its roof. Each of the gunners manned a 50 caliber machine gun. In essence, the camouflaged aircraft in colors of dark green and light brown was the weapon utilized for transporting mass destruction to far-away places inhabited, more likely than not, by a civilian population, and not by enemy soldiers.

"Land based" radiomen were not required to fly in these aircraft. Nevertheless, at our discretion, we were given once a month the privilege, if you can call risking your life a privilege, of flying one mission, which entitled us to extra pay, or "flight skins." To be quite frank, the fear of what was liable to happen and the possible adverse effects from it, discouraged me from ever volunteering to go on any patrol flights, or bombing "strikes." The fear prevailed despite the fact that in all the months I was on Palawan Island, only one B-24 was lost, not in combat, however, but because of mechanical failure. Surprisingly, I gradually grew accustomed, and somewhat contented with the routine of "standing eight hours radio watches" on the ground knowing that a little over a year remained for my tour of overseas duty to end. Thereafter, in accordance with operational procedures known as the "rotation" cycle, a radioman arrived at the base specifically for the purpose of relieving me of my naval duties, thus making it possible for me to return to the States.

It may well be a fact that a routine tends to lull the senses by our failure to realize that, no matter how familiar the situation or task may be, the unexpected is always hovering over us. Moreover, it's liable to occur when we least expect it. This can be related to the ever-present mosquitoes on the Island that were likely to attack us at any time without any prior warning. The routine was suddenly interrupted one night while walking toward the Quonset hut after completing the four to midnight "radio watch." Walking from the radio shack to the hut, which was a distance of about a mile, involved, at some point, crossing the end of the runway. As I approached the runway, ambling along in a nonchalant fashion, on a cloudless night illuminated by a full moon, I heard the first frightening short bursting sounds from the sirens. These sounds were alerting everyone on the base of an on-coming air attack by the Japanese. Surmising the most likely target for the planes had to be the runway, almost in near panic, I realized at that moment my life was in danger.

The initial reaction was to find an underground shelter, of which there were none to be seen anywhere, no foxholes, or anything resembling a hole in the ground. But what did catch my eye, and which somewhat reduced my anxiety level, was an enormous bulldozer a few yards to the left of my path. Quickly running toward my objective, and getting under the huge machine, I crouched my body between its two tracks. Moments later I heard the distinct but unfamiliar roar of Japanese aircraft engines, and shortly thereafter, the thunderous explosions from the bombs dropped on the runway. By all accounts, the air attack was a relatively small one, with one or two planes, and lasting no more than a few minutes. Yet, the steady blasts from the sirens signaling "the all clear," were not heard for another hour. During that period, in the far-way distance, most likely from someone having a portable radio in a foxhole, I heard for the first time the faint sounds of the Andrew Sisters singing "Rum and Coca Cola." This was the song in which they had created new sounds to the well known soft drink label by placing emphasis on the first letter /A/ and the second letter /O/ of the words, Coca Cola. More than anything else, what was memorable about the event was, not the air attack with the bursting bombs, but hearing the Andrew Sisters, and their rhythmic calypso sounds from that lively song. This was my first, and what was to be the last actual encounter with an enemy whom I never saw in all the months in the South Pacific; though as ironic as it may seem, I saw the Japanese everywhere in New York City before Pearl Harbor, and always lugging their expensive cameras, and taking photos of practically everything within their sight.

Japanese soldiers, or their civilian counterparts, were no where to be seen on Palawan Island, and we therefore were allowed to venture outside the base in our times of leisure, specifically, when we had no work assignments. On numerous occasions some of us left the base in search of, I don't think any of us knew. Probably, it may have been a way to relieve the monotonous of all that was familiar to us, the Quonset huts, the runway, and the seashore, which was on one side of the base. Always the same scenes greeted us on these excursions, the dense jungle with trees that appeared to be held together by a profusion of vines that surrounded them, and an occasional tall palm tree by the side of the narrow dirt road that cut through the jungle like a furrow made by a plow.

On one occasion, however, we wandered a greater distance along the dirt road than we had previously gone before. Eventually, one of us sighted a slight clearing in the jungle, which appeared to be a footpath barely visible to the eye, obviously from the lack of anyone using it. We followed it for about a half a mile, when suddenly directly ahead of us in the far distance was a large oval shaped clearing about the size of a large parking lot. Situated around the clearing's outer edges were houses, which at first glance had the appearance of dollhouses because of their extremely small sizes; all had little porches facing the open area, and appeared to be freshly painted in bright colors of greens, blues and yellows. As we approached the area and got a better view of the houses, much to our surprise, people, both males and females, including some children were on the porches frantically waving their arms outwardly for us to go. Undoubtedly they were not welcoming us, nevertheless, we kept walking toward the small houses ignoring their arm signals. At this point, as we came closer and able to hear them shouting at us in some strange foreign language, and with frenzied arm gestures waving us away, having misgivings about proceeding any further, we halted in our tracks and came to a standstill. After gazing at them and their little houses for about a minute or so about ten yards away from them, we opted to end our excursion and return to the base.

Narrating the event the following day to my supervisor, a "chief petty office," I found out our group had unknowingly intruded on the only leper colony on the Island. Strictly speaking, not one of us ever went back to get another look at those cute little house painted in bight colors. Fear from coming within close proximity of people with leprosy had been our main concern, after finding out those wretched souls, because of their dreaded, incurable and highly contagious disease, were confined to a life-long sentence in those little houses in the middle of the jungle. It's interesting to note that recent studies have shown that leprosy, in fact, is not the contagious disease it was once believed to be.

The Island's natives, unlike those confined in the leper colony were free to go anywhere. In fact, they were allowed on the base, especially if they had something to sell. Relatively short with dark skin, almost black to be more precise, and the absence of oriental features common in the people of Leyte, the Palawan natives had the facial appearances of Malaysians. They were a common sight on the base, and always peddling their wares, which were mostly necklaces and bracelets made from seashells. However, on rare occasions they had monkeys perched on their shoulders offering them for sale as pets. How they had managed to capture the wild creatures was a bit of a mystery until cleared for me by one of the pilots.

Somehow, the natives had discovered the psychic greed in the animal's nature, which ultimately led to their capture by, of all things, a coconut. A hole, only big enough for the monkey to get his paw into, was made in a large unripe green coconut. The coconut, along with the bait, a ripe banana inside its hole, was then placed in an area where primates were known to congregate. A monkey on seeing the banana, stuck his paw inside the hole, grabbed it, and instinctively attempted to remove the fruit. However, only by releasing the banana and leaving it where he had found it, was the animal able to extract his paw from the coconut. Not wanting to give-up the precious fruit, he therefore kept holding on to it; and since the weight of the coconut prevented the monkey from running or climbing trees, he was easily captured. By his refusal to release the banana, the animal sacrificed his only means of escape. In short, what is the moral of this story? Can it be that greed will get us nowhere? Nonetheless, the least we can say is that greed led the monkey, not to his freedom, but instead to his ultimate capture.

The daily sight of these natives trying to sell, among other things, all kinds of trinkets and monkeys predisposed us to some of their odd merchandise. For example, they sold, or attempted to sell, reptiles of all sizes, turtles and iguanas. However, nothing prepared me for the grisly sight encountered one day on the way to the radio shack. I had crossed the runway, and beyond it was an area used as an athletic field, or a place for hanging out watching others play ball. About fifty yards ahead, a small group of sailors had gathered, and others were running toward what was quickly becoming a crowd. Obviously something of interest was happening, and I quickened my pace and headed toward the crowd. On arriving at the scene, I saw sailors had gathered in a large circle, and some were snapping pictures of a native standing in the middle of the circle. In one hand he was holding a brown burlap bag where he had carried it. And dangling from his other hand, the man held a short piece of rope, which had been attached to the shriveled neck of the decapitated head of a Japanese. The head, most likely, must have been that of a Japanese soldier discovered wandering in the jungle. What made the sight all the more horrible was its ghastly appearance, that is, the head had swollen to almost twice its normal size. The blood around the neck where the head had been severed had become coagulated, and because of the head's rigormortis condition, it must have happened only several hours before the native brought it to the base. Notable was that the native was not trying to sell it, but merely charging the sailors a fee for the privilege of photographing him with it, or having their pictures taken holding the gruesome thing. Never mind whether there was a moral issue to consider or not, the native indeed had no problems getting customers.

In attempting to analyze the behavior of both the sailors and the native, there is, no doubt, a moral issue to be considered. To pass judgment on the native, however, may be somewhat ludicrous. Hence, we can exclude him, who most likely may have been a borderline savage with little or no sense of reasoning, no formal education, and having only the instincts of survival at any cost. His objective probably was to acquire whatever means were available to him in order to survive. Nonetheless, is there any way to justify the sailors' actions in light of whom they were, civilized human beings having some education, some form of values, and certainly, the capacity to reason. Their behavior can be analyzed, if we begin by first referring to the dictionary's definition for the word moral. There, in it broadest form, the word is defined as "conforming to a standard of what is right and good." Arguably, this "standard" cannot be applied to all circumstances, especially when we take into account the situation or setting where the incident occurred. To observe, analyze, and thereafter draw conclusions, we may discover that here we have sailors, who in all probability have experienced combat, the sight of human blood associated with it, and worst of all, may have witnessed the death of their comrades directly related to a common enemy. Moreover, these sailors, though quite civilized, with a sense of values, some education and the ability to reason, may not have been thinking about moral behavior at the moment they were willing to have their picture taken with a human head that had been decapitated. In particular, the fact that the head represented an enemy who had inflicted death and bloodshed on their "mates." Perhaps, to a lesser degree, boredom, or the lack of social activities may have contributed to the sailors' behavior. Further, their youth, all were in their early twenties, may have been another possible factor to consider.

Mortal beings that we are may shed some light on our behavioral nature. In fact, it can be said that nothing in our lives is everlasting. Whether it is depression, excitement or boredom, these feelings do tend to come into our lives in cycles. They come and go, but nonetheless, are never experienced on a constant level. Unless we have some type of mental health disorder, can we realistically say we are always depressed, excited, or experiencing some form of emotional feelings? The point to underscore is that sooner or later at some juncture in our lives, we experience these emotional disturbances. However, eventually they fade away, but only to make their appearances again at a later date.

Surprise is another one of those human emotions I neglected to mention, but which can directly relate to what follows. Indeed, surprised I was in reading the news about an Army B-25 aircraft slamming into the 79th floor of the Empire State Building. It was a foggy Saturday morning on July 28, 1945, and the plane, which had departed Bedford, Massachusetts with a scheduled stop at LaGuardia Airport, elected to divert to Newark Airport because of the adverse weather conditions at LaGuardia. Traveling at a speed of about 200 miles an hours, the aircraft struck what was at the time the tallest building in the world killing its pilot, two crew members and eleven other people on the ground.

On a special evening nine days after this noteworthy news event, the lack of amusements was made-up for, and in more ways than one with a surprise I should add. A U.S.O. troupe, (United

Service Organization,) arrived at the base to perform their spectacular rendition of the highly popular Broadway musical, "Oklahoma." Except for the vague memories of an eight year old boy viewing Spanish vaudeville with his mother and future stepfather, never before had I seen live performers on a stage, except for the previously mentioned Bob Hope troupe on Ponam Island. Spotlights of various colors were cast on the actors literally bathing them in glorious colors of greens, reds and yellows and many more, naturally adding to the evening's pleasure. The stage floor, which was actually a large plywood platform, was protected from the weather with a high oval shaped roof covered with corrugated steel sheets supported by two parallel metal arches not unlike the ones seen today at some McDonald's restaurants. At various times the stage was filled with actors performing a mixture of ballet and country style dancing with their intricate steps executed in a frenzied manner. Culminating the performance was a rousing musical score danced and sang by the entire cast.

Half way through the musical, and without any prior warning, the unexpected occurred. The colored spotlights suddenly were turned off, and the overhead white ceiling lights came on reflecting their piercing brightness on the stage. As though frozen to a stand still in the midst of their dancing, the performers came to an immediate halt. Immediately thereafter, the base commander appeared on the stage holding a microphone to his mouth. Apologizing for the interruption, in a firm clear voice he announced that he had just received an official notice that a secret weapon, "an atomic bomb having tremendous power" had been dropped on a Japanese City, Hiroshima, and most likely hostilities would come to an end with the expected surrender of Japan. As to be expected the instant response from the audience was a loud roar of approval. Soon thereafter, the overhead ceiling lights were turned off; then the colored spotlights re-appeared, and the show resumed to its exciting finale with the entire theatre company singing and dancing the musical's title song, "Oklahoma."

CHAPTER 59

In The Name of Patriotism

Three days after the bombing of Hiroshima, the Air Force dropped another atomic bomb on the City of Nagasaki. After the deaths and almost total destruction that rained on these two Cities, Japan surrendered on August 14, 1945. These two atomic bombs not only caused the deaths of vast numbers of people, but also maimed many of them, and left many others with the inevitable after-effects of cancer and other maladies from the results of exposure to large doses of radiation. This prompts one to ponder on the moral issue of an act that Admiral William Leahy called "barbaric." The label has far reaching implications, particularly when one considers its reputable source. At the end of the war, Admiral Leahy held the official rank of what is known today as "Chairman of the Joint Chiefs of Staff."

Political issues set aside, a serious question should be raised regarding the need for Nations to exercise some moral restraints when conducting their wars. Wars personify killings and destruction, and in the nature of things in the world we live in, surely, there will always be wars among Nations. Stronger Nations will vanquish weaker ones as the means for justifying their end, the acquisition of economic gains. However, does it have to involve a civilian population most likely made-up of the elderly who are physically incapable, or those who cannot participate in the wars because of age or gender? Nations should wage their wars in specific designated areas, or battlefields that are far away from the civilian population, and equally important, conducted solely with military people.

Reflecting on those events of World War II, a sense of moral outrage is perhaps the only way to describe the feelings in realizing the pervasive ways in which political leaders and their military followers exploited the innocence of youth then as, in effect, they still do today. No matter what military environment I happened to be in, whether close to an Island's battle zone, on a naval ship on in numerous classroom training sessions, the population was always the same. The majority consisted of young men in their late teens or early twenties. The minority group were the commissioned officers, (the leaders,) most of whom were almost twice our age. Moreover, it was this minority group and their political leaders who, supposedly having some moral judgment and wisdom because of their senior years, and all highly educated, procured the lethal weapons and implemented the battle strategies for young men to destroy one another in the prime years of their lives. Waving the deceptive banner of patriotism, these leaders looked-upon by the citizens as wise, intelligent and caring men, were indeed successful in leading the young and willing lambs to the slaughterhouse.

How can we prevent, if not totally at least to some extent, the exploitation of the youth population, particularly in times of wars by the older political people in power? For a start, perhaps the wise words of the Greek philosopher, Socrates may well serve as a useful guideline. Socrates, "recognized one good: knowledge and one evil: ignorance." Further, the "ignorance" the philosopher used to express his thoughts can be correlated with innocence. According to the dictionary, the meaning of innocence is "freedom from knowledge of evil." Thus we can conclude that a lack of "knowledge" about the evils of war can conceivably classify a person as ignorant of that particular "knowledge." What I'm leading up to is that with a formal education, most of us can acquire the "good," or the "knowledge," which to some degree will act as our shield for protecting us from those who may have ulterior motives, some self-interest, for example monetary gains, or instill in us patriotic ideals. To further emphasize the point, they may want to exploit, manipulate, or in some way or manner, take advantage of us. Finally, what can be said about this business of patriotism? Broadly speaking, patriotism is, indeed, a business that is often promoted by the rhetoric of smooth speaking politicians, and all the trappings associated with it, in particular, flags songs and buttons that connote one's beliefs. Patriotism, in essence, is the zealous support of one's Country, even if it means risking one's life in times of wars. In the final analysis, why risk our most valuable possession, our lives? Above all else that matters, our primary support should be directed, not toward any patriotic beliefs, especially those that involve sacrificing our lives, but rather, to anything that will prolong our temporary existence on this earth; and in one important aspect, the anything I'm referring to can be defined having the strong will to live to a "ripe old Age."

PART IV
The Post-War Years

CHAPTER 60

Some Observations

It's Sunday, well past mid-day and I'm sitting at the desk gazing out the window viewing the grayish sky, and searching for thoughts to put down on paper. Directly across the building is Riverside Park where the trees in their never-ending cycle for this time of year are gently dropping their brownish yellow leaves to the ground. Small pitch-black birds with yellow beaks can be seen flying in large clusters around the trees. Beyond the trees is the West Side Highway with its endless vehicular traffic, and automobiles passing by my view at intervals lasting perhaps no more two or three seconds. Paralleling the highway is the Hudson River whose murky waters are barely visible since the remaining leaves on the trees are obscuring a full view of the river.

The scene from the window is not a pleasant one, but one that tends to instill a feeling of sadness, though at this moment it's more pensive than sad. Musing about time, understanding that his birthday is but a few days away, he realizes all those years that have passed him by can never again be re-lived. Brushing away the melancholy mood, intuitively he becomes aware that, indeed, one can re-live the past with memories and recollections. The pinnacle point in his life has been reached, and all that remains is the downhill journey to the final end. Therefore, a firm commitment is made, to continue with his memories, recollections, reactions and opinions, which will serve a two-fold purpose: to relieve the past, but of more important to him, to leave his son a legacy of his father's life

Life is dynamic. It's a force that's physically or mentally constantly in motion, and even when we're asleep our mental capacities are active in dreams. Perhaps leaving a record of our lives' activities can be a method of prolonging the dynamics of life after death. The true purpose, however, may be to maintain the dynamics, if only in written form, so that those love ones will never forget us. Realizing that the final end may be rapidly approaching, we may try to grasp for anything that will keep the process of life from ending, grasping for those illusive "straws in the wind," a popular saying heard in a by-gone era, which suggests the impossibility of a situation. More so, once the process of life appears to be at its final phase, we're inclined to seek for causes and effects, or in a clearer sense, reasons for our total existence.

A total existence may not be the correct way to describe our lives, and a partial existence can be a better way of defining it. During sleeping periods, we are, in effect, not aware of our existence, and except in dreams, we have no recollections of life. Sleep therefore can be a form of temporary death in which the cycle of life begins only after waking up. Briefly summarizing these observations, we can conclude the existence of life is constituted in two cycles, one of which is the period of sleep when we're not cognizant of our existence; the other is during the awake cycles when our lives have meanings. This meaning varies of course, and it depends in how we perceive ourselves and our environment. More precisely, it's an on-going process whereby we attain a sense of ourselves as we live our days, months and years. As an illustration, in our formative years, in general, the majority of us are oblivious to any sort of a meaning for our existence. The main interest once we awake from our nightly sleep is focused on physical and mental activities, which will satisfy our needs and cravings for enjoying life. However, after the teen years, particularly as we grow older, we may gradually tend to dwell more on the meaning of our existence.

Answers that may satisfy us are not readily available for our quest for this meaning. Nevertheless, we can speculate about them in ways that will not give us answers, but may instead clarify some aspects in our lives. For instance, if we disregard the question why we exist, and focus in how we can prolong our temporary existence, we become aware in the essential patterns that will sustain us, and other patterns that we can apply during our existence. For a start, and this may sound overly simplistic, and perhaps it may be, nonetheless, based on past experiences, all of us are aware that we can function physically and mentally only by satisfying certain basic needs. We require oxygen, water, food and sleep in order to continue living; this is knowledge we're all familiar with, however, what we may not realize is that these vital patterns are what sustain life, and can never be disrupted. These basic patterns are what provide us with life. Failure to deny the body these needs will result in our existence coming to an end. Most significantly, without oxygen, death will indeed come to us within a matter of minutes. What we must realize is that from an analytical perspective, our existence is held in bondage by the sustaining powers of oxygen, water, food and sleep. Knowing the forces, or patterns, that will maintain our lives, we can observe other patterns in nature and correlate them with our basic ones, others observed, and apply them to improve our existence on earth.

All living matter conforms to the same cycle, birth, the growth process and death. In humans, however, the growth process is not only physical but also intellectual, and social as well. Naturally, with death the cycle ends, unless we believe in certain religious doctrines of an everlasting life after death, or Plato's philosophy of man's mortal body and immortal soul, which unlike the body, never perishes after death. The preeminent Greek philosopher believed that, "the immortal soul goes away to exist in another world." At this point the purpose is not to discuss my ambivalent feelings about Plato's philosophy, but rather, to concentrate on the growth process cycle, in particular, the intellectual and social aspects in our learning behavior attained as we grow older.

What is intellectual growth, how does it affect our behavior, and how do we attain it? To some individuals the intellectual may represent a person of superior mental attributes; or looking at it from a negative point of view, it can convey a pretentious individual who has "delusions of grandeur," and with his haughty demeanor may have contempt for others who are not like him. Nevertheless, in defining intellectual growth by which the individual develops in gradual stages the capacity to reason, the growth is based solely on prior knowledge, and not on sense stimuli; this is the intellectual man's creed, along with his awareness that emotions can interfere with the manner in which he perceives or deals with his situations. In short, the more knowledge we acquire, the more we add to our intellectual growth.

Arguably, knowledge is the driving force that generates the desire for other possibilities beyond those we have already achieved. We attain the power by disciplining and sacrificing our most valuable possession, time, in order to gain more knowledge and reap more possibilities. At this point the reader may rightfully question, why this quest for knowledge? What can be significant answers to the question is that with enough knowledge, we acquire a feeling of independence and usefulness. We get to understand our personality and make it work for us, aware there will always be more possibilities and more barriers ahead. We take risks in order to overcome the anxieties of not knowing; for we have learned that fear comes from the unknown. Further, we have learned that with an ample amount of knowledge we can become participants and leaders, rather than mere spectators and followers. Moreover, we have learned that with knowledge, intellectual energy and reasoning powers we can cope with any situations by controlling our emotions, observing listening and analyzing.

Reasoning powers associated with intellectual growth can improve as we gain more knowledge, furthermore, what will also improve is our social behavior. Once we achieve a sufficient amount of knowledge, naturally this depends on the individual, some of us may need more of it than others, we develop self-confidence and self-reliance. Our pride and self-esteem grow to far-reaching levels. More so, the shyness, which may have been caused by feelings of doubt, insecure, or worse, an inferiority complex all dissipate, and are replaced by what should be exercised with the utmost caution, a superiority complex, along with being sure of ourselves in all aspects of life. With our acquired knowledge we have learned the traits of a good personality are enthusiasm, charm, good manners and zest; formal wear is always practiced in a business setting, and informal wear used exclusively for pleasure. Our social behavior has endowed us with principles of good speech, thus enabling us to communicate and motivate sincerely and honestly, and the manner in which we use language can mean success or failure. Finally, we know the value of listening attentively, and showing courteous attention. These attributes, such as the one just cited can be the results of our intellectual and social growth.

Having said that intellectual and social growth develop as we acquire more knowledge, the question may now be raised, where, in fact, can we obtain this knowledge? Knowledge as we know is not a place, nor is it a material object, but an abstract word that expresses a certain quality in a person. The quality can, in a very broad sense, be defined as a state of knowing. More precisely, it is understanding, awareness, or simply a person's familiarity with a fact, place or thing. Not surprisingly, we have access to this knowledge from the time we're born until our lives end. Sources for obtaining it are our parents, school, books, the environment, religious institutions, or from our peers. However, there is a type, which perhaps in a truer sense can be a higher level of formal knowledge that may be attained in college and a graduate school. In these higher level learning institutions students, among other disciplines, focus on research and the cause and effects of specific situations or problems. After many years involved with formal education both as a student and as an instructor, my firm belief, and one which can readily be disputed, is that most of our intellectual growth, and to some extent our social growth are derived from these learning institutions. As a result, we become analytical thinkers, seldom accepting, but always questioning. Actions, we have learned, rarely occur spontaneously, and for every action there is always a reaction. To conclude, intellectual and social growth develop with knowledge that, among other things, can solve for us the mysteries of life.

CHAPTER 61

Taking on Responsibilities

The war's end came as an unexpected surprise. The Japanese were certainly tough fighters who from past combat experience were never known to surrender. Actually, the common belief among us was the war would last another ten years. Discharged six months after the end of the war, there were indeed surprises, or specifically, inconveniences in store for a twenty year old sailor conditioned to having his basic needs, food, clothing and housing satisfied by the Federal Government. For example there were the shortages of sugar, coffee, shoes, and in order to obtain these essentials, whether you were a recently discharged serviceman or a civilian you still needed the required ration coupons. Men's suits and white shirts were scarce to find because of their short supply; and nowhere were to be found the much in demand women's luxury item, nylon stockings. Likewise, critical shortages of rental apartments existed throughout the City; in fact, in order to accommodate the large influx of discharged military people and their families, the City had built a temporary housing complex on Glasson point in the Northeastern section of the Bronx overlooking Long Island sound using quonset huts.

At the beginning these shortages had no effect on me. These were the times that might have been described as carefree, or not having to be responsible or accountable to anyone. Residing at home again with my dear mother and stepfather, his son had already left home, and still on the Government's payroll by virtue of being a member of the 52/20 club, I was somewhat financially secured. In the literal sense, it was not a club, but instead, a name familiar to all unemployed discharged servicemen receiving benefits of twenty dollars a week for a maximum period of fifty two weeks from the Federal Government. Twenty dollars was not exactly an abundant amount, even in those times, nevertheless, it provided me with adequate money resources for not having to seek employment. As a result, I lounged about for a time, a few months more or less perhaps, doing very little of anything except to drive the 1941 Studebaker I had purchased with the money saved from Navy wages. With friends tagging along contributing to the cost of the gasoline when I was able to get it, (it was rationed,) and which was twenty cents a gallon, we explored the City, and all the surrounding areas, including Yonkers New Jersey and Connecticut. Weekends were consumed playing the glorious game of stickball on a block ideally suitable for the game because of its wide street; the block was 106th Street between Broadway and Amsterdam Avenues. And always, whether playing ball, socializing in civilian clothes, or wearing the naval uniform, I proudly displayed on my clothes what was then considered a badge of honor, the small gold colored lapel pin, "the ruptured duck," which, in effect, identified the wearer as an honorable discharged serviceman. The pin had the profile of an eagle with both its wings spread-out as though embracing the viewer. Of course, never can I recall receiving what might have been considered special treatment or privileges by wearing the pin. The fact that soon after the end of the war all young men, with but a few exceptions, were wearing them, may have been the probable cause.

Call it human nature if you will, in how some of us tend to become restless when we don't have a purpose to strive for in our lives. Idleness did eventually instill a feeling of restlessness to the point where I decided to go back to school, and take advantage of the benefits of free tuition provided by "The GI Bill of Rights." "GI" was the official name given to all servicemen, though actually, the meaning of the two letters was "Government Issue." After some months of leisure, the idea of going to college didn't appeal to me at the time, so I decided to attend "The YMCA Technical Center" at 63rd Street and Central Park West where I took courses in radio theory and improved my skills in sending and receiving the Morse code. The sole purpose for attending the Center was to prepare for two tests, one in radio theory and the other sending and receiving messages in Morse code administered by "The Federal Communication Commission, (FCC.) These tests had to be successfully passed, along with a "First Aid Certificate test," all of which I managed to pass after six months, before the applicant was issued a Telegraph and Telephone License, and a "First Aid Certificate." These FCC licenses and "First Aid Certificate certified one to work as a Merchant Marine radio operator aboard merchant ships. Most likely, it had to be a conflict of interest that the people at The Technical School had neglected to inform me that with the advent of teletype machines aboard merchant ships, the positions of radio operators had become obsolete.

Marriage vows were taken during this time, and four months after the fateful decision a child was born, my first son, Richard. However, the marriage did, in fact, have two redeeming values, It kept me out of the Korean War with a "3A" classification from the Draft Board, and provided me with a sponsor, a newly acquired brother-in-law, which made it possible to be accepted as a privilege member of a powerful union. "The Metropolitan Union of Garage Workers" had the exclusive rights to provide workers for the owners of all the garages in the City, and I was to become one of the workers. Still very much in evidence at this time was the critical housing shortages, which had an impact on those unfortunate ones who were shopping for rental apartments. I was one of the individuals who eventually had to settle for one of the units at the Veterans Emergency Housing Complex on Glasson Point in the Bronx. The development, in essence, was a large housing project, which was constructed with Government surplus quonset huts. Each of the huts was divided into two sections to accommodate two extremely small one and two bedrooms apartments. There, in one of the small units, the three of us lived for no more than a year. Ironic as it may seem now, after spending the better part of my military service time in those gloomy huts, I was once again subject to their depressive appearance in civilian life.

Circumstances at various times in our lives do influence us to make assumptions that may or may not be true. Involved in the wearisome task of looking for a large two bedrooms apartment to no avail, I gradually began to suspect that perhaps my failure to obtain suitable housing for my family and I may have been due to my Spanish surname. Consequently, I was seriously contemplating changing it to my wife's maiden name, Quinn, when I received an unexpected proposal from another brother-in-law. He was attending a Preparatory School in Ithaca, New York, and suggested that, because of my "GI" free tuition benefits, I should enroll in the same school and share housing expenses with him. He and his wife and two siblings lived on the outskirts of town in an old dilapidated Victorian house. Out of sheer desperation to move-out of the small apartment in the ugly Quonset hut, I accepted his offer, and the family and I relocated to Ithaca. "Cascadilla" was the name of the prep school, which according to its policy statement, the objective was to prepare students to be accepted at Cornell University; the following day after our arrival, I enrolled in the school. Not surprisingly, despite the enthusiasm at the expectations of some day attending the Ivy League college, the lack of sufficient income to provide for a wife and child compelled me to move back to the City after having attended the school for only a month.

Moving became readily possible when, in order to obtain a rent-free apartment, I applied and was hired as a custodian, or what was then known as a janitor, of a five story apartment building in the East Bronx; and still a member of the garage union, I had no difficulty getting temporary work at garages, until eventually hired as a permanent worker at a garage just off Third Avenue and fifty six Street that was to last almost four years. Union parking attendants' wages of $65.00 for working a six day week were considered relatively high, and more so, they were augmented by tips from the customers and the annual Christmas bonus, which averaged $250.00. However, the younger workers, including myself, were never aware of the hazardous working conditions they were exposed to as a result of the carbon monoxide fumes from automobiles. These were the times when the well-to-do had their private chauffeured limousines, and a number of their expensive cars were garaged where I worked permanently as a parking attendant. One in particular belonged to the popular singer Kate Smith, whom I never had the pleasure of meeting, but whose clear melodious speaking voice I often heard when she called by phone to have her chauffer pick her up at her Park Avenue residence. This was also the period when the unsightly Third Avenue El was to be razed, and as to be expected, there were great demands from the real estate developers for all the old blighted tenement buildings that lined both side of the Avenue as far north as 125th Street.

CHAPTER 62

The Expedition, and Leisure Activities

North of the City of Glens Falls, New York was were it happened, and a happening that sparked fresh memories of a long ago incident on Ponam Island in the South Pacific. Glen Falls, in comparison to other metropolis, was and still is today what can be more appropriately called a village. And not unlike today, its population, like most of the upstate towns, villages and hamlets, was indigent with the majority of the inhabitants receiving public assistance. The poverty atmosphere was particular evident in the Fall, and during the harsh and bitter cold winter months, most likely due to the absence of tourist dollars. A popular sport, especially for the men, and namely one that was more like an annual event of bringing meat to the family's table, was the Fall's deer hunting season. An invitation to participate in this annual event from yet another brother-in-law whose wife and in laws were all born, raised, and attended the public school of Glen Falls, was how I got myself involved in the so-called sporting event. Mainly out of curiosity for something never before experienced, I accepted his invitation to spend a few days with him and his family, and indulge in an activity that was to be my first and last hunting expedition.

Prior to the expedition, my notion of a hunt was that one or two men walked through the woods until an animal was sighted, and then shot, or literally caught alive, and taken home to be butchered. However, no such thing ever existed in the north woods of "the lake region." There, hunting deer had all the earmarks of a mismatched game in which all the players ganged-up on a helpless animal that, despite its ability to outrun any man, had very little chance of escaping alive. The players on this particular hunt were about a dozen or more men, including myself, and as it happens in all groups with some objective to attain, there was the designated, or self-appointed leader. He had the authority to assign those who were to be the "spotters," and the ones who were to be the "drivers,' usually the younger men, naturally, because of their youthful stamina; two young men and I were selected to be "drivers." As I was to find out later, seldom is the deer sighted by a "driver," but only heard so that it's usually one of the "spotters" who sights and shoots the animal. Nevertheless, nothing is ever absolute in this world, there are always exceptions, and this hunting expedition was to be one of those exceptions.

We began the "drive" walking at a fast pace, and purposely making as much noise as possible with our footsteps through the brush. The three of us, though starting together, quickly separated following the leader's instructions so that soon we lost sight of one another. Without seeing or hearing anyone else nearby, my only concern was not to get lost in those woods. I must have trampled through the brush for a good fifteen minutes when suddenly, I heard what sounded like a galloping horse. Almost immediately thereafter, I saw it, the deer directly ahead of me about twenty yards with its white tail pointing straight-up in the air, and as I had been told, a sure sign of a frightened deer. Immediately I brought the rifle up against my right shoulder, and with my left eye closed took careful aim at the galloping animal. But much to my surprise, I didn't pull the trigger as I had intended to do, instead, I merely stared at the deer, somewhat fascinated by it upright tail until I lost sight of it. Shortly thereafter, I heard the nearby sounds of gunshots, and ran toward where they had come from. Arriving at the scene almost at the instant of its happening, I saw the gruesome appearance of a young man, one of the "drivers," straddling the deer lying on the ground, and with his hunting knife slitting its belly below the neck and downward to the hind legs; then, while scooping out the animal's entrails with his hands, and the animal's blood all over his clothing, he was a grisly sight to behold. Similarly to what I had witnessed on a Navy lieutenant's face during which he was shooting a pig on Ponam Island, the young man's face had transformed into that of a sadistic individual raging with fury. Never again was I to participate in the so-called sporting event of killing a defenseless animal with a firearm.

Returning to the City, and locked into a job that was not in the least appealing, or to my liking, nor productive in any manner, except for the weekly wages, which realistically speaking, did provide for the household expenses, and other non-essentials, I eventually developed an enthusiasm for ballroom dancing; this did not come as a complete surprise however. Recalling my uncle Domingo's fondness for dancing, I may have inherited the aroused interest from my uncle, or probably from a tradition that is still prevalent today with Spanish people, especially those residing in the Caribbean Islands. The fact this was an era when the Spanish, or Latin bands as they were known, were at their peak in popularity, may have also added fuel to the enthusiasm for dancing. In general, not only the Spanish, but also young and middle age Americans were enthused with dancing to the music provided by Tito Puente, Tito Rodriquez and Machito and his Afro Cubans. The Palladium Ballroom was where it all happened. There, on weekends, but particularly on Wednesdays when one hour of free lessons was included in the price of admission, hordes of dancers first had their lessons, and then danced away the evening to the rhythmic beat of Latin music. Today this type of music is better known as "Salsa," however, in that era the various dances had names, for example, "the rumba," "the mambo" and "the cha-cha-cha;" and each one of them required a specific movement of both body and feet. After only a few years, the craze for Latin music came to a rapid end, and displaced by a new form of music derived from Jazz, and based on "The Blues," with the name, "Rock-n-Roll."

Aside from the dancing sessions, there were other leisure activities, for instance, the occasional outings to the movies, and of course, television viewing. Television was not the sophisticated "state of the art" medium it is today; rather, it was, in fact, technically inferior in its early stages of operation.

The novel aspect of what really amounted to viewing miniature movies in your living room instead of in a theatre seem to contribute to the enjoyment. And what significantly added to the pleasure was its imperfection since the black and white images were often blurred and grainy in appearance. This poor reception occurred despite the essential roof antenna that without it you were not able to receive the picture. The antenna was somewhat of an awkward shaped affair having two parallel metal rods, each one about sixty inches in length, and attached at their mid sections by a thirty inch crossbar, thus giving the antenna the form of a large letter /H/. The /H/ was supported by an aluminum pole, generally about ten or more feet in height, and secured to the roof's floor. Not surprising, a landlord usually charged a monthly fee to those tenants who had TV antennas on his roof. No doubt, similar to the monthly charges paid to a company today for having a cable attached to your TV set, and leading to a remote sight antenna miles away from your apartment.

This was the time before the advent of TV tape recording, so that what the viewer saw was what actually was being televised at that particular moment; as a result, many technical errors and actors' mishaps were viewed on the small screen. "Boom mikes" were often seen unintentionally at unexpected moments appearing directly above the performers' heads, though they were not meant to be within the range of the camera. At times, furthermore, actors inadvertently bumped into the set's props, specifically, sofas, chairs or lamps, slurred their words, or what must have been frustrating for them, forgot their "lines," and had to resort to adlibbing them. Moreover, programs on the small picture tube were limited to the hours of five in the evening to midnight. Prior to those times, the only images televised were the "TV patterns" that looked like bull eyes targets on archery ranges. Usually in the middle or below the pattern were seen the three or four letters identifying the station and its channel number. There were only seven channels in the broadcast band, one of which was a favorite of mine, channel eleven because of its "Night Owl Theatre" that began at ten o'clock at night and ended at midnight. The nightly program televised old movies, most of which were "B Westerns" dating back to the early thirties, and some vintage silent films from the mid-twenties, in particular, the films of Charles Chaplin and Rudolph Valentino.

CHAPTER 63

ARINC

Sunday was like any other day, more so since on that day garage customers, or tenants as they were known, took their cars for the customary drive to the countryside, and as a result, created lots more work for the parking attendants. However, unlike other weekdays, on Sundays The New York Times published their large "want ads" section; always I religiously scanned the "section" hoping to fine what I was looking for until one Sunday, eureka, I discovered it hidden in the smallest print imaginable. The ad had been placed by an airline agency seeking experienced radio operators with FCC Licenses.

Early the following Monday morning, and with my Licenses in my possession I went directly to the agency. On hearing I had no airline experience, the person interviewing me advised me that, because of my Licenses, most likely I would be hired "on the spot." Giving me instructions in how to get to the company, which was located in Valley Stream, Long Island, his last words were the fee would be one week's wages, but only if I were hired. Aeronautical Radio Inc. was the company's name, and used the acronym ARINC for its radio station's "call sign." The station manager inspected my Licenses, and asked if I had ever operated a teletype machine. On hearing my negative reply, he had me sit in front of one of the machines and type some words. What almost instantly came into my mind was the sentence I had typed many years earlier in the Naval Radio School to practice typing, "The quick brown fox jumped over the lazy dog's back." Because I was a "touch typist," or not needing to look at the keyboard to type, and with the teletype's keyboard identical to that of a typewriter, I had no difficulty typing a few of the sentences, and at a rather fast rate I may add, before he stopped me; and like the gentleman at the agency had said, I was hired "on the spot."

The position of radio operator, which was to last four and a half years involved sending and receiving radio messages from commercial airlines' airborne aircraft, and commercial aircraft that had just arrived, or were about to depart an airport. In contrast to the wartime experience, voiced communication was used, and not Morse code. All messages sent and received were typed on the radio station's teletypes and received on teletypes in the respective airliners' dispatch offices. Position reports were also relayed by telephone to air traffic controllers at "The New York Center." The station had four operating positions, or circuits as they were called, which were manned by radio operators "around the clock," or twenty four hours a day seven days a week. Each circuit monitored a specific route, for example, Pan American's Caribbean circuit, the North Atlantic circuit, and two circuits handling United Airlines' airborne traffic, and departure and arrival messages. To satisfy the airlines' policy, radio operators had to be fast typist in order to type the messages verbatim as they were received.

The North Atlantic position, in particular, had two aspects that in some respects made the work more interesting than the other three positions. The first one was hearing the distinct accents from the pilots of foreign "carriers." Foreign airlines were legally bound to have their pilots transmits their messages in English; the second was the position's operational features. Two small electronic boxes that had the appearance of cigar boxes were situated to the right and left of the teletype machine; having numerous push-buttons on them, each one was labeled with its respective airline's name. The radio operator, who had to wear earphones while manning the position so as to decrease the noise level in the station, on initially hearing the pilot's call-up on the frequency identifying his airline and "call sign," pushed-in the appropriate button for that particular airline. Thereafter, all that the radio operator typed on his teletype also appeared on another teletype located at the foreign airline's dispatch office at the airport. Not in the least dull or monotonous, the work was rather interesting, and at times exciting, especially when the operator was involved with messages of an emergency nature. The years of experience performing this type of work, ultimately led to procuring a position as an air traffic controller with the Federal Aviation Administration.

The position of an airline radio operator was, to say the least significantly different from the job of parking cars in a garage, and in effect, there were no ways to compare the two for similarities. One of the glaring differences was the work environment. In essence, there was no dirt to be seen anywhere in the radio station, and you went to work wearing clean clothing, and arrived back home with the same clean clothing. In fact, on the day shifts, all workers, whether radio operators or not, had to wear shirts and ties. Another vast difference was the air you breathed was clean and not polluted with noxious carbon monoxide fumes. Perhaps the only annoying aspect was the noise from the teletypes machines since the noiseless teletype was non-existence in those times. Still, seeing that radio operators had to wear earphones while performing their duties, they were not exposed to the machines' loud noises unless they removed their earphones. Also, unlike garages in the City, the radio station was an "open shop," which meant you didn't have to belong to a labor union, and therefore, no membership dues were deducted from you wages. The biggest fringe benefit ARINC offered, however, was the annual complimentary round trip fare for its radio operators and their immediate families, wives and children, on any airline to anywhere in the United States, including Hawaii, and the Caribbean Islands.

Vacations, as everyone knows can be costly, especially the ones to far-off places. Consequently, I prolonged the fringe benefit until the last year of employment with ARINC before taking advantage of the free fares the company offered the radio operators. Why I selected to go to Havana, Cuba rather than the Island where I was born, and where I experienced some of my most cherished childhood memories is still a questionable mystery even today. More so, in realizing the time was the summer of 1958, and at the threshold of my thirty second birthday, and yet, had never returned, nor had given it a thought, about going back to Puerto Rico since my arrival in the City in the early thirties. In subtle ways, maybe it may have been the lingering feelings that despite my age, there still remained some persistent self-conscious thoughts, perhaps more of an embarrassing nature than anything else, to be known as a Puerto Rican. The wisdom of being who we are, without any masks or outer façade to disguise our true identities, and recognize our culture and our heritage had yet to be acquired. In many aspects, I still had the unrealistic vision of submerging myself totally in the American culture.

My wife and I, on our arrival at the Havana airport, encountered no problems with customs. This despite the fact we had no passports in our possessions, but as I had previously found out, Americans were not required to have passports to enter Cuba. The hotel's name escapes me at this moment, though it was a modern high-rise building, and close by was "The Havana Sheraton." Notable to point out, in our spacious accommodations overlooking a plaza surrounded with palm trees, I saw something strange, and something I had never seen before, nor knew the purpose for it. At first glance it appeared to be what one always sees in a bathroom, a toilet, but in some ways it was different. Later I was to find out the white porcelain fixture equipped with running water was use for washing one's crotch and called a bidet.

Outdoors were many sights of interest, two of which caught my attention, the Coca Cola Bottling Company and the Schaefer Beer Brewery, which were located on the outskirts of the City's downtown area. Schaefer was the brand name of a popular beer known by consumers, and non-consumers as well, as a New York beer since its brewery was in Brooklyn. Further, all the automobiles and trucks seen in the short period of time we were in Havana, five days to be exact, were American made. In fact most of the products in the food markets obviously had been shipped from the States, to name three specifically, among the many others, American cigarettes, Kellogs Corn Flakes and Quaker Oats. At times the thought entered my mind, doesn't the Country produce anything except sugar and cigars? Another interesting sight that not unlike the bidet I had never seen before, and which had a uniqueness all its own, drew my attention. Located practically on every block were small stands immaculately painted in bright colors and sold only one thing, deliciously brewed coffee. The stands, which were extremely popular, never lacking customers, served mostly expresso coffee that Cubans called "negrito" because of its black color. As an added attraction, a tall glass of drinking water with ice cubes was always served with the coffee.

Havana, or La Habana as it is known to Cubans, and the rest of the Spanish speaking world was indeed a beautiful City when I was there, with its wide boulevards all lined with tall palm trees, art deco apartment buildings and family houses, most of which had been painted white, and all with bright red Spanish tile roofs. Automobiles, mostly new ones, were seen everywhere, and as previously mentioned, all, without exceptions, were American made. But what appeared to be an anomaly were the vast amounts of soldiers who armed with rifles and side arms patrolled the streets, as though on guard against a known enemy; no one was volunteering answers to my question, why the reason for all the soldiers? The populace, moreover, appeared to be unaware of the ominous political uprising that was gradually unveiling in their Country. Unknown to me at the time, and in all probability to most of the Island's citizens, Fidel Castro's forces had laid siege to Havana, and in less than six months the Country's dictator, Fulgencio Batista would go into exile, thus leaving Castro and his forces to march triumphantly into the beautiful City.

Unlike today when the expectation in any situation is always in the back of my mind, and that is, what if the unexpected were to happen. The unexpected did, indeed, occurred on the departure from the Havana Airport. I was detained for over an hour by the military authorities for failure to have any papers in my possession proving I was an American citizen. The fact that I spoke in Spanish advising them I was born in Puerto Rico didn't seem to help matters any. After a thorough interrogation, and searching our suitcases, what finally convinced them I was from the States, and not a Cuban attempting to leave the Country, were my traveling permits issued by ARINC allowing my wife and me complimentary fares to Miami, and then on Cubana Airlines to Havana. Explaining my predicament at the airport to an American passenger who was also on board the Cubana flight that had just departed Havana bound for what then Idlewild Airport and not Kennedy, I learned that Cuban citizens were not being allowed to leave the Island because of the Country's political turmoil. Ramifications of this political situation, which eventually led to the breakdown of diplomatic relations between the United States and Cuba, and which has yet to be resolved, were to directly affect me two years later after my vacation trip to Havana.

CHAPTER 64

A brief interlude

Anticipating what is liable to occur in any situation, or the thought of what if the unexpected were to happen, arguably, can be said to be activated by the mind. Further, the power to reason, the capacity for thinking, and the ability to imagine and conceive ideas all derive from our thoughts, and these thoughts originate in the mind. Scientific studies have found that the mind is directly linked to the brain by nerve cells, which stimulate the brain into some action. For example, if I stub my toe, the mind sends a message to the brain, and in a matter of seconds I experience the pain. This is common knowledge that we're all familiar with, of course. Likewise, we can accept the fact that the brain is made-up of matter, or a complete whole, nevertheless, the same cannot be said about the mind. In short, the mind is the abstract part of our physical being.

Having said already that the mind stimulates the brain to a specific physical action, by contrast, we can further say thoughts can remain solely in the mind without a person acting them out physically. Therefore, we can conclude that the protagonist, the main character, or in the context of this discussion, the driving force playing the leading role in our lives is not the brain but the mind. The question that may now be raised is where, in fact, does the mind get its power, or the source energy to develop thoughts? Two answers that readily come to mind are: 1. The power is implanted in us by an All Mighty God. 2. Learned behavior may instill humans with the power, or the capacity to have thoughts. The former answer can be a simple one provided we believe in an

All Mighty God as the creator of all phenomena, all matter, and all that is living and non-living in the universe. But as has been previously stated, what about the non-believers in a God, or those of us who are agnostics and have yet to find our God? Most likely, we may never find the answer to the question, where does the mind get its power?

One thing we know for sure, and that is our ability to think. Another is that we know what our thoughts are every conscious moment of our lives; yet, we can never know what other individuals' thoughts are, unless they choose to disclose them to us. Nonetheless, we still may not be sure whether they are revealing to us true thoughts or false ones. The fact of the matter is we never truly know other people's thoughts, except our own; we are indeed masters of our minds. However, there is an element of human individuality that should be considered. For instance, my thoughts, or at least most of them, may not be the same ones as those of others. What should be noted, further, is that there appears to be a correlation between thoughts and experience. Experience does seem to be an individual factor in what manner we react to a situation. Considering everything, however, we do have rambling thoughts about practically anything, about the known and the unknown, but these do not necessarily influence our behavior. It is debatable, naturally of course, that experience appears to be what affects our manner of thinking.

Our thinking, as has been said originates in the mind, specifically, in the conscious mind, and may be influenced by prior experience. On the other hand, arguably, the brain might possibly be what stimulates thoughts and links them to the mind. To the reader this line of thinking may sound like that old perennial question, what came first the chicken or the egg? Suffice to say that both the mind and brain may be directly involved in the thought processes of humans. A final aspect to consider is that the mind and brain are two separate entities. To say it once more, the mind is the abstract thing that's in our human make-up, nevertheless, we can never see it; whereas the brain is an organ made-up of matter, has substance, and can be seen.

All that has been said up to this point has related to whether our thoughts have their origin in the mind or the brain. This brings us back to the original question, which has now been slightly altered, where does the mind or brain acquire its source of power, or the energy to generate our thoughts, and if not from an All Mighty God, then from where, and for what purpose? Perhaps a way of approaching the question may be to examine our rationale for seeking answers to them. Suppose we were to fuse these questions into a whole, and label the whole a cause and effect syndrome. This label can then be defined as the malady some of us are afflicted with that results in the compulsive desire to seek-out reasons for causes and the effects from these causalities. Of course, the disease is by no means terminal, and if we classify it as an attribute, it can have redeeming values that can be of some benefit for us. Nevertheless, the sickness may have ill-effects in ways that we may not always realize.

We may, for example, tend to become obsessed with the basic principle that nothing can exist or happen without a cause. Shouldn't we be asking ourselves, isn't there some exceptions to this principle? Why must there always be a cause and effect, and purpose for everything in our lives? In essence, we may be attempting to find answers to questions that may never have answers. However, we can, nonetheless, theorize about answers to these questions. For instance, it is conceivable that from the results of "the big bang," the spontaneous action of gases produced one cell that multiply itself into many more, which gradually matured and developed into humans having the capacity to reason and to think. This action may have been how life evolved, not only in humans but in animals and plants as well; furthermore, these living things are still reproducing and developing from earlier forms, and all with a temporary life. And once again, we arrive at the key question, for what purpose was this evolution? The answer may be satisfied by another question, and that is, is there ever a purpose for what results from a spontaneous action? To conclude, certainly there is no wrong in striving to find answers to questions that confront us, even profound ones such as the origin of our thoughts, or the evolution of life. Our objective should be not only to become knowledgeable in all aspects of our lives, but of more significance, to cast away those fears that stem from the unknown. In the final analysis, what needs to be considered is that there may not always be reasons for the causes, or answers readily available to our question

CHAPTER 65

Unfamiliar Surroundings

It never occurred to me that someday, despite the satisfaction with the work, I would resign my position with ARINC. The intent to leave was aroused by a new order issued by the company shortly after my arrival from Cuba that all radio operators were to be scheduled to visit The New York Air Route Traffic Control Center at Idlewild Airport. The visit to the Federal Government's Facility was indeed a learning experience in more ways than one. Actually, the building was a huge hanger with an oval shaped floor area roughly the size of a football field. The hanger housed over three hundred men, most of whom were involved in controlling air traffic. Controlling air traffic was performed with the aid of console tables, about the size of studio upright pianos, and which were located around the oval floor area. Vertically posted on the consoles, or boards as they were known, were metal "strip holders," each one 1X12 inches in size in which strips of papers were inserted containing letters and numerical data. On entering the huge room what initially drew my attention was the room's total darkness, in fact, the entire area was almost pitch black, with dark curtains on all the windows shutting out the outside light. As I was to find out later, darkness was an essential part of the environment enabling controllers a better view of the "targets," (aircraft) displayed on the few bright green colored radar scopes in the room.

The luxury of silence that at times can bring about moods for thinking, or reveries of agreeable things was nowhere to be found. Instead, the large room appeared to be an area consumed in almost chaos with men issuing orders in loud excitable voices, and at times resorting to yelling, or screaming four letter word epithets at one another. The exciting atmosphere of the place, and that I had found out the Facility was seeking air traffic controller trainees, but most of all, The Federal Aviation Agency, (FAA,) had a wage scale structure that would enable me to ultimately earn a salary twice the amount I was receiving from Aeronautical Radio Inc., prompted me to submit the job application. Much to my surprise, three weeks later I received a telegram at the radio station advising me that I had been hired for the position of air traffic controller trainee, and the date for my scheduled interview.

Reflections of memorable happenings of thoughts about life in general can re-awaken the human spirit, even at a ripe old age. Notable in some respects, was the incident, or more to the point, the learning experience that occurred sometime during the interim three weeks prior to receiving the telegram from the F.A.A.. A telephone call from my sister-in-law about nine o'clock one evening was how it all began. Detecting an urgent need by the sound of her voice, she advised me she was having labor pains and would I drive her the hospital. Knowing her husband worked nights, and except for her two pre-school aged children, she was all alone, I droved as fast as I could to her apartment.

Arriving at the apartment approximately thirty minutes later, I ran the doorbell numerous times without receiving any response. The door was unlocked, and on entering I heard her moans coming from the bedroom, and telling me not to come in. Realizing she was in need of help, I walked in the room and found her lying across the bed in a nightgown, and with her legs tightly crossed as though trying to prevent the inevitable from happening. Recalling what I had learned long ago in the first aid course, I quickly went to the bathroom, washed my hands thoroughly and returned to her. Her main concern was expressed in a few pleading words, "please, don't look at me," as I told her to uncross her legs lift the nightgown and allow the baby to be born. All the while groaning slightly, she obeyed my commands. No one, however, not even the instructor at the first aid station, had prepared me for what I was about to witness at that moment. Her pelvis was in a spontaneous pumping action, or moving up and down, and the vagina was expanding gradually. In the middle of the opening I saw what appeared to be a round black spot the size of a half dollar coin. At first I was somewhat puzzled at what I was seeing, however, as the spot gradually grew larger, I realized it was the baby's head covered with black hair and mucus. With the baby's head almost in full view, I kept encouraging her to "push harder." She obviously was experiencing a great deal of pain, and to relieve her agony I attempted to extract the baby from the womb by grasping its head with both hands only to release them immediately on feeling the baby's head; it felt as though I were grasping a ball made of jelly. Somehow, at that moment I realized what I was attempting to do the mother was able to do it without any help from me.

The baby was born within a matter of minutes crying loudly, which I knew was the sign of a normal birth, and with the mother asking whether it was a boy or girl. The umbilical cord was wrapped around the baby's trunk so that I had to pick-up the new born and rotate it several times to unravel its cord before I was able to see that it was a girl. The mother laid on the bed thoroughly drained of all energy as I contemplated cutting the cord. What gave me second thoughts about performing the procedure I knew had to be done was the cord's surprisingly large size. Appearing nothing like a cord, but more like a chain, it was about two inches in diameter and approximately three or more feet in length. With its hollow area filled with blood, which felt extremely warm on feeling it, the notion of cutting the umbilical cord grew into a formidable task to think about. It was at that instant that I got on the phone, called the police, explained what had just happened, and asked whether I should cut the cord. Apparently, I had caught the policeman answering the telephone by surprise, and in an excited voice ordered me not to hang-up but to "stay on the line until he got back to me." I held the phone to my ear for what seem like a long time, but actually was no more than a minute or so. On hearing his voice again, he advised me not to do any cutting, nor anything else for the mother, that a doctor was on his way, and arriving in fifteen minutes. An unfamiliar surrounding it was, and most definitely one that can only be defined as a learning experience. Never before had I been aware of the painful ordeal of giving birth to a child can be for a woman. A final note about the event, on arriving home late that night, and my wife not knowing what had happened, became overly alarmed on seeing the front of my white shirt almost completely covered with blood.

The other unfamiliar surrounding, of course, was the initial experience with the F.A.A.. The transition from an airline radio operator to that of an air traffic controller trainee, or "developmental," the Federal Aviation Administration's label for those trainee aspiring to become full-fledged controllers, was not an easy undertaken, to say the least. Trainees were classified as temporary employees until they successfully passed the four months course requirements at the F.A.A. Academy in Oklahoma City. Specifically this meant scoring a seventy percent or better on all tests, and demonstrating to their instructors the ability to perform the work with simulated operational problems conducted at the Academy's laboratory. Any trainee failing to meet the training criteria was "release from service," and no longer on the Federal Government's payroll. Naturally this was of major concern for trainees, thus raising their anxiety level worrying about all aspects with respects to training, and particularly whether they still had a job at the end of the four months. Moreover, once the training phase obstacles at the Academy were overcome, there still remained the requirement of having to become "a journeyman," or a certified controller at a Facility within a period of three years, otherwise you were terminated, or eliminating the technical words, you were out of a job. Apart from these requirements, however, a supervisor, if he saw some potential in your capability to pass the training requirements, had the power to sign a waiver authorizing you more time in which to complete the training program.

Stresses, rather than subsiding, instead, increased to a higher level, in particular, when performing the grueling work of controlling large volumes of air traffic; what's more, you were held accountable for all "systems errors." A system that, indeed, had all the earmarks of having flaw in the way it was conducted, and predisposed controllers into making mistakes. A more comprehensive discussion on this issue based on an in-depth study for a doctoral dissertation will be taken at a later time.

On the job training, (OJT,) commenced at the New York Air Route Traffic Control Center after arriving from the Academy. Issued the title of Assistant Controller, and assigned to a twelve men crew working a rotating shift, that's exactly what I did, assist controllers in their work. In essence, this involved calculating aircraft's estimated times of arrival over compulsory reporting points, or "fixes," writing the times on strips of papers that had been inserted in "strip holders," and posting the "holders." The "holders" were posted in vertical bays on upright consoles, or "control boards,' with each bay representing one of the various "fixes" an aircraft would traverse in that particular control "sector;" New York Center had a total of thirty six domestic control sectors. A crucial aspect of the work load was calculating the correct estimated times, which had to be within a three minute tolerance of an aircraft's arrival over a "fix." Small round calculators made of cardboard or plastic were the tools used for accomplishing this remarkable feat. Of course, nowadays computers perform this function, nonetheless, in that post World War II era, the age of computers and electronic hand-held calculators had yet to arrive. A final note associated with the job description of an assistant controller, if two or more strips reflected aircraft arrival times over a "fix" of less than ten minutes, assistant controllers had to print /Ws/ in large red letters on the right side edges of the strips to alert controllers scanning the boards of potential "conflictions," the system's euphemism for mid-air collisions.

Training was usually conducted on the mid-shifts when air traffic was minimal allowing controllers time in which to administer simulated control problems to the trainees. The entry grade level for a trainee was a "GS-5," however, after completing the four months training course at the Academy, the trainee was automatically promoted to a "GS-6." Significant to note, there were no women controllers or assistants at the Academy, and years were to slip by before I saw a female trainee at the New York

Facility. The final promotion for an assistant controller was the GS-8 level, but only given after the trainee received his "security clearance," which normally took six months to arrive from Washington D.C.. All controllers and assistants were required to have "security clearances' in their personnel folders, and as fate would have it, six months elapsed, and a year and more, and still my security clearance had not arrived.

One morning my supervisor with a quizzical look on his face, as if questioning the reason for it, tells me the "chief," (the Center's Administrator,) wants to see me. With some misgivings as to his reasons for wanting to see me, I enter his office, the "Chief" greets me, points to an adjacent room, and advises me two gentlemen are there waiting to see me. On entering the room I see two tall men standing alongside one another, rather than sitting behind their desks. Immediately I sense the two men have no interest whatsoever in my training, nor my work ethics, but in something of a more serious nature. Introducing themselves by flashing shiny gold badges, they tell me they're from the Federal Bureau of Investigation, (FBI,) and are going to ask me some questions. However, prior to their interrogation, and perhaps as a way of alerting me they knew of all my previous movements, cite among other events, the year I had arrived in the Country, whom I had lived with, schools attended and my service record in the NAVY. Then, as though attempting to surprise me into not giving them false answers, the questioning begins, in rapid succession, first from one agent and then from the other. Specifically, the crux of the questions deal with my purpose for going to Cuba; for example, what was my purpose for going, what did I do during the time I was there, who were "my contacts," and did I have any relatives or friends residing on the Island? At the time of this event "The Bay of Pigs military operation in which Cuban exiles funded by the Central Intelligence Agency,(CIA,) invaded Cuba for the sole purpose to overthrow Castro's Government, was still a year or more away from becoming a reality. Nevertheless, the military operation may have already been in the planning stages, hence the reason for the FBI agents' concern about my trip to Cuba. Ultimately, my answers, apparently satisfies the two agents, with the results that three weeks later I receive my "security clearance." Recollections of the FBI affair reminds me of George Orwell's symbol for a fascist government in his novel, 1984, "Big Brother." To be sure, never did I realized until that incident how much "Big Brother," (our Government,) in essence, was involved, and in all likelihood still is today, in spying on its own citizens.

PART V
The Turbulent 60's

CHAPTER 66

A System's Error

Unvarying procedures tend to become routine, particularly in one's work setting, nevertheless, this was not true at the New York Center. Though the operating criteria and procedures seldom varied, for instance, the separation standards, and the method of monitoring aircraft along their flight routes, always the unexpected errors seem to occur. Always there were the miss-posted strip holders in the wrong bays, which identified the "fixes," wrong altitudes written on the strips, incorrect calculations of times on strips resulting in a plane reporting over a "fix" ten or more minutes before the time written on the strip, thus creating a potential "confliction;" or what made matter worse, dealing with a plane that had declared an emergency, and had to be given priority handling over all other aircraft. The yelling screaming and cursing from controllers, especially during peak periods of air traffic, in a huge room that because of its darkness was known as the coal mine, didn't really help working conditions any. High volume of air traffic, in effect, was the system's Achilles' heel; it had the effect of disrupting all sense of order both in the system and in the controllers. And as to be expected, the high volume of traffic made its customary appearance whenever adverse weather conditions in the form of low clouds and poor visibility moved into the area; the result was like stirring a hornet's nest. Pilots who normally flew in "visual flight rules," conditions, (VFR,) were no longer able to maintain forward visibility and came on the frequency to request "instrument flight rules clearances, (IFR,) in order to fly by referring to the aircraft's instruments, and be safely separated from other air traffic. These conditions, which undoubtedly increased the work for controllers at the New York Center, were known as "IFR days."

It was on one of these "IFR days" realizing all too well that it was snowing, the sky was overcast with low clouds, and it was Friday, only nine days until Christmas, I decided to call-in sick on my eight o'clock morning shift that would end at four o'clock in the afternoon, and of course, pleased to be missing a hectic day of work at the Center; that memorable day was December 16, 1960.

The early morning was cold and dreary, and after making the call to the Facility I went back to bed. On rising about eleven in the morning and looking out the window, I saw the light snow still coming down with about a half inch coating on streets that already had mounds of it on their outer edges as a result of the seventeen inches that had fallen on December eleven and twelve. The day certainly was depressing, with the sun nowhere in sight. Music had to be the remedy to relieve the situation, and turning the radio on heard the soothing sounds of a string quartet. Suddenly, the music was interrupted by the announcement that an apparent mid-air collision between two commercial airliners had occurred moments ago over Staten Island, "to stay tuned for further details," and then the music resumed. The first reaction was to call the Center to find out if my crew had been involved, but realizing I was suppose to be sick and in bed, refrained from making the call. Instead I tuned to a news station, but the only known reports available were that a DC-8 jet bound for New York International Airport,(Idlewild,) and a piston engine Constellation scheduled to land at LaGuardia Airport had indeed collided in mid-air over Staten Island.

In the following days to come, details about the accident were read in newspapers. Oddly enough, the people whom I worked with, particularly crew members who had actually communicated with the DC-8 were not volunteering any information. In all probability, they were given orders not to divulge anything to anyone as a precautionary measure against any future litigations. What follows is a brief summary of the catastrophic accident that happened on the morning of December 16, 1960: AT 10:33 AM a Douglas DC-8 jet and a Boeing piston engine Constellation aircraft, both of which were commercial airliners flying in IFR conditions, and following directions radioed by ground controllers collided in mid-air. The Trans World airline Constellation on initial impact broke into three sections and plunged to the ground crashing in Miller Army Air field in Staten Island. Desperately struggling to maintain altitude, the United Airlines jet continued on course attempting to reach its destination, Idlewild Airport. Losing altitude rapidly, the jet's left wing dipped and struck an apartment building on 70th Avenue in the Park Slope section of Brooklyn and slammed into "the Pillar of Fire" church engulfing it in flames. Ten other brownstone buildings were totally destroyed in the aftermath of the crash by the ensuing fire. All 128 passengers and crew members on both aircraft perished. This was the worst air disaster at the time.

As to be expected, speculations for what caused the mid-air collision ranged from various theories, which namely dealt with pilot errors, controller errors, or perhaps a mechanical malfunction aboard one of the aircraft. However, it was not until a year and a half after the accident had occurred that the Civil Aeronautics Board, (CAB,) released its findings in June, 1962. Despite the lengthy report, it had had little or no bearing on the actual collision. For example, it cited, among a lot of other data, the point of origin and destination of both aircraft, weight, cargo, and the names of crew members. But what was significant in the report was that New York Center had cleared the United jet to the Preston intersection, and to descend to 5,000 feet. After the flight had reported passing thru 6,000 feet it was advised to contact Idlewild Approach Control. Thereafter, the DC-8 jet called the Approach controller and announced that it was approaching Preston at 5,000 feet; this was the last transmission heard from the jet. The TWA Constellation was cleared by the New York Center to descend to 9,000 feet and to contact LaGuardia Approach Control. Acknowledging the clearance, the aircraft advised it was leaving 10,000 feet and going over to LaGuardia Approach. In communication with the TWA flight, LaGuardia Approach cleared the aircraft to descend further to 5,000 feet on its final approach for the landing at LaGuardia Airport, and issued a "traffic advisory," "in the vicinity of a northeasterly heading." Following this transmission, the radar targets merged on the controller's radar, and communications with the TWA flight were lost. The Civil Aeronautics Board concluded that "the probable cause" of the accident was the United DC-8's failure to hold at the Preston intersection, its "clearance limit," and instead overshot, or flew beyond the intersection and penetrated the TWA Constellation's flight path.

For those who may not be familiar with air traffic terminology, a "clearance limit" is the fix to where an aircraft is given a clearance. On approaching the "fix," and receiving no further clearance, the aircraft must commence to hold at the "fix." To begin the hold, the pilot must fly no more than five miles beyond the "fix" before executing a 180 degree right turn, thus reversing its course, and fly outbound from the "fix" for twelve to fifteen miles before repeating the maneuver. In essence, the pilot continues flying a pattern resembling a horse racing track awaiting further clearance. The report also disclosed that the DC-8's high rate of speed approaching Preston was another contributing factor. From this, one can infer that even if the jet had intended to hold, its high speed made it impossible for the DC-8 not to fly beyond the "fix's" five miles restriction.

What appears to be questionable in the report, and certainly open to discussion is shifting the blame for the catastrophic midair collision on a pilot, rather than on the F.A.A. The glaring fact, and one not mentioned in the report, is that the FAA's air traffic system did have the legal responsibility for maintaining the two aircraft separated from one another. A question that should have been raised is why was the pilot held accountable, in particular, when he was flying his aircraft on instruments, and assuming the controllers on the ground were performing their job responsibility of keeping his DC-8 separated from other aircraft. For the sake of argument, lets assumed the pilot flew beyond his "clearance limit," but whether done intentionally, or a careless oversight is not known.

What in fact is known is that the jet was in "radar contact," meaning the aircraft was being visually monitored on radar by a controller. Therefore, why was the pilot not alerted, if and when he flew his aircraft beyond the "fix," and neglected to hold at Preston? Moreover, if the DC-8 was being flown at a too fast rate of speed, why didn't the controller advise the pilot to decrease the speed of his aircraft?

Pointing out what appear to be inconsistencies in the report is not meant to cast judgment on anyone in particular, that is, unless we begin by pointing fingers at the F.A.A. and its air traffic system. It's highly probable that after advising the United Airlines jet to contact Idlewild Approach, the controller discontinued monitoring its flight path because he was busy controlling other aircraft. In effect, the high volume of traffic on the controller's frequency may have acted as the catalyst for the air disaster. At this point, what should be considered is that, in general, we tend to view Federal Government Agencies as structures whose prime purpose is to regulate systems so as to maintain or improve their standards of operation. Further, we're inclined to prejudge them as entities that due to their huge budgets, large bureaucratic framework and vast amounts of skill workers are infallible, and will seldom, if ever, make mistakes. One of human nature's basic laws is that no matter how sophisticated a system is, it is always prone to technical breakdowns, system failures, and of course, human errors. Twenty eight years after the air disaster this writer collected extensive data for a doctoral dissertation that dealt with a case study of the problems of the FAA's controller training program. The results of the study are too massive in context, and beyond the scope of this work. Nevertheless, two of the concluding factors in the findings were the Agency's emphasis on training individuals to control large volumes of air traffic as the criteria for certifying them. The other was the Federal Aviation Administration's failure to project the rapid growth of air transportation.

CHAPTER 67

Searching For A Purpose

No pun intended, but surprising to note how the mid-air collision can be related to the beginning of the first "big bang" of the turbulent 1960's. In the early 1960's a cultural revolution was about to begin in which student rebels, civil right marchers and anti-war protesters were challenging the authority of the family, the police, the military government and the university. The 60's were indeed years of drastic changes, males let their hair grow to their shoulders, sex was freer, soldiers were dying in Vietnam, and the use of drugs became the standard bearer for the youth culture. It was an era of violent killings, occurring not only in the distant war, but also from the results of the political turmoil at home. The President, John F. Kennedy, conspired with the Mafia to have Fidel Castro assassinated, yet ironically was assassinated himself riding in a motorcade in Dallas, Texas on November 22, 1963. In 1965 Malcom X A minister for "The Nation of Islam," also known as "the Black Muslims," was gunned down as he began to deliver a speech in a ballroom in upper Manhattan. Martin Luther King, the civil rights leader was shot dead in Memphis, Tennessee as he stepped out of his motel room on his way to dinner in April, 1968. And completing the cycle of bloodshed inflicted on public figures in the 1960's, two months later on June 5, 1968 in a Los Angeles ballroom while campaigning to become President of the Country, the former President's forty two years old younger brother, Bobby Kennedy, was shot dead by an assassin.

The needless killings of public figures were followed six months before the end of the decade by, no, not another killing, but by what may have been this Nation's biggest folly undertaken, the Moon landing. In July 1969, after lavishly squandering billions of the taxpayers' dollars, the Country succeeded in landing two men safely on the Moon's surface, and returning them back to earth. These huge money expenditures were implemented solely to beat the Russians "to the punch," and whom the American politicians and their military figureheads had surmised were planning a Moon landing. The Russians, as we were eventually to discover, had other ideas in mind. For purposes of having suitable areas in space for their "cosmonauts" to conduct studies, the Russians were involved in developing and placing platforms in space. The Moon landing proved to be nothing more than a media spectacle with photos of the actual landing beamed back to earth and shown on television. And as for the redeeming values, over thirty years have elapsed since the event that the media described at the time of its happening as "man's greatest feat," and yet, all the Nation has to show for it today is a bunch of useless rocks. One of these rocks, which I saw on display at the White House in Puerto Rico, made no lasting impression on me; it was just an ordinary common brown rock the size of a grapefruit. A final afterthought, why weren't all those billions of dollars applied toward better worthwhile causes, for example, research to find cures for two of man's biggest killers, cancer and heart disease Certainly, in more ways than one, the 60's were also years of changes, or on a more personal level, the awakening years for a man approaching his forties, and beginning to have philosophical reflections, two of which were his future and the purpose for his life. For the first time in his life he found himself alone, and enjoying every moment of it. Divorced, and with a son who had been drafted into the Army, and sent not to Vietnam as the father had expected, but to Germany, he resided in an old Victorian house in Patchogue, Long Island, which he was able to purchase with his GI Mortgage Benefits. Never at the time did he imagine that he was to live in that old and somewhat dilapidated house for almost ten years. There, aware that he was at the threshold of his mid-point in life, he began the search for the illusive answer that has baffled Western philosophers for centuries, the purpose of life, but more specifically, his purpose in life.

Certified as a "manual controller" working the "control boards," the next phase, and one that had already been pre-planned for him, was training to become a radar controller. That he knew for a fact the work was to be grueling and much more stressful than that of a "manual controller," didn't help his cause any. He had no other options other than to conform to the FAA's training requirements; and that was that all "manual controllers" had to be certified as radar controllers. And from the very beginning of the training, he encountered difficulties that he sensed stemmed from his age, which in accordance with FAA standards, he was too old for a "journeyman radar controller." Sluggish to react to control situations, perhaps due to poor reflexes, and the psychological awareness that, except for the supervisors, all his co-workers were younger than he was contributed to his eventual transfer to a non-traffic control Facility. Nonetheless, though at a slow pace and with little or no progress, his training continued, with him all along realizing it was just a matter of time for the transfer to become a reality. Still, all through this training period there was always the nagging question, what's the purpose of his life? Surely he kept reasoning, there must be more to life than just doing the type of work he was involved with? As a result, he seriously began contemplating becoming involved in some purpose, some activity in which to accomplish some realistic objectives of which he had no idea whatsoever what they were to be.

First there were the ballroom dancing lessons at an Arthur Murray Studio in Brentwood, Long Island, all of which dealt with basic steps in the various popular dances at the time. Consequently, I quickly lost interest in an activity that was already familiar to me, and aside from that, the lessons were too expensive. And then there were the flying lessons, which much to my surprise, I found them to be rather dull and not to my liking, especially when I discovered my eardrums were overly sensitive to the loud roar of the small plane's engine. After the first solo flight, or the one in which I flew the aircraft alone without the aid of the instructor, I lost all enthusiasm for flying that pre-dated to World War II. Finally, there was music that all along had invariably been imbedded in the back of my mind, but never had the money or the time to become involved with it.

CHAPTER 68

Brief Notes On Music and The Guitar

The awakening period actually began with the beginning of music pursued more as a diversion and much less as purpose for accomplishing something in life. However, not listening to it as the reader may have assumed, but producing musical sounds on an instrument, on a classical guitar, which is sometimes referred to as the Spanish guitar. Before discussing briefly the awakening period, what I propose to do now is to focus on some general aspects of both music and the guitar, which may be of some interest particularly to the layperson. Music theory, learning to read musical notations, and playing a musical instrument can never be compared with learning to fly or dance, both of which after a certain number of lessons, depending on the individual's ability, the learner is able to perform adequately what has been taught. By contrast, in learning to play a musical instrument, the learner must practice consistently everyday in order to gain proficiency in his playing. Some instruments require more time than others, however, with the classical guitar it usually involves daily hours, and years of practice, especially if the learner has aspirations of becoming a professional musician. I did not have those desires, and therefore, after almost six years of total dedication with taking formal lessons, and spending four or more hours each day practicing I gave up taking the music lessons. Finally, I realized the endeavor was too demanding on my time, and surely I thought, there were other activities to be become involved with rather than only music. And that's when I stopped taking guitar lessons, and began the lengthy academic studies by enrolling as freshman at a college.

Those years occupied in total solitude practicing on the guitar implanted in me what was lacking, and not aware of it at the time, the discipline for acquiring the patience to think, listen and observe the world around me. This issue will be discussed more in context at a later time, but now the focus will be on a bit of information concerning music and the guitar. For a start, what may come as a surprise is that there are only seven tones in music, which sometimes are referred to as sounds. The infinite number of ways in varying these tones by making them higher or lower and combining them, in essence, is how music is created. Unlike ordinary noises, tones are distinguished by their regularity of vibrations, their frequency, or what is known in music as constant pitch. Specifically, what the person playing a guitar does is play these seven distinct vibrations in a sequence of various combinations of high and low tones by shortening and lengthening the strings to produce an arrangement made-up of pleasing sounds known as the melody.

Basically there are three types of guitars, the electric, acoustic and classical. The acoustic guitar, not unlike the electric guitar, has steel strings, but the sounds are not amplified electronically. The tones of an electric guitar, however, are electronically amplified, and the strings in both the electric and acoustic guitars are set into vibrations with the aid of a pick, which is usually a small triangular shaped piece of plastic held with the thumb and middle fingers. By contrast, a classical guitar is always plucked because of its nylon strings. Unlike the electric and acoustic guitars with their steel strings, using a pick to play a classical guitar will rapidly cause the strings to break. Further, what gives the tones their brilliance in a classical guitar are the player's long finger nails purposely grown on the plucking fingers in order to create the beautiful and sometimes haunting melodious sounds of the instrument. Any guitar can be played by simultaneously strumming all six strings, thus playing chords; a chord is a combination of two or more tones. This method, though highly popular, most likely because of its simplicity in playing the instrument, is limited to accompanying a singer, groups of singers, or what is very common, the player sings and accompanies himself with the guitar. The other method of playing the instrument is by picking or plucking individual strings. Obviously, it should be noted that playing individual strings is significantly more difficult than strumming chords.

Difficulties in the beginning, to put it mildly, were numerous and lasting almost a year. Consequently, the high level of frustrations was causing me to think seriously about giving up the whole idea of learning to play the instrument until the unforeseen occurred toward the end of that year. The happening justifies a brief narrative, if only to underscore the point that a problem can indeed be resolved provided we know what the problem is. I had been getting lessons from an American man much younger than I, and a student himself taking guitar lessons. During a lesson session one day, he told me he was going to Spain for a month to, among other things, shop for a guitar and suggested I take lessons with his teacher while he was away. Right then and there, I though about quitting, nonetheless, after spending so much time struggling with the instrument, I decided to prolong my agony a bit longer, and took his advice.

The day I met his teacher, and had my first lesson with him was a disappointed experience that added to my frustrations. Nevertheless, I persevered with what was to eventually become a pleasurable pastime. His name was Juan De Lamata, a Spaniard and professional musician who at the time was the Flamenco guitarist at the renown nightclub, "The Havana Madrid." During the course of our years of teacher and student relationship, I learned he had toured world wide with the popular Flamenco dance team of that era, Rosario and Antonio as their guitarist. Moreover, I also found out he had been playing classical and Flamenco music on the instrument since the age of nine, and as a young man had graduated from "The Spanish Conservatory of Music" in Spain. His ability to hear the true pitch of musical tones bordered on uncanny attributes. As an illustration, there was the time he invited me to a concert at "Town Hall" where his close friend the famous Flamenco guitarist Sabicas was performing. Sitting alongside each other and about eight rows from the stage, with a slight smile on his face whispered to me that his friend was playing with a guitar that was slightly out-of-tune. Further, there was the lesson where I had wished to learn to play a particular song he was unfamiliar with, and had me hummed the tune for him. Humming the song softly, I observed him jotting down musical notations on a pad. When I had finished, he took his guitar and referring to the music he had written on the pad, proceeded to play the identical melody I had hummed for him.

The first lesson on that fateful day, as all others were to be thereafter, took place in his studio with him sitting with his guitar, and I also with my guitar sitting directly across from him. He said, "play something, anything." Struggling with a "piece" I had been practicing for months, he kept observing me, with his eyes almost glued to the movements of my plucking fingers. Finally, after a minute or so, he stopped what may have seen to him, and quite rightfully, my arduous ordeal, and began asking me questions. The questions dealt with, among others, the length of time I had been taking lessons, what specific method, if any, was used, and the type of music played. There followed a lengthy discussion, in Spanish of course, we always conversed in what was his first language, about aspects relating to the theory of music; and I all the while wondering, why doesn't he have me play more? A lapse of memory at this moment prevents me from remembering what I had said to him, however, as soon as I had said it, he snapped his thumb and middle fingers and said, "that's it, that's your problem." He had discovered from whatever I had said that I was left handed, yet had been playing the instrument right handed.

To clear-up what to a person not familiar with the instrument, might sound like a hazy statement, I was plucking the strings with the right hand, and pressing down on the strings at the "neck" of the guitar with my left hand. He asked for my guitar, and promptly proceeded to re-string the instrument; why he did this requires some explaining. When playing the guitar right handed, the "neck" is on your left side, and the body of the instrument is on your right side. To continue what I hope is a clear explanation, the nearest string from your view is the sixth, or low sounding base string, and the one furthest from your view is the first, or high-sounding string. However, when you reverse the strings in order to play the guitar left handed, the strings will now be in reversed order, which enables you to play left handed with the "neck on the right side, and the body on the left side. Of more importance to the left handed person, you plucked with the left hand, and press the strings on the "neck" of the instrument with the right hand. It's quite obvious that a guitarist playing right handed cannot play the instrument unless the strings are reversed. But what should be noted, however, is that the beginner, or in my case near-beginner, has to re-learn all the "pieces," or songs he has learned playing right handed in order to play the same "pieces left handed. Realizing this fact, I was on the verge of giving-up the whole business when he handed me my guitar with the strings not where they had been, but which were now in reversed order. By the expression on my face, he must have surmised how discouraged I was at that moment, and advised me not to give-up hope, adding what eventually was to become a fact, that in three months I would be playing, and much better, all that I had previously learned. Then, to my surprise, he turned his swivel chair around, and pointing to a large rectangular black box resting on a shelve on the wall said, "with that I'll teach you in five years what took me over ten years to learn." The box was a large tape recorder, the type seldom seen nowadays, with its two seven inch spools for winding the magnetic tape. In a literal sense, the recorder served as a hearing aid for his students. A typical lesson initially began with him sight-reading the "piece" from a book while simultaneously playing it. Thereafter, he and I sight read and played the same "piece" but at a very slow tempo, with him correcting me whenever I made a mistake. Finally, he turned the recorder on and taped the "piece," again at a very slow tempo. He then handed me the large spool with instructions to take it home and practice the "piece" by sight-reading it from the book and at the same time playing it reproducing the same sounds and tempo heard on the tape. Naturally, a prerequisite was having a tape recorder, and of course, I purchased one almost identical to his, and costing three hundred dollars, which was a rather large sum of money in those days. Diligently applying his method, which, in essence, involved not only having Mr. De Lamata at his studio, but also at home with me, I practiced, learned and played for about six years; and during the course of those years, much to my satisfaction, I acquired the skills to play classical and Flamenco music, not in a professional manner of course, but to the extent that listeners did enjoy my playing. He once said to me what have been true words of wisdom that I have invariably applied in all other succeeding endeavors. Always remain relaxed, and don't create any tensions while you're playing; as long as you're relaxed and maintaining the tempo you will play, and your musical sounds will please others. In the last analysis, this is quite true. Tensions and nervousness tend to interfere, and act to impede us from whatever we're attempting to accomplish.

CHAPTER 69

Observing, Listening, and Discovering

A while back I referred to an awakening period, which no doubt needs to be narrowed down in some manner. To be more specific, this was a period in which I gradually became aware of my surroundings. Again, this is yet another general statement that should be specifically illustrated. To begin, this enlighten period can be directly related to the six years involved with studying music, which most certainly gave me the human attributes I was not aware I was lacking. These attributes that I have a firm conviction we should all have, enable us in some ways to better understand our world. The attributes, or better yet, discipline, to have the patience to observe, to listen and to think for hours on end, were acquired during the many hours consumed practicing playing the guitar. Moreover, listening skills, which were an enormous asset at a later time in college classrooms were developed at home to such an acute sense where I was almost able to visualize the actual vibrations of strings to their very last ending sounds when I strummed them on the guitar.

I was, furthermore, able to observe objects carefully for their forms, colors and sizes, and even to visualize them when I closed my eyes. The powers of observation had taken hold of me to the point where I found myself observing everything in sight for all their minute details. For instance, something I had never done before, I watched birds, particularly those in the backyard of the house for their appearance, colors, size, movements on the ground, and listening to their unique chirping sounds. The leaves of trees, which were no exception, were thoroughly examined for their forms, size, color and texture. Much to my surprise, I made the discovery that, though the forms of leaves and colors vary, depending on the type of tree, what appeared to be a common trait among all leaves, no matter what type of tree they came from, were their pistils, or what looked like a series of veins, which had identical forms, and from their centerlines other veins extended outward to form what looked like a series of /Vs/ one above the other. These keen observations of not only living things, but also objects, which I had totally ignored before becoming involved with music were the reasons why I had my son begin piano lessons at the early age of eight years old. Another result, and perhaps of more significance to some degree, the study of music and learning to play a musical instrument instilled in me, and hopefully will do the same for my son, the self-assurance and self-esteem I was lacking.

Shifting topics from observing and listening to that of discovering, which in actuality was a mid-life discovery, and one that in my adult years I had begun to suspect. More so, in a moral sense, the discovery was indeed demeaning for my mother. In many ways it helped to explain her tolerance for her husband's psychological abusive behavior toward her first son by another man. The affair unraveled itself with the urgings from a young lady whom I had met six months earlier in Brentwood, Long Island to visit her during the time she was taking courses at The University of Puerto Rico; the young lady had returned to the Island to resume her studies at the University. Thus, after almost a forty year long span, I decided to return to the land where I had had many happy experiences as a very young boy.

What was for a young boy a five day voyage by ship in the early thirties was now in his manhood years a mere three and a half hour flight from New York City to San Juan, Puerto Rico. My arrival was uneventful except for one pleasant surprise. No sooner had I arrive at the airport than memories of my early childhood years were re-kindled on detecting the distinct and unique scent most likely coming from the Island's rich soil. That first night, after so many years, I heard again the familiar sounds of the little nocturnal frog "Coci," which periodically during the night hours makes its presence known; the rather soothing sounds it makes, "coki-coki-coki," are similar to its name. During the brief two weeks visit there were, among others, the well known sights seen as a young boy in a long ago era, banana tree, palms, sugar cane, the beautiful flaming red hibiscus flower, and the ubiquitous lagartijas, the small lizards that are seen everywhere throughout the Island.

A special event during those two weeks was meeting Anabel, the young lady's friend, and a girl no more than eighteen years of age from well-to-do parents, her family owned a shoe factory.

Anabel, a highly intelligent young lady, had already earned her baccalaureate, and was working towards her Masters. On my return to New York, we began to correspond frequently by mail for about a year. One day I received a letter from her, not from Puerto Rico, but from Barcelona, Spain telling me that her family had re-located to the Spanish City in order to be near their new shoe factory. Moreover, she was planning a month long backpacking journey to North Africa, and advised me to obtain a passport as soon as possible and accompany her on the trip. Eager to see her again and participate in what appeared to be an exciting adventure to far-off lands never before seen, Spain and North Africa, I rushed downtown to obtain the passport. At the immigration office I was told my discharged papers from the Navy were not valid proof of citizenship, and what they required was either a birth certificate or a baptismal certificate. Confronting my mother with the need for one of these documents, she declared they had been lost long ago in Puerto Rico. In the end it took me almost six months to acquire both documents, and much to my regret, I never got to go to Spain, nor take the backpacking trip to North Africa with the lovely Anabel.

Nonetheless, what I did discover from the episode, and not to my surprise I may add, was the reason I had my mother's surname, Santiago, instead of my father's, Solano, was that I was born out of wedlock; and as was probably the law or custom in those times, and perhaps still is today, both documents reflected the child as having no father. Familiar with what the certificates contained, my mother tearfully pleaded with me for forgiveness when she found out I had them in my possession. To this day, I still don't believe she ever accepted the fact that it didn't matter to me she had not been married to my father; what did matter indeed was that I had been very fortunate to have her as a mother who loved me dearly.

Why is it that religious doctrines and government laws imposed on us what may not always serve our best interest? Predictably, what they my tend to do if we disobey them is, not unlike what they did to my mother, foster a guilt complex in us. Do these institutions have the right to morally condemn a woman for having a child with out first taking her marriage vows? Doesn't she have the right, considering the fact it's her body, to bear a child, care for it and nurture it without being held accountable to anyone? This situation may yet be rectified in the future to conform with some third world Countries where these religious and government laws are not practiced.

PART VI
A New Beginning

CHAPTER 70

Weather, and City Happenings

The end of hostilities in Vietnam, after what appeared to be an endless war, finally came to an end. Shortly thereafter, my son was discharged from the Army, and soon after married his high school sweetheart whose parents were known to be one of the few rich families in Patchogue; and both relocated to Tampa, Florida to begin their married life. Also coming to an end were the turbulent sixties, and though I had no notion of it at the time, a new beginning was in stored for me. Actually, it began in the early seventies, and resulted in ending almost ten years of bachelorhood. Further, after twelve years of working in Long Island, but no longer having the physical reflexes demanded for the job of an air traffic controller, I was transferred to a "Flight Service Station" in Teterboro, New Jersey on March, 1971. Soon after arriving at the Station, I was sent to the Academy in Oklahoma City for six months of intensive training in all aspects of weather phenomena. After being certified by the U.S. Weather Bureau as an "aviation weather briefer," I returned to "the Flight Service Station." The foregoing may read somewhat like a resume, and it may well be, a brief summary of the training required for what the job entailed, briefing pilots with weather information along their intended route of flights. However, what I was not aware of at the time was that "The Flight Service Station" was to be my home away from home for the following nineteen years.

Adverse weather conditions, and knowing the causes for them can be of some interest, in particular, how the elements of nature can unleash their powerful forces on us. I can still recall the small boy in Puerto Rico fondly believing his dear mother telling him during a sudden outburst of thunderstorms that the reasons for the sound of thunder was that God was angry at us; but what in fact causes thunderstorms and their thunderous sounds, which are always likely to be heard soon after we see the lighting? And what about this lighting, what in fact causes it? Before proceeding further, however, the intent here is not to perhaps bore the reader with an extensive and dull exposition of weather, but merely to discuss briefly some aspects of weather that sooner or later impact on us. To begin, what exactly is wind, moreover, what causes rain, snow, and as previously mentioned, thunderstorms, their thunderous sounds and lighting?

Wind, as the reader may have suspected all along is only air in motion, and the stronger this motion is, the more we feel the wind. However, what causes the motion is more complex in nature, and far too wide in scope to explain in the context of this brief narrative on weather. Suffice to say that the rotation of the earth plays a significant role in causing the motion. Rain and snow are the results of variations in temperatures, both on the surface and in the atmosphere. Oversimplifying the explanation to some degree, once the water vapor, or the invisible water that's in a volume of air rises to a particular area of cold temperatures, the water vapor condenses and eventually becomes rain, or water droplets; and if the water droplets descend through temperatures below the freezing level, they turn to snow. Finally we have the thunderstorms, which are extremely hazardous to aircraft in flight, and their lighting strikes can be dangerous to people on the ground, especially those who may choose to shield themselves from the lighting beneath trees. Noticeably to all of us, thunderstorms usually occur during the months of summer. Why is this so? Heated and moist surface air from the hot sun becomes buoyant and is forced upward by cooler denser air. The rapid accent of this moist unstable air into cooler temperatures aloft condenses to form cumulonimbus clouds or thunderstorms. But what are the causes for the lighting and thunder? The lighting flash we see are the tremendous surges of electrons flowing down or up a path, (the circuit,) or the "lighting channel," generated by electrical charges of unlike polarities, negative and positive, from the cloud to the ground, or vice versa. An analogy of this action is the electrical energy, or the flow of electrons produced by the negative and positive charges of a battery. The crash and rumble we hear soon after the flash of lighting are the results of the flood of electrons rapidly heating the air in their path causing the air to expand in all directions faster than the speed of sound. Temperatures increase along the "lighting channel" to about 30,000 degrees Celsius, (five times the surface temperature of the sun,) instantaneously, and almost as quickly the temperature cools resulting in great sound vibrations. Knowing these facts about the weather as a very young boy would have surely removed the fearful thoughts I had concerning God's anger toward us whenever I heard thunder.

Ending the brief exposition on weather, what follows may also be said to be brief narratives about City happenings. No longer the need to be residing near the place of employment, Long Island, I moved into a lovely studio apartment on 90th Street between Riverside Drive and West End Avenue, only a mere twenty minutes drive to "The Flight Service Station" at Teterboro Airport. Indeed, I was glad, not only to have become a City dweller again, but also to have finally gotten away from the somewhat depressive years on Long Island that, in essence, offered no activities to arouse intellectual energies, for example, no theatres, concert halls or museums. Most significantly, however, the depression stemmed primarily from the years of periodic loneliness experienced as a bachelor; an experience that perhaps all long-term bachelors can relate to. Furthermore, this nagging experience was to hover over me for another year in the City. Recalling those years at this moment, the realization comes to mind that the human being is indeed a social animal; we do in fact need intimate relationships to nurture our soul and our physical needs. In gradual stages, as the years passed by, I gradually became aware that the absence of a meaningful relationship was the missing link in my life. As an after thought, the loneliness made its presence known not at night before going to sleep, but surprisingly, when I least expected it to happen, during the solo evening meals in restaurants. Having to eat alone without the companionship of someone, preferably of the opposite sex, to share thoughts with, smile at or just joke with can be a horribly lonely experience. Thus, coming to grips with myself, and realizing my situation, I seriously began the search that ultimately was to end in a marriage.

Considering the fact it was her first marriage, the wedding was a relatively small one, (she didn't want a big wedding,) with only the immediate family attending the ceremony at an enchanting small "Meditation Chapel" in Riverside Church; the event happened on a brisk winter evening on December 28, 1971. Due to the vast differences in our ages, I was twenty three years older than my new bride, I had mixed feelings about the union lasting, perhaps no more than two or three years, yet it has lasted for more than thirty years thus far. No one seem more happier at the wedding than my dear mother who most likely realized at the time of its happening, and rightfully so in my opinion, that after so many years alone, her first born son was to finally settle down with a wife, and no doubt, having visions of a grandson in the very near future. As a write these words, it saddens the senses in remembering that her vision was not to appear for another fourteen years. On May 7, 1986 her grandson was born, one month after her life had ended at the age of eighty nine from the aftermath of a severe stroke suffered three years earlier.

Her stroke was not an unexpected occurrence, but one that I had suspected all along might happen when I found out from a surgeon doctor that she had an erratic heart beat. The discovery warrants a further explanation, if only to highlight what may arguably be a fact; and that is, some doctors can, in particular situations, lack moral judgment. In a clearer sense, they may have ulterior motives in the treatment of a patient, for instance, to express it bluntly, fattening their wallets rather than caring for the patient's well-being.

It had its beginning, like many incidents do, with a telephone call. My mother, who was eighty five years old at the time and living alone, her husband had passed away eight years earlier, called to tell me she had discovered a small lump on her breast and desired to see a doctor. I took her to a surgeon doctor who, on examining her, insisted that if the growth was malignant, she would have to undergo an operation for the removal of the tumor; afterward, he told me about her heart condition. I agreed to the simple biopsy test to be performed, but ordered him that if the growth were cancerous, under no circumstances did I want my mother subjected to what may be a life threatening operation, especially in her late years of life. He insisted that it was a customary procedure to remove a malignant tumor immediately after the biopsy. I held my ground, and emphatically told him that if it were cancer to leave it were it was, but she was not to be operated on. Surprisingly to me at the time were the results of the biopsy test, which revealed no cancer cells in my mother's breast. Yet, he had the audacity to, not only call me at my home a week later urging me to consent to the operation, but also had his assistant call me explaining that they had to explore deeper into the breast to see if there were any cancer cells that did not show-up in the biopsy analysis. Notable was the fact that this operation was to be done on a woman who was only a few months from her eighty six birthday. I was infuriated with those two supposedly professional individuals and their lack of ethical standards thinking all along, and I may have been wrong, that inasmuch as they were both surgeons, there was no money to be had unless they performed the operation on my dear old mother. The incident did have somewhat of a happy ending. The growth never grew larger, nor did she ever experienced any pains on her breasts during the few remaining years of her life. Her stroke occurred about a year after this incident.

CHAPTER 71

Morocco and Spain

The honeymoon was of course in Puerto Rico, and initially it had its unfulfilled beginnings. A day after our arrival, my bride suffers second degree burns on her body as a result of a two hour exposure to the tropical sun at the beach. So severe is the sunburn that I have to take her to a local hospital for treatment, and follow-up visits. As a result, during the entire week of the honeymoon I'm unable to caress my bride in any manner whatsoever. Nonetheless, a new era had begun for us in playing the roles of husband and wife. What we did all those fourteen years prior to the birth of our son, and why we waited all that time to have a child is another story that in due time will unfold itself during the course of the writing project. In general, however, we involved ourselves with work, school, and of more pleasurable activities for us, we traveled extensively throughout Western Europe, and the exotic lands of North Africa.

Those were the first years at "The Flight Service Station," and though the work was never as stressful or as exciting as controlling air traffic at the New York Center, still, in other factors it did have its merits in ways that were never experienced at the Center. Principally, this was because throughout the work day we were involved talking to pilots in person and not by voice transmissions as I did at the New York Center. The verbal encounters primarily dealt with the various natures of flying, and of course, briefing them with weather data along their flight routes and at their destinations. In contrast to this type of work, my wife first worked at the New York Public Library, and for a brief period of time during the Christmas holidays at Tiffany's, the world renowned jewelry department store on Fifth Avenue. After the Christmas holidays she was hired as an apprentice social worker by a Foster Care Agency where she was employed for about a year. This experience helped her to get accepted at New York University's Graduate School of Social Work; Her graduate work at the university eventually led to her professional career as a Master Social Worker," (MSW.) After work and school there were the vacations, most of which were consumed exclusively in what neither of us had ever before done, tour the countries of Western Europe and North Africa.

Vacations to far away lands, and what is there about this almost magical phrase that instills in some of us mental images of remembered vistas of places never before seen; This is a glorious period in time during our moments of leisure when we are fully able to experience all that is new to our eyes, and yet old, actually hundreds and thousand of years before the discovery of the Americas. Surely, as if my magic, vacations to far-away lands can transport us to magnificent sights that reflect not only the age of time, but of more value, what man has been able to create despite the lack of machinery and other modes of technology not accessible to him at the time. Vast cathedrals, Aqueducts, castles, monuments, and roads that have withstood the ravages of time, and are still standing are proof of man's creative abilities. Moreover, from the earliest of times, dating back to the stone age, man has left on earth his mark of artistic creations, as an illustration, the animals with their beautiful colors painted in caves that are still there for the eyes to behold in parts of France and Spain.

Following this path of artistic designs further, after those paintings left for us by people who lived in caves, man has left us marvelous examples of his imaginative powers, some of which are Stonehenge in England, the Parthenon in Greece, the Rome Forum, the Pantheon and the colossal Coliseum in Rome, Italy. In some aspects, this can be viewed as an example of succession, or simply, something coming in sequential order. For instance, the old towns of Spain in which each one has a church or a cathedral facing a small plaza are almost identical in design with what is seen in all the towns of Puerto Rico today. Perhaps in somewhat of an awkward manner, what I am leading up to is this: All artifacts perceived are pre-conceived from other origins. And if we go back to the cave paintings, and dwell momentarily about the old adage that everything has a beginning, what indeed came before those paintings, and where was man before wondering the face of the earth, and living in caves? Reverting to a theme that seems to be prevalent in this work, someone or something must have created man, or did he just evolved from an ape? And if a God created him, what was God up to, and what in fact was he doing before he created man? This leads us to further profound questions, what is man's origin? And if we accept the belief that God created him, what was God's purpose in creating man? These questions have confounded man since the beginning of time, whenever that was, and may never have answers. Suffice to end the metaphysic reflections with the basic premise that everything has its origin, including man, and wherever that origin stemmed from is still to be answered.

At any rate, a lighter side to resume focusing on, and one that will raise no profound questions, and get mix-up with metaphysics, are sights and happenings that occurred on vacations; these happenings may not always be pleasant ones. They can in fact develop into uncomfortable circumstances beyond one's control. A case in point was the incident that had its beginning on a ferry that had departed Algeciras in Southern Spain bound for Tangiers, Morocco in North Africa. Shortly after boarding the ferry, we were asked by an Arab soldier for our passports. After inspecting them, the soldier gave my wife her passport, but held on to mine, and not until we had arrived in Tangiers two hours later did I get back my passport. Aware at the time of the happening that without the document would have made it impossible for me to return to Spain, to say the least, I was quite anxious during the two hours on that ferry. The fact that my hair was down to my shoulders, and I appeared to be Jewish may have given the Arab soldier cause for believing he had an undesirable young man in his midst. That we were not detained on shore after disembarking led me to believe the matter had come to its end.

Days later, however, on our return to Tangiers to board the ferry back to Algeciras, on presenting my passport to a custom's agent, two soldiers grabbed my arms and escorted me to what looked to be a walk-in closet, but was actually a very small room without any windows. There I was handed over to, not another soldier as I had expected, but to an extremely tall and slim Arab whose ancestors most likely may have come from a Watusi tribe. He must have been all of seven feet tall, and with his head almost reaching the small room's ceiling. Wearing a long dark brown woolen robe reaching down to his ankles, and with a slight grin on his face, as though purposely showing me his platinum capped teeth, he motioned me to remove my shoes, and then raised my arms above my head. Thereafter he proceeded to search, or frisk may be a better word to describe it, every inch of my body from my head to my toes. Somewhat disappointed in not finding whatever he was looking for, but only my wallet and some coins, he opened the small room's door and turned me over to the two soldiers. The two soldiers then led me back to the custom's agent. Later aboard the ferry I found out from another tourist that the Arab who had searched me was looking for drugs in my possession, and if he had found any, Morocco's military police would have locked me up immediately and "thrown away the key." The incident was certainly not a pleasant one for us, and very much relieved in knowing we were returning to a friendlier and less hostile surroundings.

Undeveloped is the word commonly applied nowadays to define the North African Country of Morocco. When my wife and I visited the Country in the summer of 1974, a more appropriate word to describe it ought to have been primitive. Except for the modern City of Casablanca, which with its art deco architecture, tall date palm trees lining the broad avenues resembled Nice in Southern France, a squalid environment throughout the landscape greeted the visitor to Morocco. Signs of widespread poverty, filth, flies, men and children beggars, but what was a worse eye sore, pitiful women holding infants on their shoulders and with an arm extended asking money from the tourists. All had a forbidden look about them, with their faces partially hidden with cloth so that only their eyes and foreheads were in view. Children, in particular, made a nuisance of themselves following you wherever you went offering their services as tour guides, and all wanting to take you to the Casbah. No, this Casbah bore absolutely no resemblance to the one with the intricate network of winding pathways seen in the 1938 movie, "Tangiers," with Charles Boyer and Hedi Lamarr, but simply a market place for shoppers. However, what appeared to be an exceptional attribute among the children of school ages was they spoke and understood four languages, their own Arabic language, English, French and Spanish.

Noted also in our travels south of Tangiers were the magnificent mosques, at least when viewed from the outside; unless you were a Moslem, you were not allowed to enter them. Once we found ourselves in rural areas what appeared odd to us were women and not the men working in the fields, some with the aid of camels and donkeys rather than with tractors, or any other type of modern farm machinery. The men, for the most part, were seen lounging around the small outdoor cafes along the roads drinking and playing cards, and what seem to be in fashion, most of them had their teeth capped in platinum. Somewhat of a comical sight were the rest rooms in the roadside cafes, which may best be described as quasi-modern plumbing. They were not the conventional type latrines, but instead, outdoor shacks with toilet bowls in them, but had no running water. The strange and funny aspect, at least from our point of view, was that no sooner had the patrons left the small shacks, little old ladies dressed in black and carrying pails of water entered them and flushed the toilets manually. What was not comical in any sense of the word, but rather a frustrating fact to a shopper was that whether you were in a store or dealing with a street vendor, you always had to negotiate the price for an item you desired to purchase. All things considered, the overall experience in our travels in Morocco was not a pleasant one. In particular, from the very first moment of our arrival in Tangiers, we had the keen sense to realize we were not welcomed visitors. This fact was confirm by the tour guide on our bus trip to Marrakech who cautioned us that Arabs hated the Americans and regarded them as "dogs."

Contrary to the Arabs' attitude, the people of Spain had the welcome mat out for all tourists, including the Americans who visited their Country. And it certainly appeared to be a banner year for the tourist trade, especially with the large influx of English, Germans, and Scandinavians who traveled to the Country in flocks taking advantage of Spain's crippling economy, which with its extremely low cost of living, made it ideally suitable for the low budget travelers of Northern Europe. It's incredible to note that in the month's time in the Country, our total expenditures amounted to less than one thousand dollars. Spain, though ruled with an "iron fist" by the dictator, Generalissimo Francisco Franco, and politically isolated from the rest of Europe, nonetheless, was a friendly Country, and what made us more self-assured was that both of us were fluent Spanish speakers.

One notable factor not common in all other Countries of Western Europe, or in North Africa where it might have been expected, was that all policemen carried machineguns strapped to their chest with chains, nevertheless, there was no cause for alarm, inasmuch as never did we have any encounters with the police. The closest we ever came to one was witnessing a brief altercation between a policeman and a young Englishman traveling with us who decided to take a picture of a police officer issuing a traffic summons to a motorist. On spotting our English companion and what he was doing, the officer rushed over to him grabbed the camera, opened it, removed the roll of film, and then returned the camera to the young man. Thereafter, a verbal reprimand ensued in Spanish in which I had to serve as the translator for our English companion.

Traveling through Spain, the visitor soon discovers that most of the rural areas, especially in the southern part of the Country, are blanketed with olive trees. But more appealing to the tourists are the many castles that dot the landscape, and all dating back to the middle ages. What's more, near Granada there is the artistic beauty of "Alhambra," the palace built in the thirteen century by the Moors who occupied the Peninsula for over eight hundred years. And then, of course, there are the traditional bull fights, which are held in huge stadiums named "Plazas De Toros," or bulls' plazas. Another tradition is the "Siesta," or the early afternoon nap, which is practiced religiously by most workers. Essentially, it's not the nap that's important, but the hours of leisure usually between one and three in the afternoon, and because workers are not held accountable to their employers for any work. As a result, most of the stores and restaurants are closed during this time period. The custom, however, does have its drawbacks; in order to compensate for the lost selling time during the "Siesta," working hours are extended so that a work day does not end until eight or nine o'clock in the evening. Most likely, that's why Spaniards customary have their evening meal, their "Cena," around ten o'clock in the evening, or thereafter.

The custom is adhered to throughout the land, especially in the urban cities, for example, Madrid, the Country's capital. Madrid architecturally, and with its subway system known as "the Metro," and its crown jewel, the Prado museum, in some ways resembles Paris. The rather small museum cannot be compared in size and the vast quantities of art objects that the stupendous Louvre houses. Nonetheless, what it lacks in quantity more than makes-up for in quality with its abundance of classical paintings, some of which are by Velazquez, Goya and El Greco. Many wonderful sights never before seen captivated my eyes on our travels through Spain; but not one gave me the emotional impression that a small plaza in Sevilla did. People of all ages were strolling along the square, which overlooked the City's cathedral, and white pigeons were seen everywhere on the ground, as though accompanying the pedestrians. The plaza's outer edges were lined with small trees looking more like shrubs than trees, and literally covered with miniature ripe oranges about the size of plums. On viewing the scene, instantly memories of a long ago bygone era came to light recalling the time when as a young boy, no more than five or six years old I had seen a small plaza lined with orange trees in front of the massive cathedral in Caguas, Puerto Rico, and almost identical to the small one in Sevillas; yes, memories do linger on.

CHAPTER 72

Our Travels Continue

Italy, or more specifically, Rome, Florence and Venice, not unlike Spain, welcomed the tourists, and especially in Rome hordes of them were seen everywhere. In fact, at times it appeared as though there were more tourists than native dwellers ambling along the City's streets, and they were amply rewarded with the many attractions, notably antiquities that Rome had to offer them. One peculiar sight that caught my attention, odd as it may seem, was the large amounts of cats roaming around the Forum's ruins. My wife's reaction to the scene, and she was earnestly serious about it, probably because even in those times she was a devoted lover of cats, was that most likely they were spiritual animals from another life seeking their ancestral homes. Another odd sight was the one I gazed at from the roof of St. Peter's Cathedral. Standing beside one of the huge angel statues that surround the roof's perimeter, I saw what could only be described as an ironic scene, totally out of context with all the splendors of the cathedral. Vast slums literally covered the land directly beyond and around the church, circling it as though asking for some help from an obvious source, the riches of St. Peter's. At this moment I'm tempted to speculate that this dichotomy between the rich trappings of a religious order and the slums of the poor may have been purposely created in order to enhance the opulence of St. Peter's Cathedral and Vatican city.

Florence and Venice were then, and may well still be today two cities as different as night and day. One presented the visitor with what can be described as daytime activities, and the other with the nightlife. Florence offered the tourist the experience of viewing renaissance marvels of churches, palaces and the creative genius of Michelangelo's sculpture of David. David, according to the Bible, was a young shepherd boy who with a stone hurled from his slingshot slew Goliath the giant. The majestic form of the big huge statue, which is fourteen feet tall, and thus twice the height of man, can be viewed in the City's main square. By contrast, Venice's enchanting beauty was fully appreciated only at night. The thousand or more lights reflecting on the canals' dark waters gave the City the appearance of a carnival in full swing, with revelry and feasting on-going throughout the night hours. In particular, this occurred in St. Mark's Plaza with its numerous restaurants and cafes, and where live music from the orchestras in the Plaza never ceased to charm one's soul. Unlike the nights' festive activities, the days were rather gloomy with the ever-present fog hovering overhead and lingering in the City for many hours. The offensive foul odor emanating from the ebb tide, which usually occurred during the day, moreover, contributed to the depressive atmosphere. And then there were the pigeons, hordes of them swarming and cooing over practically every foot of walking space on the Plaza. And as to be expected, leaving their droppings, and in general, creating a nuisance for tourists who had to be extra careful for fear of stepping on the droppings, or what may have been worse, one of the birds. Recently my wife, son and I took a tour of the City, and not to my surprise very little had changed since I had last seen Venice more than twenty five years ago.

The French speak nothing but French. A perceptive statement no doubt, also redundant in form, and does indeed need clarification. In essence, what is meant is that, in general, the French refuse to learn and speak any other language but their own. English and German, needless to say, were frowned upon. However, what surprised me to some extent that summer of 1974, was that the French, and again I'm speaking in general terms, didn't speak Spanish, nor did they have any desire to learn the language; yet their Country bordered on a Spanish speaking Nation. This refusal my have had it origin from what, arguably, they appeared to be, highly independent and stubborn individuals who saw and reasoned only through their own lenses, and were easily intimidated by values different from their own. Nonetheless, what may be seen as highly controversial attributes cast on these people, we cannot deny the fact that the French, to some extent, have been the great innovators of our time.

To begin with, they have been known for generations to be the producers of fine wines, perfumes, and have introduced to the world trend-setting fashions, and not to be left out, gourmet dining. The French have even devised a novel way to serve a frankfurter, or the hotdog, as it's commonly known in America. Of course, not the ordinary way with mustard and sauerkraut, but they seem to have improved its taste by doubling the size, serving it on a large bun, and smothering the meat with melted cheese. Moreover, they had added a new feature to compliment women's footwear fashions. A common sight in Paris in 1974, and one never before seen in the States, women wore high boots to just below their knees. Another novel aspect was the manner in which waiters tabulated your bill in some restaurants. Naturally with pens or pencils, they merely itemized the bill on the dining tables' paper tablecloths, added a fifteen percent gratuity charge, and, voila, you paid the bill directly to them and not to a cashier. And as for popular attractions, among many others, and especially geared for the tourist trade were "The Louvre, which is an ancient royal palace that has been converted to a museum, "Versailles Palace" with its beautiful "hall of mirrors," "Notre Dame," the famous early gothic cathedral, and what has become the capital City's landmark, "The Eiffel Tower."

Also worthy of mention that year was their relatively modern subway, with their first and second class passenger cars, and known then as it is still know today as "The Metro." Some of the newer cars had rubber wheels rather than steel, thus the system was much quieter than the noisy New York subways. More impressive though, was the manner in which they had developed a method for entering the stations' platforms without the need of coins or tokens. Of more significance, it should be noted that a similar method, the "Metro Card," was not introduced to New Yorkers until almost twenty five years later. The person purchasing one, or a booklet of ten "garnets," which were rectangular shaped yellow tickets about the size of domino pieces, by merely inserting one of these "garnets" into the turnstile slot enabled the person entrance to the platform. Not to be overlooked before leaving France for Amsterdam and England, the French have had their illustrious military strategist and Emperor, Napoleon the first, who as a result of his military victories extended the Nation's territories to what came to be known to all Frenchmen as "The glorious French empire." The popular saying, "leave it to the French," may have had its inception with Napoleon. The great warrior had one of his favorite white horses stuffed by a taxidermist, and was on view in 1974, and I believe it still is at "Le Pantheon Des Grand Hommes De France in Paris; and noticeable to everyone, who comes in sight of them are the large /Ns/ carved on the sides of the bridges on the "Seine River." No doubt, they are there to commemorate France's popular military hero.

Amsterdam, the commercial capital of the Netherlands, and better known as Holland, is not the quaint town with windmills and Dutch people wearing wooden shoes one has read about, but instead, a modern metropolis with over fifty canals with their enchanting small arched bridges. The many small charming little bridges, most of which are only for pedestrians, crisscross the canals' water throughout the City. At night especially, the numerous lights from the bridges reflect on the dark waters giving the viewer the appearance of twinkling little stars that have fallen from the sky and are now floating on the glowing waters of the canals. Amsterdam's population, most of whom not only spoke their language, but also English were extremely friendly people, particularly to the tourists. In 1974, and I don't know if it's still in effect today, the public transportation system consisted of "trams," better known to the tourists as streetcars. And one of the surprising aspects was the large amount of people riding bicycles, not for pleasure as one might have expected it but as their means of getting around the City. Most likely, the land's flat terrain and the absence of strong winds, which tend to prevent physical exhaustion, provided the people with what appeared to be a popular mode of transportation.

Two of the popular attractions in the City were the VanGogh museum named in honor of their favorite native son, the world renowned impressionist painter, and the "Anne Frank House." The house is where thirteen year old Anne and her Jewish family went into hiding from the Nazis in World War II. During this time the young girl kept a diary, which has been read by millions of people throughout the world, and is today still considered an important document from the War. Our visit was a brief one, lasting only four days, during which we stayed at a lovely four story white "canal house" overlooking the waters of one of the canals. On one of the days, we went on an all day joyous bicycle tour with a dozen other cyclists viewing many sights, and including a walking tour to a small farm house. There we saw what all of us thought was the highlight of the tour, how they made Holland's world famous Goda Cheese. Whenever I have Goda Cheese nowadays, there are times when memories tend to linger on that glorious bicycle tour, especially to the small dairy farm on the outskirts of the City of Amsterdam.

The final stop on our first vacation to Morocco and Western Europe was to England, a Country that some Americans, or perhaps a good majority of them consider their mother Country. And what can be said during that particular time of June, in 1974 when low clouds blanketed London, the sun seldom showed its face and the relentless drizzle presented a scene of dreariness to the visitor? Nevertheless, to say the most, there were the popular sights, "Buckingham Palace," "Hyde Park," "the tower of London" and "Picadilly Circus," which somewhat compensated for the depressive weather conditions. Most surprising though, was the native population's manner of speaking, not as I had expected, for example, people sounding not unlike the voices of the English actors Ronald Coleman or Robert Morley, instead, most spoke with a cockney dialect that, because of the loss of the initial /H/sounds in words, was rather difficult to understand, particularly on first hearing it.

To cite some popular sights outside of London, among others, there was "Stonehenge," the prehistoric stone structure on the plains of Salisbury, the City of Bath with its ancient Roman Baths, and the thatch cottage of Jane Austen, the novelist who wrote, among other novels, Pride and Prejudice. And not to be omitted were the popular theatres of London where a ticket for a matinee performance generally cost no more than three dollars. After the theater the places to go were the pubs, which were numerous enough for one to be on practically every corner of the City's downtown area, and all serving food and about thirty varieties of beers and ales. Finally exhausted but contented after the month's vacation to Morocco and various other countries in Western Europe, we flew back to the U.S.A.. Arriving at the John F. Kennedy Airport in Queens, we took a Carey Bus to New York City, the Big Apple, and our home.

CHAPTER 73

Another Brief Encounter, and Fears

In years to come there would be exciting trips to other countries, among them, Brazil, Greece, and especially to Mexico where we toured the Country for a month's time from Mexico City to the Western part of the Country, and then eastward to the Yucatan; there, we viewed the famous Mayan ruins of Chichenitza. However, despite all our travels to distant lands, no trip was as rewarding to the inner senses as the one taken to Puerto Rico, specifically to meet for the first time a certain someone; and what might have been the origin of that forthcoming meeting? And how did it all come about?

For many years, as far back as my early childhood, I had heard rumors from various family members relating to the existence of that certain someone. Nonetheless, confronting my mother about the rumors, she, much to my frustration, always denied them. The meeting had been arranged by my cousin Federico, who had written advising me that the person was in Puerto Rico and desired very much to meet me. On that fateful day, staying at a lovely guesthouse by the ocean just south of the Condado area in downtown San Juan, my wife and I waited patiently at the guesthouse's patio for our visitor. According to prior arrangements made by my cousin, she was to arrive around noontime. Some moments after twelve noon, my eyes caught sight of a somewhat youngish woman who appeared to be in her early sixties, and no more than five feet tall. As she approached us walking along the gravel path that led to the patio, I noticed she was wearing a strangely beautiful turquoise colored turban. As she came closer, I was somewhat stunned by the sight of a person whose facial features were almost identical to mine. At that particular moment, it seem as if I were looking at my reflections in a mirror. The lady was Josefina Solano, my long lost sister. As I was to learn from her during the course of our lengthy meeting, our relationship was that of a brother and sister having the same father but different mothers. There in that patio the three of us chatted for hours, with her and I reminiscing mostly about our past lives. The meeting finally ended with her having to leave for the airport to board a flight back to Miami where she lived. Despite my not realizing it at the time, our meeting was similar in one respect with the brief encounter I had previously had with my father, Fidel Solano, many years earlier in Puerto Rico when I was no more than five years old. The meeting with my sister Josefina Solano was the first and last time I was to see her. She passed away suddenly a year later after a short illness.

I had no premonition prior to its happening, and therefore there were no fears involved. The fears were to come much later, which before narrating them, a brief discussion relating to fears may serve as a primer for the narrative. "The only thing we have to fear is fear itself." A rather ambiguous statement perhaps, despite its popularity when it was first made by President Franklin D. Roosevelt at the outset of World War II. Why ambiguous we may now ask? In the attempts to answer the question, it may be noted that the statement does not give us a clear definition of what, in effect, fear is. What I'm suggesting is that there are indeed many ways in which we can define fear, and a prime example is the common one, fear of the unknown. Depending on the individual of course, fear can be experienced in various ways, or expressing it differently, what may be fearful for one person may not necessarily have the same effect for another. It may be enough to say that fear for most of us means the presence, or nearness of danger. Further, it can reveal itself as apprehensions to what may happen, and yes, even a feeling of terror. And as has already been said, fear may be experienced as a feeling of anxiety for what may be liable to happen. At times, it may develop into panic that can cause unreasonable fears, which may lead to irrational or senseless behavior. Up to this point, what has been discussed seemingly borders on semantics, and that it clearly has. Nevertheless, the brief discussion can perhaps function as a suitable introduction for what I'm about to describe, the type of underlying fear I experienced after almost thirteen years of marriage. I am not the least superstitious, which leads me to believe the number thirteen had absolutely no bearing whatsoever on the circumstances that were to unravel that year.

The beginning, like some unexpected happenings, occurred on an ominous note. After years of giving me subtle hints about her desires, she finally resolved the matter for both of us. During the course of the many hints, I attempted to reason with her that she still had to complete her graduate work, and the burden would indeed curtail our freedom to travel. However, of more important to me, and most likely not to her, I tried explaining how the added responsibility could have an adverse effect on us, for instance, draining our money resources. To no avail, I kept emphasizing to her that our freedom from any obligations except to ourselves most certainly would nurture our marriage into an everlasting happy relationship. The true fact from this verbal conflict was that I was not about to take on responsibilities that for me had ended long ago. Probably, being the social worker and therapist she had finally become after years of studies, my wife saw through my thinly disguised excuses and gave me her ultimatum. Her years were rapidly approaching that phase in life for a woman when it was not possible to conceive, and she was well aware of that fact. "I'm getting on in years and desperately want a child, and if you're not prepared to be a father, I have no other recourse other than to divorce you and find and marry a man who will grant my wish." Those were the words that gave me the fear of losing her, and the fear in realizing her determination in proceeding with the divorce if I didn't comply with her wishes.

Months passed by without her becoming pregnant, and suspecting the probability of some physical defect as a result of my advanced years, she advised me I had to have my semen tested; but on hearing the laboratory's results that the specimen submitted was normal, she had herself examined. The prospects of any unforeseen problems never occurred to her, and was quite upset on finding out there was a blockage in her fallopian tubes. Somehow relieved when I heard the lab's report, I nevertheless underestimated her strong desires to have a child. Signing herself into a hospital for the needed operations, within two days she was discharged with the blockage cleared. After her second miscarriage, I had reconciled myself to what appeared to be the inevitable, the impossibility of her becoming pregnant. Nonetheless, the fear irrupted again when I noticed the first signs of her pregnancy had begun to show. To my amazement, I found out she was already six months pregnant, and realized, correctly I may add, she was not going to lose the child. To some extent, I did become fearful dwelling on thoughts of the added responsibilities, and especially on becoming a father again at the ripe old age of sixty one. Yet what followed seem to allay most of the fears I was experiencing. She agreed to my suggestion, much to my surprise, that if the child should be a girl, she could name her whatever name she chose; however, if it were a boy it was to be named Fidel.

Our son Fidel was born at about 9 AM on May 7, 1986, three days before my wife's birthday. That she had previously selected Gabriela as the name for the baby girl, prompted me to compromise by agreeing with her desires to select Gabriel for the baby boy's middle name. Given the privilege to be by her side at the time she gave birth, I was quite surprised when the doctor asked me if I wanted to cut the cord. With the doctor holding the baby by the ankles in mid air so that the infant was upside down, and with cries piercing my ears that only a newborn can make, I cut the umbilical cord with a pair of surgical scissors. What ensued I certainly was not prepared for, nor did I expected it. Blood from the cut splattered the front of the shirt I was wearing. To this day I still regret not saving that shirt as a token of the actual moment of my son's birth. Another unforeseen happening occurred all during his infancy and toddling periods. And as a result, I always experienced an inner glee in telling people whenever they said it, which was often enough to become annoying, "What a lovely grandchild you have," that I was the father and not the grandfather. It happened so frequently that at times I was tempted to buy a top, (T-shirt,) with the words, "I'm the father" engraved on it.

CHAPTER 74

A Mother's End

Death was not imminent, but what can be worse, a prolonged agonizing effect in knowing there could never be hopes for her recovery. The end happened eleven months after the birth of my son, or to be more precise, in April of 1987. For me especially, it was indeed a sorrowful ending, though not an untimely one, and there are times I can still recall the first warning signs of her impending misfortune. Three years before she passed away I made my customary weekend visit to her apartment, and on seeing her immediately suspected something was ailing my mother by the expression on her face. She showed no semblance of her happy disposition when greeting her number one son. What I saw at that moment was a sad looking old woman with a forlorn appearance that perhaps reflected a sudden ailment had occurred. Not to alarm her in any manner, I merely asked her how she was feeling, and if there were anything she needed? Her replies were, "fine," and there was nothing she required, adding that she was just feeling a bit tired and depressed, nothing more, and there was no need for me to come the following day to visit her. I didn't object, inasmuch as Sunday was the day to take my son to the park on his stroller. The visit was rather brief lasting no more than an hour, and when I left her, my last words were I would call in the middle of the week. At that moment, never did I realized that was the last conversation I was ever to have with my mother.

Scheduled to begin work Monday at four in the afternoon, but still concerned in how I last had seen her the previous Saturday, I decided to call just before leaving for the "Flight Service Station."

315

The telephone rang and rang numerous times, and I waited patiently, knowing she was a slow walker, and the phone was in the kitchen; the fact that she was blind also contributed to her slow pace. The phone kept ringing and still there was no answer. Aware she was housebound, and never left her apartment, I knew for certain there had to be something wrong, some mishap, or perhaps some fowl play, and I must go to her quickly. Despite having a key to her apartment, I purposely knocked on the front door several times without getting a response, or anyone attempting to open the door. Letting myself in with the key, I called, "Momi, Momi," and receiving no answer proceeded directly to the living room and then the bedroom. Not finding her in either one of those rooms, I approached the bathroom, which was closed and pushed the door open. I found her slouched on the floor with her back leaning against the toilet bowl, and still wearing her nightgown. With her glazed eyes wide open and eyelids not blinking, the expression on her face was that of a person who had been hypnotized. The lower part of her face appeared to be dropping slightly giving her somewhat of a distorted, or deformed appearance. From that moment until the final end, that expression never left her face. I spoke to her several times without getting any response, and she kept staring straight ahead without making any eye contact with me. I attempted to lift her, but realizing she was too heavy, I called the police. Arriving a short time later, they placed her on a stretcher and carried her to the waiting ambulance.

All that evening I was with her at the hospital, and not being told about her illness despite my repeated questions, but all along suspecting the obvious, that she had had a stroke. Within the next few days other minor strokes were to occur, and as a result, my mother never returned to he apartment; instead, in a matter of weeks she was transferred to a nursing home in the Bronx's Pelham Bay area. My dear wife's concern with the long distance my mother was from us prompted her to seek another nursing home where she could be closer to us. Applying her social worker's expertise, within a short time she succeeded in having my mother placed in a home a mere four blocks distance from our apartment.

I always had the notion a nursing home was a convalescent environment where people went for their gradual recovery after a serious illness. Nothing could be further from the truth. Emphasizing the point, she never did recovered, nor for that matter, probably neither did all the other thin, hollow eyed and emaciated patients supposedly there convalescing until their recovery. Without exceptions, all the patients were extremely old, who appeared to be more dead than alive, and within a year's time my mother was to become part of this group, wasted almost beyond recognition. Invariably, I remembered her as a tall buxom woman with hefty legs and an abundance of black hair. Despite her age, and until her stroke, at least once a month she went to the hairdresser to have her hair and fingernails done; never can I ever recall seeing my mother with gray hair. However, gradually, within the first months at the nursing home, I began to notice her black hair turning white, but far more disturbing, she began to lose a lot of weight, and the always enigmatic blank stare never left her face. A great deal of my visits involved speaking to her constantly hoping to receive some verbal, or at least a body language response from her, but never did I get it. Adding to my distress, they cut her hair very short without my consent, and when I questioned the reason for if, they justified their action by telling me it made it easier for them to comb her hair. Naturally, I was furious with what they had done, however, what was I to do, her hair had already been cut, and to make matters worse, her hair never grew back to its original condition.

There came the time in the last year of life when her physical appearance changed drastically into that of a person almost unknown to me, resembling not the mother I used to know, but a shriveled little old lady looking more like a living skeleton than a human being, and worse, her face had become almost completely distorted; a face contorted by a sagging left jaw as though she no longer had stamina left in her to hold it up in its normal way. Her small body was always in the fetus position like she had regressed to the unborn phase of human life, and a feeding tube had been inserted in her neck to furnish her with the nutrients she no longer was able to take by mouth. Her condition had deteriorated to the point where she had lost the use of her mind and body, and all that was keeping her alive was a tube hooked up to a machine. Many were the times I was tempted to disconnect the feeding tube, or pay someone to do it for me, and let her die in peace, but my wife discouraged it by advising me it was against the law.

Ultimately, I was no longer able to bear the sight of seeing my mother in that horrible condition, therefore, during her last six months of life, my wife visited her while I remained downstairs in the nursing home's lobby waiting for wife's report on mother's condition. Finally, the evening before the end, I received a telephone call from the nursing home advising me she had pneumonia and were rushing her to the hospital. The following morning about 6 AM the phone ran giving me the notice I had expected all that previous night. At the age of eighty nine my dear mother's life had come to its end. An after thought occurs to me as I write these words, strange as it may seem, there are occasions when we think we're prepared for the inevitable, yet we still fail to grasp what our reactions will be, or to be more explicit, how we will conduct ourselves when the actual happening arrives. Hearing the voice on the other end giving me the news, I hung up the phone and stood there for about a minute or so, thinking about what I cannot recall now, but what I do remember after receiving the call was locking myself in the bathroom sobbing with intense grief for five or ten minutes, and all the while my wife asking me from the outer hall, "Fidel, Fidel, are you alright?"

CHAPTER 75

Emotions, and The Ravages of Time

What is it that instills in us feelings of emotions for loved ones when we realize they will no longer be with us when death arrives for them? On the other hand, there are some of us who tend to be overcome with emotional feelings that tears are actually shed when viewing a landscape, a painting, or what may be more common, viewing a particular sad scene in a movie; and then there are those exhilarating joyful moments when emotional tears of happiness appear before our eyes on meeting a loved one not seen in a long time. Finally there are the emotions resulting from the frustrations for our failure to achieve what we desire, or the emotional reaction, the anger cast on others for the physiological or psychological hurt they have imposed on us. What in fact does cause us to experience these emotions?

Evidence has shown that for anything happening in our conscious mind, something must have occurred in our brain to trigger the emotions. Therefore, we can concede that the brain must be the driving force acting on our consciousness. This is a recurring theme no doubt, and one that to some extent has been previously dealt with. Nevertheless, to expand on the theme, or to repeat unintentionally what may have already been said, the discussion on human emotions will continue. Keeping in mind that the brain is the stimulus for our feelings, a good example can be offered. If I accidentally bang my finger while hammering a nail on a wall, and nerve cells fail to transmit the impulse to my brain, I would feel no pain on my finger. Further with this line of thinking, emotions have to be relayed to the brain before we can experience them. However, unlike the hammer striking the finger, feelings of emotions may not be the result of a physical act, but more of a psychological occurrence that impinges on our behavior. It may be thought of as a kind of dormant thing deeply submerged that surfaces at times when we least expect it, takes hold of us as an uncontrollable force, and not easily contained as much as we may attempt to do it. Not withstanding the fact that our individuality plays a significant role in the way we behave, or clearly stated, what may raise emotions in one person may not do the same for another, what should be accepted is that something does indeed trigger our brain; but what can that something be? And if not the results of an All Mighty God, who according to the beliefs of the atheist or the agnostic does not exist, then what? Can this something that causes our brain to react possibly be the result of a spiritual thing? But what if we don't believe in spiritualism? To be over simplistic in drawing conclusions, we can resort to the adage that the something is part of our human nature; for sooner or later, to be sure, we do experience emotions. In any case, to bring these metaphysical thoughts to a close, the question of what causes us to have emotions most likely will never have conclusive answers.

Human emotions can be like thunderstorms, which suddenly make their appearance on bright sunny days by stirring up strong winds, dark clouds quickly form shedding torrential rains, the sounds of thunder are heard, and flashes of light illuminate the sky. However, unlike thunderstorms that rapidly dissipate, and the bright sun reappears to resume its normal function, emotions can linger on for moments, hours, days, and at times recur at regular intervals for years. These emotions generally generated by frustrations did in fact linger on-and-off for almost two years primarily caused by my failure not to realize the obvious. Why is it we don't always seem to perceive what stares back at us every time we look in the mirror? How this all came about happened a year after my mother's death when I found out the "Flight Service Station" was scheduled to relocate in the Spring of 1990. The Facility was to consolidate with other small "Flight Service Stations" to form "A Hub Facility" in Millville, New Jersey. The town of

Millville is a three hours drive from the City, and as a result, commuting to work made it almost impossible for me. Consequently, for the following two years prior to the Facility's movement, I submitted over twenty five "bids" every time there was an opening in "The New York Region" at the J.F. Kennedy Airport; the airport was only a thirty minutes drive from my apartment.

A "bid" is the Federal Government Government's jargon word for what in essence it is, a resume, except that you state your qualifications, the required experience for the position and your education on a standard form. If your "bid" impresses them in any manner, you will be called at the Facility and scheduled for an interview. The interviews, to say the least were many, but always there were the rejections that I was over-qualified, or under-qualified lacking the required experience; and what was amazing, the fact that I had a doctoral degree didn't seem to matter to them. Indeed, after receiving numerous rejections, I began to get the impression the degree actually represented a threat to the people interviewing me. What I mean by this is, they may have been fearful that if they were to hire me, some day in the near future, I would displace one of them because of my education. At one memorable interview a male acquaintance who had worked at the Teterboro "Flight Service Station" was one of the members on the panel interviewing me. After the interview I had the feeling that all had gone quite well, yet I got the usual rejection. The consensus of the panel was that I didn't have enough experience for the position. Walking out into the hall, and naturally, highly disappointed, I was soon approached by the acquaintance. After getting me to promise not to divulge it to anyone, adding it would jeopardize his job, he said, "despite you having met all the requirements, the panel felt you were too old for the position." Never did I realize until that fateful moment that at the ripe age of sixty four I was no longer a young man. Yes indeed, at times we do tend to become blind to what stares at us in the mirror, the ravages of time.

Six months before the actual moving date all personnel at the station received the official written notice that Teterboro "Flight

Service Station" was to relocate to Millville, New Jersey on March 1, 1990. Reconciled to the fact I was not to attain a position at "the Regional Office," I called the president of "The Spanish Coalition of Federal Aviation Workers," and explained my plight to him. Fortunately, I was a charter member of the labor group's Eastern Region, which had close to five thousand Spanish Federal Aviation members, most of whom were Mexican Americans from the southwestern part of the Country. He was instrumental in getting me transferred to the "Bridgeport Flight Service Station" in Connecticut. Unlike Teterboro, which was a branch of "the Eastern Region, and only twelve miles from the City, Bridgeport was part of "the New England Region," and was a distance of sixty eight miles by car. Nevertheless, my problem of having to move from the City had been resolved, and on March 1, 1990 I reported to the "Bridgeport Flight Service Station." I was to complete a four year stint at the Station before retiring from Federal Government Service.

Reflecting on the frustrating experience now, the thought occurs to me that we should realize that, indeed, there are powers in numbers. What I mean by this is that in a sense, striving for something we almost desperately need, without an outside force for support can predispose us to failure. Working alone in my attempts not to have to go to Millville, I was never to succeed, nonetheless another person working on my behalf was successful. That this individual represented a large body of workers most certainly was a contributing factor in my getting transferred to Bridgeport. If there is anything to be learned from the experience, it's that in our endeavors, particularly in the business world, we should, if the urgent need arises, never attempt them alone, for sooner or later we are going to need help from a support group, whether it's a coalition, association or a labor union, otherwise we're most likely to fail.

CHAPTER 76

The Bridgeport "Flight Service Station"

In general terms, a blessing in disguised is one of the ways to define the new working environment, and a satisfying one that was to last four years. Specifically, however, what is there to say about Bridgeport, or what in fact was the "Flight Service Station" like? Foremost, the Facility was one of the only two "Hubs" providing aviation weather to pilots flying from the New England States. Unlike Teterboro with its outdated teletype machines, Bridgeport had a marvelous computerized system that merely by pressing a button gave you access to actual weather and forecasted weather around the world; also, it was much larger than teterboro having over fifty "aviation weather briefers," not including the administrative staff. A bigger advantage from my point of view at least, was that soon after arriving at the Facility, I was appointed a "Training Specialist," which set the stage for acquiring the background experience for the future second career, teaching in a college classroom setting.

In essence, the work of a "Training Specialist" entailed training new workers in the skills required for the type of work the job demanded, and which I had been doing for many years. Another part of the work, or what were called "duties" involved conducting "refresher training" in standard and new procedures to all "weather briefers." Though driving sixty eight miles five days a week to work on the Connecticut Turnpike quite often taxed the nerves, the opportunity to train young men at a relatively new Station was challenging, but more so, rewarding to the senses. Moreover, I was blessed with a station manager who admired me for my conscientious work, all my years of experience with the Government Agency, and perhaps also because of my academic credentials. Indeed the last four years of employment with the Federal Aviation Administration at the Bridgeport Station were the most rewarding and enjoyable ones.

Long past the age of retirement, still, I had never given the matter much of a thought until an unexpected incident occurred off the Connecticut turnpike on my way home from work. The cause for the happening undoubtedly was the effect from the constant humming sound from driving on a highway. Feeling extremely drowsy, and fearful of falling asleep while driving, I had the good sense to drive off the Turnpike and onto a service road leading to a McDonald's restaurant to get a coffee. The last thing I remembered was driving on the service road; on waking up sitting behind the steering wheel, the first reaction was to look at my wristwatch. I had been asleep for almost ten minutes, yet had managed to park the car in one of the designated parking stalls in the parking lot. How I accomplished that remarkable feat while asleep still remains a mystery to me till this day. Right then and there a firm commitment was made to work at Bridgeport no longer than the three years remaining to complete my forty one years tenure with the Federal Government, thus entitling me to the maximum retirement benefits, eighty percent of my base salary.

Months later rumors began to circulate around the Facility that the F.A.A. was planning to offer a "buy out" to those employees with thirty years or more of "service time," as an incentive for them to retire; or to put it in a more forceful manner, as a method for getting rid of them. The "buy out," or lump sum of money, was a concept devised by the private sector and adopted by the Federal Government as a cost-saving factor. The Agency's intent was to eliminate the high salaried old employees, and hire new workers who, once trained, were able to perform the work at half the salaries paid to the old timers. Naturally, what was of prime interest to the old timers with thirty years or more of service, one of whom was this writer, was how much was the F.A.A. planning to offer us. The answer arrived sooner than I had expected it via a long distance telephone call from the Station Manager. While vacationing with my family in Mexico early in March, he called to advise me that the "buy out" was "official," and the Government had offered us, (he was planning on retiring,) twenty five thousand dollars. However, he also declared that a one month restriction had been imposed for accepting the offer, which essentially meant I had only until the end of April to submit "the paper work." After computing the numbers, I discovered that if I were to retire within a month's time, the retirement benefits would be seventy six percent of my salary, rather than the eighty percent I was striving for. Reasoning that the lump sum would make-up the four percent difference, I cut the vacation short, returned to the Facility and submitted the retirement papers. What I had failed to take into account in my computations until after retiring on May 1, 1994, was the fact that eight thousand dollars from the lump sum would be deducted for taxes, and as a result, I only received seventeen thousand dollars. Broadly speaking, with one hand Uncle Sam gave me money, and with his other hand took part of it back. Wouldn't it have been more honorable for the Government to had declared that taxes were to be imposed on the lump sum of money allocated to the retirees.

The period of retirement was to last a mere three months before I was to resume toiling away in the fields. Coming to grips with myself that a life of idleness with little or no purpose whatsoever, other than to look for anything to occupy my mind was not for me, I began mailing out resumes to the local colleges. There was the possibility, so I had assumed, that with my academic credentials I might be able to obtain a teaching position. An idle mind is the devil's advocate, so the saying goes, and I was not about to play his game, notwithstanding the fact that I was, and still am a no-believer in a heaven, hell or a devil. Hell in my opinion is right here on earth, and indeed, sooner or later has the tendency of making an appearance on our lives in aspects we can at times relate to as a living hell. Seeing that my assumption was right on the mark, in a period of two weeks, I received what in fishermen's language can be expressed as not one but two bites, St. Francis College in

Brooklyn, and Mercy College in Dobbs Ferry, New York called me by telephone to set-up the dates for the interviews. Both schools appeared to be in need of my services, though in two departments as different as night and day. Since it was closer to home, I opted for St. Francis for the first interview. All of my years of experience in aviation apparently had influenced the interviewer into believing I was the suitable candidate for teaching business courses in the various fields of aviation. However, on finding out my degrees were in education and not business, he advised me that the Department was, in essence, looking for a person with a Masters Degree in business administration. My only other recourse, therefore, was the interview with the Dean of the English Department at Mercy College. On looking over my resume and credentials, he discovered we had both graduated from the same school, Columbia University, and accepted me as an Adjunct Professor.

Fidel Angel Santiago, Madison, Wisconsin—1943

Father, mother and I (mother is pregnant)—1924

Fidel Angel, Puerto Rico—1931

First communion

Mother, brother and stepfather, mother's friend is on the left.—1946

Mother, baby brother, Henry, and a friend—1945

The writer on Ponam Island in the Admiralties, South Pacific—1944.

At the right is the writer with friends at the Havana Madrid Nightclub, New York City—1946

Mother—1950

The writer and mother at his brother's graduation from Manhattan College, New York City—.1963

Fidel, cousin Federico is in the middle, and a friend—Caguas, Puerto Rico—1968

The writer, his stepfather's brother and his daughter in front of the Empire Hotel, across from Lincoln Center, New York City—1966

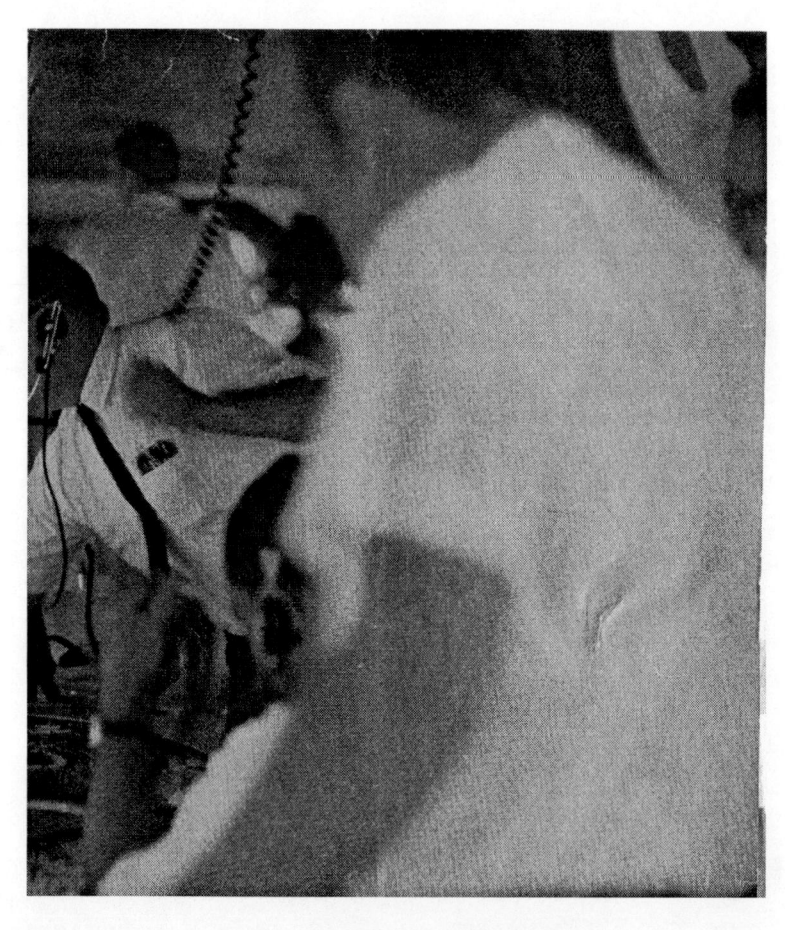

Taken at the Federal Aviation Administration's New York Air Route Traffic Control Center, Islip, New York—1968

The writer's wedding to Elizabeth Payne Santiago on December 28, 1971 at Riverside Church, New York City

Fidel Santiago, air traffic control specialist at Teterboro's FSS, has been with the agency since 1960. Prior to transferring to Teterboro, he was stationed at the New York Air Route Traffic Control Center.

Over the past twelve years, Fidel has remained active in developing his educational skills. He has instructed at Columbia University, Queens College and LaGuardia Community College. In 1978, Fidel was accepted for Columbia University's Master's Program and received his degree in June 1980. Two years later, Fidel attained his degree in Education. He is presently working toward his doctoral dissertation at Columbia.

Fidel Santiago

EASTERN REGION INTERCOM

The article and photo are from the Federal Aviation Administration's Eastern Region Intercom monthly newsletter—May, 1984.

Father and son on Prince Edward Island, Nova Scotia—August, 1988

Mother and son, Prince Edward Island—August, 1988

Graduation from Columbia University—May, 1988

Fidel Gabriel Santiago, 15 years old—New York City

Father and son at home—March, 2001.

At Xavier High School. Son is a member of the Junior Officers Training Corps. (JROTC)—March, 2001

PART VII

A New Career

CHAPTER 77

Some Opinions On Public Schools

Teaching college students is an entirely different process from the one I had applied as "A training Specialist" at Bridgeport. For example, the basic approach used initially at the Facility was to explain the function thoroughly, and quite often with the use of visual aids, the chalkboard, or an overhead projector. This first step was followed by actually doing the particular task for them, or as it was known, "modeling." Thereafter, the new workers, or ones with previous experience were required to do, or mimic what I had "modeled" for them. Success was attained only after they had demonstrated their ability to perform the task. Even if only one trainee failed to execute the function adequately, the training process was repeated, quite often several times, until all were well versed in the task. By contrast, the primary objective pursued by college professors is to get students to think, and exercise their minds. Above all else, emphasis is placed on this notion once the students' skills in reading, writing and manipulating numbers are developed to levels higher than were acquired in the high schools. In teaching English courses the old adage of "practice makes perfect" is used to develop the reading and writing skills. Further, reading essays, novels, plays and poetry, are the means applied in which to get students involved in classroom discussions and writing college papers focusing on critical analyses of what they have read and discussed in the classrooms. This approach is used solely for the purpose of developing the students' intellect capacity, for instance, their ability to reason, or rationalize, and draw conclusions from what they have read. Once these skills are achieved, students can applied them away from college, or in the outside world.

The years at Mercy College teaching students, some of whom have been Afro Americans and Hispanics has had, to some extent I must admit, bearings on the following observations and reactions cited dealing with conditions affecting the City's public schools. For a start, what obviously has been one of the most glaring problems with the system is the apparent flight of the middle class from the public schools; and as a result, with very few exceptions, these parents' children attend private schools. Consequently, a somewhat blighted landscape pervades over the public schools made-up primarily of students from the minority sector whose parents are at, or below the poverty level, and living in ghettos, or run-down neighborhoods. Thus, what is lacking in the public schools' classrooms, and which can be of some significance, are children who can serve as role models for inspiring or motivating Black or Hispanic kids into doing more and better work in the schools. There is no denying the fact that these children who can served as role models, in particular those coming from Jewish and Oriental homes seldom, if ever, become high school drop-outs, and in general, go on to colleges. Arguably, what may be another problem for the public schools, and which in all likelihood will generate adverse reactions from these families is the lack of academic orientation of Blacks and Hispanics, some of whom come from the Caribbean Islands. Moreover, what may further add to the problem is that, except for Blacks, these school age children generally speak their parents' native language in the homes. The final results are the kids fail to acquire a sufficient amount of practice in the second language, especially when English is spoken only in the schools. Barring perhaps those children whose parents come from Haiti, or other non-English Caribbean Islands, Black children of course speak English at home. Nevertheless, their overall difficulties in the schools appear to originate from their failure to read more at home, and maybe in having parents who may not have gone beyond the grade school levels.

These problems can indeed create barriers in the learning process, which can take years to overcome. How are children going to learn sufficiently if they are deficient in English? Indeed, I can relate to those unfortunate circumstances vividly recalling all the learning problems encountered in the public schools, and all due to my lack of English language skills. Furthermore, what will most likely create an insurmountable situation for the public schools is that it's highly probable in years to come the Black populations will increase significantly, and the large influx of Hispanics, and to a lesser degree other non-European immigrants will, more likely than not, grow at a rapid pace. What also seems to interfere with what the City's public schools are striving to do is that the learning process that takes place nowadays in the classroom for children, particularly teenagers, has become a bastion for what these children relate to as normal standards. Their sole intent appears to be that of upholding a milieu in which learning is frowned upon, and the few desiring to learn, study, and who, furthermore, speak proper English, are perceived by their classmates as weird individuals having unnaturally strange behavior. The only things that seem to matter for them are admiring show business celebrities, sports personalities, consuming electronic gadgets, movies, television, and what may be of most importance, the necessity for wearing the latest teenage fashions. A case in point, and one that was somewhat of a surprise for me on hearing it, was the occasion during our meeting when the student confided in me by declaring her high school years consisted, "only of one big fashion show." Little wonder is therefore aroused when one reads in The New York Times, (the issue was published the first week of November, 1999,) that in the "tough new state standards on tests, 77 percent" of the eight graders attending the New York City public schools had "a failure rate in mathematics combined with 65 percent failure rate in English."

The City schools are obviously not preparing young people with the educations they will be required to have in the business world, nor are they preparing them for college. The question most likely to be raised at this point is how can this problem be dealt with? A solution that may seem rather drastic but one that should better meet the educational needs of children, is to eliminate the public schools, and their politically motivated bureaucratic dealings and replace them with private schools. Yes, let's do away with them, and have the Federal and State governments allocate taxpayers dollars to maintain the private schools. In turn private schools will be held accountable to the Federal and State Governments for their overall operations. Private schools have always had a favorable reputation for providing children with a good education. This may sound like a blank statement, or values judgment, with no supporting evidence. True enough perhaps, but why is it the well heeled and middle class residing in large cities never send their children to public schools? The obvious answer can be seen in the final results, which is, these children never become school dropouts, and in general, most go on to colleges after their high school years.

The problems facing the City's public schools significantly affect the colleges directly, in particular those ones having an open admission policy. Open admission makes it possible for students without high school diplomas to attend colleges. As a result, these schools find themselves overwhelmed with students who are academically not prepared to do college work. What may further complicate matters is that a large number of these students are lacking English language skills. The only recourse left for the schools, therefore, is to become involved in remedial teaching, which realistically speaking should have been taken care off in the high schools. And as for the students, many of them realizing their academic inadequacies get discouraged and eventually become college drop-outs. To cite a good example, and one that apparently is a precursor of this situation, Ms. Lucie Laposmky, the new President of Mercy College, which has an open admission policy, was quoted in the school's newspaper, (October 2, 1999 issue,) that, "one of the priorities she plans to deal with is unraveling the mysteries behind why so many students never graduate." The "mysteries" can obviously be solved by the President realizing students who never graduate should have never been admitted to the school in the first place, since they were not academically prepared to do college level work. Rather than admitting all students, these open admission schools should, instead, raised their admission standards by admitting only those students who have graduated from High school, and have demonstrated in assessments tests their ability to comprehend what has been read, write "clear error free sentences," and skills in the ability to manipulate numbers.

Nowadays, it appears to be a fashionable way of thinking that in order to be successful in life, defined in the context of this work as the ability to make lots of money, young people need to have a college education; this concept is far from being true.

College does instill in us, among other practical attributes, the ability to reason, and do our own thinking without anyone manipulating us, unless we allow them to, but it's not always the road for getting rich. If this is what parents desire for their children, there are other ways of attaining wealth, or at least acquiring the comforts of middle class stature that is only possible in our society by having a surplus amount of money. However, what parents should realize is that all children do not develop to become what in academia is known as "College material." In fact many of them as they mature into adulthood acquire the capacity to do more skillful work with their hands rather than with books. And furthermore, more likely than not, they enjoy what they accomplish with their hands to earn a living. All things considered, "the college experience" may not be the suitable approach for everyone, including, of course, a good many of our young people. There can be other options for those who either have no desire to attend college, or are aware they haven't the academic background to succeed in these schools. A technical school may be the other alternative, which does in fact trained people in skills that are marketable in today's business world. Predictably, financial success can be achieved by our ability to attain a profession in graduate schools, or develop a skill in technical schools. And if in some manner this should fail us, we can always try going into business for ourselves.

As a last measure, perhaps the Government should do what Japan has done for centuries, and this is, the Nation has sole control of its educational system. Specifically, our Government would phase-out all the public schools, and contract them out to the private sector for grade levels kindergarten and up to the twelve grades. Schools will administer semi-annual achievement tests to assess the progress of the children. On completion of the eighth grade levels, they will be given standardized placement tests. Based on the scores on these tests, some children will be placed in specialized high schools having specific curriculums, for example, among others, engineering, mathematics, sciences and medicine. Supplementing the specialized schools will be the technical schools where students who have scored below an established standard will be relegated to, in order to learn specific skills, for instance, among many others, computer technicians, carpentry and plumbing. The concept of the Government implementing socialized education can be the only way to enable children from poor families to attend private schools. Education in private schools does indeed benefit children from middle and upper class families that can afford the high tuition for these schools. The rationale, therefore, may well be, why not have all children attend private schools with tuitions funded by the Government and not the parents.

CHAPTER 78

The Past, Present, and A Racist Society

A writing project, whether a brief one or a long term undertaken must eventually come to its end; and there is nothing on this earth that is yet to be found, or made that has everlasting life; clearly, this is not a profound observation, but simply a mere fact of life. The work has indeed been a long one, longer than I had ever anticipated it to be, and what may be said in racetrack jargon, it is on its final lap. After starting what had begun as a search for thematic topics, but soon developed into recollections from the past, along with opinions and observations, like everything else in life, will ultimately come to their end. Befitting to know, however, that what began with philosophical thoughts, and the conditions of the public schools in the 1930's should end at the threshold of the new millennium with reactions about the deplorable state of these same public schools. Indeed, we are a mere three days away from the new years 2000, and the beginning of a new thousand years. Yes, time does march on relentlessly, and there has yet to be found a way of stopping it. And after all the many years on its travel, time for us seems to have arrived at a point, where my cousin Louis is fond of saying, "we must take one day at a time." The realization that a lifespan may be approaching its final end has without a doubt, implanted itself on the senses; nonetheless, it's a hopeful sign to note that one never knows when, in fact, this end will occur. And still, it's a comfort to realize I'm not alone in my ripe old age.

I have a wife and son, who at the age of fourteen appears contented in knowing he has a father and mother who love him dearly, but who has become a compulsive consumer of CDs, (computer disks,) and video games, and yes, claims to know all about life. The behavior is clearly a phase he is going through in the human growth process we can all relate to. Not to be denied mention, there is also my dear wife who since our marriage over three decades ago has had the patience to endure my not always proper behavior as a husband. Thoughts at this moment about my son's large collections of CDs prompts remembrances of a long ago era before this Nations' relentless progress in the electronic age, and the far reaching ramifications this progress may be having on us. It was the period prior to World War II, at the height of the great depression, and during which the majority of the City's population was poor, desperately poor that is. Yet people, in general, seem to be happy, and somewhat satisfied with the bare necessities they had, warm shelters, and food on the table. Of course, there existed the color barrier where Black people were confined to an area having clear cut geographical boundaries. Nevertheless, outwardly at least, there was no widespread violence, and therefore some type of harmony appeared to prevail between the Blacks and the Whites. Unlike today, where it is quite evident to perceive, the deep hatred Blacks have for the White man, this hatred had yet to surface in those times. This critical issue of racism in our society deserves further discussion, which will be taken-up at a later time.

To return to that period before World War II, people during that era were not bombarded with what today is regarded by the masses as entertainment, mind numbing television programs, video games and all the many electronic gadgets. It's hard to believe there was a time when family members were not dispersed in various rooms of the home viewing their favorite shows on television as, in general, the custom is nowadays. Rather, in times of leisure the family engaged in, among other activities, playing musical instruments, for instance, the piano, (yes in those days lots of homes had old uprights,) the accordion, board games, or simply indulging in family conversations, and quite often lasting for hours. Further, building model airplanes and model ships were popular hobbies with young people that provided them activities with which to build with their own hands; and of course, households had lots of books, magazines and comic books available for reading. The only source of entertainment, which originated far away from homes were the programs transmitted and heard on homes radios. What appears to be the obvious today, though most likely people were not aware of it at the time is that, unlike television with its visual images, only sounds were heard from the radio, which actually had the long-term effects of improving one's listening skills.

At this point the reader may get the impression the writer has failed to be aware of current social realities, and instead, is preoccupied in dwelling on the past, rather than focusing on the present. True perhaps, therefore, in order to more or less comply with the reader at this moment, the overall vision the writer has about the present is that we seem be living in a mindless age where everything is created and packaged for us. Moreover, we appear to have a population of young people seeking instant gratification with movies, electronic games, sporting events, and not to be omitted, computers. Clearly, computers have some redeeming values, among them for example, their abilities to perform complex mathematical calculations in seconds, which before their advent, were impossible to do in that incredibly short period of time; furthermore, personal computers have replaced the typewriter as a more efficient method for writing. Nonetheless, their abundance of video games and "the internet," in which people have access to vast amounts of almost any information desired, including the all-important feature for both the buyer and the seller, what to buy and where to buy it, have become a time consuming obsession for a vast majority of people. Except for allowing time for using their computers, they have no other time for anything else, for instance, reading, or just contemplating and thinking. They merely push buttons and observe the results on a small screen, which to this observer is, arguably, strictly a passive process. And if the practice of viewing a computer's screen for any prolonged period of time while its power is on, it may be harmful to the eyes. By sharp contrast, family members in those times, especially in their homes, were actively involved in activities, some of which were building or doing things with their hands, playing musical instruments, playing cards, board games and with having lengthy conversation with other family members. Rather than contented being mere spectators, instead they were actively involved as doers, as participants.

Unlike the past during which poverty ran rampant throughout the City during the 30's and early 40's, the City today is flourishing with prosperity. These prosperous conditions have been caused primarily by Wall Street's bullish record that has lasted for almost a decade. People seem to be accumulating wealth at a rate faster than ever before, yet the poor are not getting their share of it. On the contrary, only those who have the surplus dollars to invest in the stock market are reaping the economic advantages of the times. These are the people whose children attend private schools, own their own apartments, have summer homes, own or lease new automobiles, and all have one or more personal computers. Why can't this wealth, at the very least to some degree, be distributed equitably? It's quite evident our society has failed to breach the economic gap, which now exists between those who have more money than they can spend in their lifetime, and their unfortunate counterparts, the poor. And what seems to be adding fuel to the situation is the City's relentless population growth of Blacks and Hispanics, most of whom are at the lowest rung in the economic ladder, and to a lesser extent immigrants from Asia. It is this population growth that may be the catalyst for what makes-up our racist society.

Indeed, we are a racist society, however, most of us already know this fact. No doubt, it's an easy matter to know or to point out a problem does exists, nonetheless, it tends to become complicated once we attempt to find solutions for resolving the problem of racism. Call it human frailties if you will, that to be prejudiced appears to be part of our human make-up. To be sure, there will always be preconceived unfavorable attitudes about races different from ours. The fears, suspicions, intolerance, and at times hatred for other races are what constitute racism, and people's refusal to acknowledge the fact that in some ways they are prejudiced toward Blacks, Hispanics Jews, Orientals, or others, are deceiving themselves. What I'm underscoring is that prejudice may never be totally eliminated. This can be classified as a maxim, and if this is true, what, in effect, is a minority to do in order to cope with race prejudice?

From a personal point of view, in all the many years residing in this City, I have discovered a key factor related to this prejudice. Clearly, to be accepted by the majority, the common herd if you will, we must know what they know. Expanding on this general statement, we must learn to conduct ourselves as they do, learn what they value and emulate those values. To state it in a more cogent way, it's simply conforming to that old adage, "when in Rome do as the Romans do." Obviously these are rather broad guidelines, therefore, to be more specific, education is the main road to take, which can eventually lead us to achieve some salvation from race prejudice. I can almost guarantee the results that once we become educated to a level where we have earned college degrees and have attained some profession, even if our skin is apple green in color, they will accept us, not totally of course, but we will become a part of them, members of their group.

The past is dead so why dwell on it. These words I have heard many times from various sources, and true to their mark, the past can never be re-lived. Nevertheless, in some instances recalling the past is a way, so to speak, of re-living one's past. More or less, this has been the purpose for the writing project, which before ending it, should be referred to by what originally it was intended to be, memoirs from the writer's recollections, knowledge and critical reflections. Memories from the past do tend to become more vivid as one allows the mind to drift back to the past, especially when one becomes older. Perhaps this is the reason why people, in general, who are getting on in years write memoirs. In the writer's situation, it's the realization that "time is running out," and the memoirs can serve as a legacy for his son.

Yes, as one becomes older reflections from the past seem to form vivid mental images. Why is this so? Can it be a way of grasping, or attempting to hold on to something as elusive as the past, which can never again be experienced except with memories. At this very moment memories of the small farm in Puerto Rico where as a very young boy I lived with my uncle Cirilo and his family for a number of years, and thoughts about my father, whom I saw only once and only for brief moments, rouses unfulfilled desires and intentions. To once again see the small farm and visit my cousins, but most of all, to find out where my father is buried and locate his grave will be the sole purpose of my next visit to the Island. Further, attempts will be made to verify whether the rumors I have heard are true about my father's father being a French Jew who migrated to Puerto Rico from the Canary Islands, and changed his name from Solomon to Solano.

Critical reflections about the here now can be similar to getting a sense of ourselves in relation to the present. Of course, reflections naturally vary according to how an individual perceives things, so that others are welcome to disagree with what I am about to say regarding our present situation. All things considered, I have some misgivings about what is happening now as we begin a new millennium. For starters, do we really need all this progress, new technology, a good deal of which we can actually do without? Progress may be literally killing us. Why are we being subjected to all the various forms of cancers, and heart disease? Do we really need all these non-essential electronic gadgets, for example, cellular phones, "walkmen," and all the computer games to amuse children as well as many grown ups? And what about all the vehicular traffic, in particular the diesel buses and trucks congesting our streets and highways polluting the vital air we must breathe in order to stay alive? Why not switch to electric buses as some other cities have done, and revert to the railroads as the means for transporting interstate goods? And as we embark on the new millennium, there are some precepts we should think about. To begin with, the Government should disband the National Rifle Association, and hunting animals for the sheer sport of it should be outlawed. No one has the right to bear arms unless he or she is misinterpreting the Nation's Constitution. The tobacco industry should also be outlawed, and drugs should be legalized. Legalizing the selling and consumption of alcohol worked for the Country during the great depression, so why shouldn't selling and using drugs such as heroin, cocaine and marihuana be legalized?

To end this particular discussion at this time, some moral thoughts may be in order with the following that can serve as words of wisdom. The words are from The Dalai Lama who is the fourteen in line of spiritual leaders of Tibet going back six hundred years. The "universal ethics for living" should be based "on common sense rather than religious traditions." Our lives should be involved in "obtaining peace and purpose, rather than expectations of an afterlife."

CHAPTER 79

The Relentless Passage of Time

The previous chapter was to end the writing project. However, after a three months hiatus without any success of having a literary agent become interested in the manuscript, I have decided to continue with the work in hopes of someday, in the not too far future, getting it published. This may never be realized, but hopefully I'm wrong in saying this, in light of today's literary market situation where there are currently no demands for memoirs from a Puerto Rican writer. Still, lingering on this situation, the word that readily comes to mind, and one that can be associated with success is perseverance. In effect, applying perseverance in all our endeavors will eventually reap for us, if not always total success, and least some partial rewards.

Today is the 28th day of April, which to keep tabs with the calendar, we're just about four months into the millennium. Indeed, the passage of time never ceases to march-on relentlessly, and when will it stop only the future can project its end. Nevertheless, in considering all the historical events that have met their end, can we conclude with what may seem a profound statement, though it's a fact we're all familiar with, that all forms of life will ultimately also come to their end. This is A true observation no doubt, and one that can also apply to human life. Recalling what my fourteen year old son, and soon to be fifteen said to me last night at the dinner table, words to the effect that I was too old to still be working, and why I didn't retire, is a stark reminder that I'm an old man, seventy five years old. And at this ripe old age, one tends to periodically have thoughts about the eventual end, which can happen at any hour, in particular, when one is cursed with high blood pressure; or it can happen, naturally with my blessings, many years from now. The point to underscore is that no one lives forever, an awareness people, especially the elderly seldom if ever fail to realize. Thus reflecting on this thought, what has evolved in the years involved with the writing is a concept, an idea, which by the way has already been mentioned, that the finished work can be a legacy for his son composed of a written testament describing happenings, reactions and philosophical thoughts. In due course on becoming a man, an adult having the intellectual capacity, he will read the work, and understand the meanings, particularly the underlying ones experienced during his father's lifetime. Ever fearful that a catastrophic stroke may be lying in the wings waiting to pounce on me in the not too distance future disabling all physical and mental faculties, my firm conviction at this juncture in life is to work as long as I have my health, and continue writing until the day arrives when I can no longer hold a pen in my hand.

Today is May 6th, and tomorrow my son will have completed fifteen years of his young and healthy life. Writing specific dates, for example first April 28th and now today's date, is not meant to begin framing the work into a format resembling a diary, but rather, a sharp reminder that time is marching on, swiftly I might add. However, of more significance at this time, tomorrow is my son's birthday, and a joyful day it will be, I'm quite sure of it; one in which both parents and son will celebrate the event with activities yet to be determined. At this particular time in his life, the boy has grown taller, in effect, taller than his father, and nothing resembling the puny wisp of a teenager I was at his age. Aside from comparing his stature with mine, how can a love best be described that an old father has for his son who will be fifteen years old tomorrow? In terms of time the tendency is to reflect on his younger years as a starting point when he was an infant toddler, and the pre-adolescent period. And indeed I will move in that particular direction shortly, however, these recollections will not be associated with specific times and settings, but rather, ones strongly relating to an old father's unfolding love for his growing son. At the mention of the word love, the mental image that comes to mind is of a movie, which I happened to see many years ago titled, "Love is A Many Splendor Thing." In essence, what the movie did was to convey to the viewer the meaning of love by projecting on a screen various settings occurring at different times in the tryst encounters in Japan between an American soldier and an Eurasian woman. A somewhat similar approach, though applying words instead of visual effects, will be attempted to define love as described by the experiences a father shared with his son.

CHAPTER 80

Defining Love

To begin with, the love never blossomed at the very beginning, nor soon after his birth. All that troubled my mind at that time were thoughts about the added responsibilities of having to care and support a child, especially at my "senior citizen" level of sixty one. Not suddenly but rather gradually, nonetheless, these thoughts began to fade away, so that by the time he was a year old, my only concern was for the child's welfare; and as the common saying goes, all thoughts of responsibilities "went out the window." Almost constantly, particularly during the first few months, I observed his facial features with the sole purpose of discovering some resemblances between the two of us. Even though ever so slightly, there was indeed some likeness, which not to my regret, reminded me of my brother Henry when he was a toddler; or was I the least disappointed in realizing his appearance resembled that of the mother.

The first three or four months seem to be the most trying ones for the parents. Somehow his time cycle had yet to adjust to the normal way of being awake during the day and sleeping soundly at night. Instead, both mother and father had to endure with his behavior of sleeping all day and fully awake at night crying relentlessly until picked-up from the crib and walked from one end of our bedroom to the other. The parents slept in what can be described as hourly shifts by walking him every other hour and alternating the hours of sleep with one another until the early morning. This nightly ritual had the effect of my periodically dozing-off at work from the lack of sleep the previous night.

Surprising to me, the ordeal of getting only a few hours of sleep at night was not annoying; I simply had to do it out of concern for my son's need to be walked. Can this have been some sign of a father's love for his son?

    Naturally, by the age of ten months, and no longer wide awake during the nights, his days were spent with the babysitter, Ceserina. A responsible and caring young Indian woman from Peru who became very fond of the child, Ceserina wisely always watched his constant movements, whether playing in his favorite spot, the sand box playing with other toddlers, or everywhere else in the park's playground. The evenings, when not involved with water-playing in the kitchen sink as his customary nature was, he amused himself by sitting on the kitchen floor rattling pots and pans, which at the time seem to be his favorite toys. The noises didn't annoy me in the least, knowing that my son was contented in what he was doing. Another one of his noisy activities was racing up and down the long hallway as though it was a racetrack in his "baby walker." The ingeniously made "walker" most likely was what caused him to begin walking at the early age of eleven months, and does merit describing it. The "walker" essentially was a hoop having a circular bar to which four legs had been attached with wheels at the ends of the legs. Inside the hoop, and supporting himself with the circular bar, seldom did he walked, but instead ran with it, and with the "walker's" plastic wheels rumbling loudly along the wooden floor. With sheer delight I often observed him in his act making eye contact with me as though pleased in showing me how well he was handling his toy, and always with the familiar smile on his face.

    Strange so it appeared to me at the time, already the father of a grown son, and having some knowledge of a baby's growth cycle, he never did crawled. To compensate for this oversight, so it seem, perhaps he wittingly chose to take his first steps when his father was near him. The joyful moment occurred in his playpen, which was always in the middle of the living room. Normally when not sitting in it playing with his toys, he either walked or ran to another side of the playpen, but always holding onto the pen's bars for support. On this particularly happy occasion, however, looking at me and smiling, he suddenly dashes on his wobbly small legs diagonally across to the opposite corner of the playpen without holding on to anything. He must have realized what he had accomplished at that moment and repeated his performance several times, possibly for my benefit, before I picked him up, hugged him tightly against my chest, and called the mother who all this time had been in the bedroom, to tell her what I had just observed.

One thing he didn't like was the toddler car seat, which in accordance with a New York State law all children four years or younger had to be in the seat when riding in automobiles. With its seat belt strapped across his small thighs restraining him, he naturally became rebellious by screaming anytime I attempted to put him in it. After a few unsuccessful attempts, never again did I subject him to the ordeal. Of course my luck eventually ran-out in Kingston, New York where I was issued a traffic summons for not having my son in the toddler seat. By contrast, what he did like were fire hydrants and tractors. Never did he failed to run immediately toward a hydrant on spotting one, inspecting it with his little hands while at the same time walking around the object that seem to fascinate him, a fire hydrant. Similarly, but obviously to a greater extent, tractors had a special attraction for him. In Central Park, the country, or anywhere for that matter, on seen one he quickly ran towards it, and once there, if the tractor was unattended, I had to lift him up and place my son in the driver's seat. Thereafter, experiencing great pleasure in what he was doing, I watched him move the steering wheel first one way and then another, and with a beautiful smile on his face, pretending he was driving the tractor. During the Christmas holidays when he was about four years old, it was my good fortune to find the ideal beauty of a gift for my son, and one which he still has and cherishes it, a red tractor made of sturdy plastic with a seat, steering wheel and pedals to drive it; the toy tractor was the envy of all the children in the playground. At the time of purchase, the toy, which had been manufactured in Germany, was the only one in the department store, and to this day I have yet to see another one like my son's red tractor.

Our nightly and daily rituals were never dull ones, in fact, just being near my son was enough to lift my spirits. Evenings when I didn't have to work, I read to him. His favorite book, or I should mention the only book that had to be read to him was Richard Scarry's, Cars and Trucks and Things That Go. A delightful, though somewhat surprising episode occurred one day that directly related to these reading sessions. The grandmother was visiting us, when suddenly, with his favorite book held in his little hands tells her, "Nana," as he always called her, "I'm going to read to you." Much to her amazement, her grandson proceeded to read her passages from the book. She had actually believed he had learned to read at a very young age, not realizing of course that my son had memorized particular passages from the book as a result of the many times he had heard them read to him by his father. The weekdays rituals involved walking him to his kindergarten classes, and during the course of our walks, invariably singing to him, "you'll take the high road and I'll take the low road, and I'll be in Scotland before you," while hobbling along by placing one of my feet on the sidewalk and the other one in the gutter. "On The Road to Mandalay" was another song he seemed to enjoy whenever I sang it to him. After his school hours, I had to take him to a playground in Central Park and 86th Street, just off Fifth Avenue where there were long ropes dangling from a crossbar and a sandpit below them, which served to cushion children's legs on releasing their grips on the ropes and landing on the ground. Here was where my son played the role of a boy Tarzan by swinging back and fourth on one of the ropes until dinnertime when it was time to go home. After his evening meal and before the readings, I helped him to memorize the multiplication tables with the aid of index cards.

Of course, not all father and son outings were enjoyable ones. A vivid example was the frightful experience, which even to this day the mother is unaware of its happening. The potential for a horrible accident to have occurred was what made it all the more frightful. The place of the unforeseen happening was Prince Edward Island in Nova Scotia where I had rented a small cottage to accommodate the three of us during a week's vacation. Beyond the front of the cottage was a large treeless open field, which had the appearance of a huge green lawn. At almost the middle of the field was a volley court with its net strung-up and supported at each end by a water pipe about two inches in diameter, which had been imbedded into the soft ground, (it had rained the previous night.) Rising upwards to approximately fifteen feet, on the upper ends of the two pipes were large cement balls the size of basketballs used to add weight to the pipes imbedded into the ground. The cement balls and pipes gave the volleyball court the odd appearance of two giant lollypops standing upright connected by a net. The morning's blustery wind was whipping the tall grass from side-to-side, and the boy and I were walking in the field when he spotted it, and quickly led me to the volleyball court. The net was too high for his small hands to inspect, and as a result was hovering near one of the pipes when it happened. At that particular moment, and of course very near him, I was looking away at the distant horizon; and that's when I heard the loud thud like the sound a large heavy object makes plunging from high above and striking the ground. Immediately turning toward him, I saw the cement ball still attached to the pipe lying on the ground barely a foot away from his small body. Instinctively, I picked him up and hugged my little boy tightly; I stood there as though frozen with fear holding him, and realizing the cement ball had missed striking my son by only inches. Many hours were to pass before I recovered from the memory of that frightful experience. Needless to mention, after the distressful event never again did I take him to the volleyball court during that week's vacation on Prince Edward Island.

What was to erase almost completely the memory of that near fatal accident were the memorable years, which began when I first started observing him play ice hockey on an ice rink in Central Park, and baseball with the West Side Little League at Riverside Park. Delighted in having been selected a coach of his team, which was part of "The Pewee League," and his initial phase in the game prior to moving up to a Little League team, I thus became an active participant in my son's baseball games. It was during this first experience as a team member of "The Pewee League" that my nine year old son began to develop gradually into a good baseball player. To add on to what has been previously mentioned, the two things my son did not enjoy whatsoever, were playing the piano and horse back riding. Little Fidel completed over four years of formal piano lesson with various teachers at "Mannes College of Music," and with me constantly pleading with him to practice; ultimately, I realized that playing the piano was not his forte. Someday perhaps he will resume his playing, a wish that I sometimes dwell on despite the fact he has not even touched the piano keys since discontinuing the lessons many years ago. And as for his lack of interest in riding horses, conceivably, it may have originated in the genes inherited from his father. Of course this is not be true, nevertheless, for some unknown reason, or more likely than not the discomfort felt from the impact of my buttocks bouncing off the animal's back, after the initial experience, I never again had any further desires to ride horses. Finally, to come to what may seem as an abrupt ending to the topic defining love, as the result of searching ways in which to define it, the preceding happenings have notably been experiences with my son, which in some ways or manner may define the word love as it applies to a father's love for his son.

CHAPTER 81

Further Reactions Relating to The Public Schools

Realizing that my son is at the threshold of becoming a freshman at a Jesuit High School in two months prompts me to react to a rather disturbing situation, the present conditions of the City's public schools. The issue has been previously discussed, however, this was prior to my teaching experiences as a college professor. Most likely, having direct teaching contacts with college students has fueled the mind with more adverse reactions against the public schools, some of which may have already been discussed. From a college instructors point of view, and based solely from teaching at two learning institutions, college students who have recently graduated from high schools are experiencing all types of learning problems in coping with their first year of college work. These problems, to some extent, may be directly related to the public schools' failure to adequately prepare them for college. This situation may have derived from various sources, some of which are language difficulties, the home environment, and perhaps of most significance, the serious discipline problems encountered by parents, teachers and school guards from the students' behavior. Not until these conditions are dealt with in a constructive manner will we have the ideal setting I experienced in the City's public schools prior to World War II for learning to take place in the classrooms.

Public schools in that era, or at least the ones I attended predominantly consisted in a faculty of Jewish teachers born and educated in the City, but some of whose parents had been immigrants. As a child arriving in the Country knowing absolutely no English, I was exposed to those teaches, and to a teaching system which in later years was to become known as a process of submerging foreign students into English. Bilingual programs of course were non-existent at the time, and it was this fact that most probably helped me to grasp the language quickly, or at least the verbal aspects of English. Unlike the submergence system, in today's public schools children arriving from foreign countries, most of whom are Spanish speaking students from the Dominican Republic, are immediately placed in a bilingual program where they are compelled to begin learning school subjects in Spanish, and as a result are literally held back for years from gaining proficiency in English. Reflecting on my problems with the English language in public school, within a matter of months after beginning school I was able to communicate in English. However, failure to realize I was lacking in reading and writing skills were the main cause of my learning problems in grade school. What probably prolonged my frustration in the failure to learn was that not only was Spanish spoken in the home, but also my mother and stepfather knew very little English. Nevertheless, what did help me was my motivation in desiring to learn, and becoming aware in how well versed in academics were most of my classmates, the Jewish kids, and in particular, the German refugee children.

As a college instructor, I still marvel at the thought of how well prepared and determined to learn those children in the grade school were before World War II. It didn't take me long to realize that learning for them was not as difficult as it was for me, especially for the German kids whose first language not unlike mine was not English. Many years were to pass before I finally discovered the reason for this; in the German schools, as most likely still is today, children were taught English as a second language from the first grades and until they had completed high school. Also, what may have been a positive factor in the learning process of the New York City's schools were the teachers who were highly prepared not only in one subject, but also proficient in various other subjects. For example, in the sixth grade I had to address one of my teachers as, "Dr. Kruger." Moreover, teachers had full control of the students in the classrooms, and serious discipline problems seldom occurred. This effect was obviously caused by the fact that corporal punishment was legal, and a common practice in the public schools. However, what may have been more significant, principals had the authority to expel permanently from schools students who habitually disrupted the classrooms with their inappropriate behavior. The final results were that the learning process indeed succeeded despite the foreign children who populated the public schools, most of whom were German refugees.

English language disability appears to be a widespread factor influencing how foreign children perform in today's public schools. Unlike the German kids who had already developed a good foundation of English language skills prior to enrolling in the City's schools, foreign students today, a good majority of whom come from the Dominican Republic, have had little or no exposure to the English language before entering the City's schools. This is common knowledge in the school community, however, what may not be, specifically, with non-Spanish speaking teachers, is that these children, at least most of them are seriously lacking in Spanish language skills. They do speak their language fluently of course, but have little or no idea how Spanish language is grammatically structured, thus to many of them words such as subjects, verbs, adjectives, and many others are meaningless. This appears to be the English language problems confronting students from the Dominican Republic who have not acquired the language skills in Spanish that most likely will make it easier for them to learn English. Indeed, proof of this fact are Cuban children arriving in this Country who have good skills in Spanish grammar, and seem to encounter very little problems in learning English in the American schools.

Students, whether natives or foreign born, in essence, must have mastered the English language preceding their entrance into colleges. This should be the precedent if they are to succeed rather than become dropouts after their first or second semester discouraged with their inability to do college work primarily because of English language difficulties. By placing the responsibility of teaching English solely in the hands of the public schools and not in private or City colleges, this problem may be resolved. It should also eliminate the task facing college professors and instructors nowadays of having to be involved with remedial language teaching. To be sure, discipline in the classrooms and the home play an important role in helping children with the learning process in the public schools. Further, in homes where the language spoken is not English can, in fact, hinder a child's progress in schoolwork. To conclude, the truth lies in the old proverb, "practice makes perfect," proficiency in any language is improved by practice, not only in school but also in the home where another language may prolong the process of learning English.

CHAPTER 82

Opinions

Not knowing the writing aspects of a language, whether the language is English, Spanish or any other for that matter may not always give us the inclination to put our thoughts, or critical reflections on paper; rightfully aware that others will eventually read what we have written. This can, to some degree, predispose us to be viewed as borderline illiterates. Inasmuch as we may have the urge, we still refrain from acting it out, frustrated perhaps in realizing that written words are a means of recording the past, or one's lifetime experiences. This lends itself to the awareness in how important the written word is. In a clearer vain, not photos but what we have written is what gives the reader insights about a sense of ourselves in relation to what we have experienced in life, for instance, our philosophy, critical analyses of past events, and general thoughts, among others, about our love ones. No, it's not true, "a picture does not tell a thousand words."

This was brought to light not too long ago by what was observed in a funeral home I had gone to offer my respects for a man who had arrived at the end of his life's cycle, my wife's uncle. Surprisingly, what greeted me on entering the funeral parlor were the photos that were on displayed on a table not too far from where he laid at rest in his coffin. Among the photos were pictures of the man's wedding, his three sons at various ages, and photos that had been taken during family vacations. One photo in particular caught my attention, which was a photograph of the ordination of one of his sons to priesthood. This happy event for the family was to have a sad repercussion in years to come, especially for the son. The following day at church after the previous visit to the funeral home, I witnessed the priest, the deceased man's son, red eyed, and with tears flowing down his sad face presiding over his father's funeral. At this moment I'm thinking about the sorrowful happening at church, and those photos at the funeral home that essentially showed the viewer only momentary glimpses about the man, and nothing about his inner nature, his opinions, reactions, or some of his philosophical thoughts during his lifetime. Notably what should be noted is that written words and not mere pictures are what can yield for us some insights about a person's character.

The events at the funeral home and at the church were, and still are, stark reminders that indeed, death awaits us all. This occurs more so as the years pass us by, so that old age tends to sneak-up on us, and we dwell more about it than we did in our glorious youthful carefree years. Our main concern in those times was thinking up ways in which to amuse ourselves. Nowadays, this cycle in life appears not to have change that much for our youth who seem to crave for instant gratification anywhere it can be had. What has changed, in fact, is the primary source for their indulgence, or our present day pervasive electronic culture that merely by pushing buttons have converted people, in particular our youth, into passive individuals. Is this what life is really all about? From a passive person's point of view, this may be accepted as true.

Focusing on the purpose of one's life reminds me of words once said by one of the first Greek philosophers, Boehme, "He became free at the moment of creation," and "claims he is not in this universe to carry-out any prescribe order laid down by God." A religious person may view these remarks as having tones of blasphemy from a reckless individual's failure to measure his words. These words, nonetheless, can provide us with answers for our purpose on earth. In a literal sense what they mean is that we have the will, or choice to select our purpose and act it out. What this purpose may be will rest solely on our shoulders. Continuing with this line of thinking, another early Greek philosopher, Epicurus, defined pleasure as "as a state of happiness." Simply stated, our pleasures result in our happiness, and who can argue that seeking happiness lies at the root of our being; which at this point brings me to, yet, another philosopher, Henry Bergson, a Frenchman who said, "philosophy is not worth one hour of trouble if it has nothing about the 3Ws, where do we come from, what are we doing here, and where are we going?" These questions, undoubtedly, will never have answers. What does matter, nevertheless, is that we are indeed here despite the fact it's only for a limited time. And having no purpose in our lives is like a ship floundering in the high seas with no course to follow nor a destination to go to. Suffice to realize that we do need a purpose in life, but how can we define and achieve this purpose? Specifically, a purpose can be made-up of activities, and our purpose on earth should be to seek-out activities, which in the words of Epicurus, will result in our pleasures, or our "state of happiness."

Our health and our well being of course are the essential prerequisites before becoming involved with activities. To digress a bit at this point, a line from "Do Not Go Gentle Into That Good Night," Dylan Thomas' memorable poem about dying, "Rage against the dying of the light," expresses cogently what may well be the creed for old age. We must, as long as we possibly can, attempt at all cost to overcome the obstacles, which in some manner may tend to put out the flame of life within us. However, once we have our health, we can then search for those activities that will reward us with pleasures and "happiness." Justifiably, the question that may now be raised is, what may in fact be some of these activities? Before proceeding further, a reminder may be in order, and this is, in experiencing our preference for a particular activity, what may be pleasurable for us may not have the same effect on others. Bearing this in mind, the following activities, which have been previously discussed at some length, will be highlighted again as mere suggestions, and not "the rule of thumb" for the attainment of pleasures; and perhaps more to the point, these suggestions come from an old man's point of view, and may not always filter through the lenses of others.

Activities are so numerous that in the scope of this work all are quite impossible to mention. Nevertheless, there are those special ones that have appealed to the writer as a result of having participated in them, or what has already been defined as the hands-on experience. The ones that come readily to mind are sporting activities, in effect, those of which place physical demands on our bodies, for example, baseball, basketball and my favorite for many years, tennis. At the mention of the game of tennis, what is obvious is the painful awareness in realizing that old age does take its toll on our bodies, and as a result, limits our capacity to indulge in strenuous activities, and seeing that my legs will not allow it, I no longer play the game; still, we can actively pursue those that are not too demanding on our bodies. One of these can be building model airplanes as I once did in my youth, and in later years my attempts to build a sailboat within the limitations of a small apartment. The project never went beyond reading the schematic diagram once I discovered the hull's large width would not allow me to carry the boat through the narrow front door entrance of my apartment. What's to keep in mind is that building objects from wood, whether small or relatively large ones, for instance, model airplanes, model boats, chairs, a table or a desk can be liken to individual creations, which tend to reward our senses with pleasures.

Then there are the activities similarly to the ones previously mentioned that also allow us to become actively involved as participants rather than mere spectators. I'm referring to two in particular, painting with oils on canvas, or with watercolors, and playing a musical instrument. These can become hobbies, or recreational pastimes for the sheer pleasure of enjoying them, and not necessarily with the intent of developing anyone of them as a profession. What can deter you from becoming involved with drawing or painting as a hobby may be feelings of doubts that you can draw. For starters, what you actually need is time and patience to observe, paying close attention to the subject's features you're going to draw, carefully noting its angles, curvatures, and vertical and horizontal lines. Thereafter while observing the subject intently, you copy its features on canvas or paper. Following this procedure should result in a reasonable facsimile of your subject. A case in point is the fact that I was never blessed with the talent for drawing;

yet, by observing carefully, I have managed to attain good results with my drawings, even going as far as drawing a true likeness of my facial features by observing them reflected on a mirror. As an after thought, in attempting to draw your face, a good method I recommend is to begin with the eyes before proceeding further with the other features. After finishing a drawing, whether it's a landscape or flowers in a garden, embellishing your drawing with colors is a matter of choice; for example, dark or light shades just as long as the colors appeal to you. Worthy of mentioning is that whatever the finished work may be, a painting, a chair, a desk, or whatever, most likely a sense of self-satisfaction is experienced in knowing you have created a work that reflects your individual taste and no one else's.

By contrast, music, not unlike painting, can reward us with joyous pleasures. Naturally, we don't see the results of our achievement as with a painting. Still, there is the gratifying sense experienced, especially after listening to a tape recording of what we have played. The realization that we have indeed become doers can be an exhilarating experience, rather than mere spectators, as with viewing a landscape painting at a museum, or listening to music in a concert hall; more precisely, I'm referring to painting on canvas or playing a musical instrument instead of indulging in an activity of just viewing and listening. Ideally, the intent to learn to play a musical instrument should begin by initially working with an instructor who can teach you the instrument's features, and sight reading, or reading musical notations. On the other hand, if you have the ability to play what you have heard, or what's known as playing by ear, and also the all important aspect, able to maintain the tempo, (rhythm,) there is no need to take private lessons, especially as a beginner. If you do have this talent, you will, to some extent, attain success. For an illustration, I have an upright piano, and though I have had no formal training, nevertheless, when I strike keys that sound pleasant to my ears, and careful to maintain the rhythm, people who hear me play are surprised when I tell them I have never taken lessons. In short, the ones cited are but a few of the many activities that are at our disposal to indulge ourselves in whatever gives us pleasures. These pleasures, or what can arouse "happiness" in us is what we should strive for before the coming of the fate that awaits us all, "the dying of the light."

CHAPTER 83

Hazardous Work

Thus far, or at the very least, in the last chapters what has been discussed were happenings, which except for a father's pleasures in being with his son, have been random thoughts and reactions about the present state of the New York City's public schools. What I propose to do now in the spring of the years 2001 as a way of varying the events is to return to a long ago bygone era, the early 1950's. Physical hardships were indeed endured during those years in a rather unhealthy environment, and all for the sacrifices of supporting a wife and a young child. By the way, the situations I'm about to narrate were briefly mentioned earlier in describing the first permanent job lasting four years after my discharge from the Navy. At this moment, recollecting those experiences a thought comes to mind, and that is, never did I realized then as I do now the physical rigors endured those four years working in garages. This can be like realizing true happiness not while it's happening, rather, post facto, when one reflects on it and becomes aware that, in fact, happiness was experienced at that time of its happening.

Winter's cold weather is not conducive to starting the Harley three wheeler motor cycle. My 125 pounds frame makes it quite difficult to "kick start" the cold machine by pushing down on its starter lever with my leg. Cautious of the fact the lever at times kicks back, particularly in this kind of weather, I apply all of my skinny body's weight to it, always hoping the lover doesn't kick back and injure my leg. After about ten attempts, the motorcycle finally starts with a loud roar and I'm on my way with the bitter cold wind violently blowing on my face. The mission is to pick-up a car parked on the street by attaching the three wheeler to its rear end bumper and then drive the car to the garage. I hope the car has been left double parked providing for less work by not having to drive it out its parking space, which is usually between two cars, before completing the attachment.

The mission is accomplished, and back in the garage I'm thinking why did I ever have to volunteer to be a "pick-up motorcycle garage attendant" when no one else wanted the job; and why don't they supply heat to this building? The cold in my bones never seems to leave me, and here comes the foreman approaching with what I already suspect are orders to take the elevator to one of the upper floors and bring down a car a customer has called for. Not surprisingly, the car is buried, which in the work's jargon means a number of other cars must be moved to make it possible to drive it out of its parking place and onto the elevator. Breathing carbon monoxide fumes as a result of driving cars in an enclosed area and later the prolonged headaches from the exposure to the toxic fumes are some of the ordeals I have to contend with. Others are the automobiles, most of which are the large variety types, Cadillacs, La Salles and Buicks, and parking them places intense strain on the body, (power steering is still a thing of the distant future.) The elevator is narrow, so narrow in fact that there is barely room to open the car's door, and literally squeeze-out my body so as to get at the elevator's handle and lower it to the main floor. The elevator is now stopped, and again I squeeze my body into the car, put it in reverse gear and drive it backward onto the main floor. Parking cars indoors and breathing carbon monoxide fumes, when not going out on a pick-up with the motor cycle is no easy work, and knowingly, the results after finishing work will be neck pains from constantly twisting it from side to side while parking cars in reverse motion, and always the headaches.

On some days I'm sent out by the Union on jobs as an "extra," or one day's or night's work, and most of them involve relieving the old timers of some of their workload washing cars at night. Naturally, the job involves working with water, and arriving home late at night in wet clothing does not contribute to one's health, especially in the months of winter. I see the pale faces and hallow cheeks of the old timers, probably the results of years of exposures to the fumes, looking as though they are already half dead, and wondering if that's the fate that awaits me. The soap is strong, and always I wear rubbers gloves to protect the hands from the strong chemicals. And the white walls, why is it that all the cars, with very few exceptions, have white wall tires? Bending down to a crouch and scrubbing them with a wire brush and soap is part of the job, but knowing I will earn twelve dollars for the night's work helps to cope with the ordeal. The tires are cleaned, and what remains is drying off the car's body with a towel, and then rubbing its metal surface with a chamois cloth until it glimmers before starting on another car. Hours seem to be going by quickly, it's now almost 2 AM, and then off for home, remove the wet clothing and hop into bed. Tomorrow I must be at the Union no later than 2 PM to "shape-up," or be there ready to go to work, and hopefully, "a Union rep" will select me to go out on a job. At the risk of repeating it, it's no easy work, but the pay is good, pays the rent, and that's what keeps me going. Someday, perhaps in the near future, I'm hoping to fine work in the one skill I have, a licensed radio operator with experience in communicating in Morse Code.

The third Avenue El is being razed, and beyond the rubble is the garage Union's hall off Third Avenue and ninety second Street, which is directly across from the Ruppert's beer brewery. Jacob Ruppert, better know as the beer baron, owns not only the brewery, but also the New York Yankees baseball team. All garages in Manhattan have been unionized by the Union, and affiliated with The American Federation of Labor, (AFOL;) and not surprising to the members, its president is an ex-convict who has served time in prison for extortion. The daily ritual is to "shape-up" between the hours of two and four in the afternoon in hopes of going out as an "extra," or part-time worker for that night, or the following day. Aware that Black members are sent only to the garages in the Bronx, I know that if selected for a job the garage's locations will be in Manhattan, and usually in the theatre district where most of them are located. Few chairs are in the large Union hall so that most of us numbering about one hundred men must stand in rows extending from one end of the hall to the other waiting patiently for a "shop steward" to approach one of us with "a job ticket." On most occasions I'm chosen, a fact I'm later to find out is because of my youthful years, and the "shop steward" surmises, here's a member with lots of stamina and able to perform the hard work. The night shift pay, (5 PM-2 AM,) with one hour off for lunch is ten dollars for attendants and twelve dollars for washers. This wage scale is only for "extra" workers, and not for the full-timers.

Though the job of garage attendant is considered hazardous work due to the daily exposures to carbon monoxide, I've opted to risk my health in order to reap the high wages and lucrative benefits the job offers. It's like a deep sea diver who risks getting "the bends," or cramps from going too quickly from a place having abnormal atmospheric pressure to one of normal pressure, and all because of the high wages. A full time worker, as I was to become after only three months in the Union earns sixty dollars for eight hours a day six days a week, plus tips, and a share in the Christmas Fund. Also, the job is selective, in effect, only Union members are allowed to work in garages, and I'm a Union member only because I was sponsored by an old time member, my brother-in-law. Broadly speaking, the Christmas Fund is a method of coercing the garages' customers into donating money for the workers during the Christmas holidays, or run the risk of having their automobiles damaged. A month before Christmas, or soon after Thanksgiving, a large cardboard sign with its four borders enclosed with clusters of Christmas lights, and all the customers' names printed on is posted at the garage's main entrance, (the customers' entrance.) When a customer makes a donation, which is usually one hundred dollars, the amount is written next to the customer's name. A week after Christmas the money collected, which is know as the Christmas bonus, is divided among the workers into full, half or quarter shares, depending on the length of time a worker has been employed at the garage for that particular year.

A full share, which was usually about three hundred dollars was an amount in those days that today is the equivalence of almost one thousand dollars. Needless to say, money was the incentive that kept me from seeking other work of a less hazardous nature. Nevertheless, always I read "the want adds" in the New York Times in hopes of someday finding what I was looking for. That day was finally to arrive almost four years after working in garages as a parking attendant.

CHAPTER 84

A Vacation

Prior to the departure in time to a long ago era, the early 1950's, discussions centered primarily on activities, and how to involve ourselves with them as outlets for engaging in life, rather than with the passive unreal distractions that, among others, movies, television and computer games offer us. One of these activities can be the recreational pleasures derived from traveling to foreign lands, or for that matter, to distant places in one's Country for the sheer joys of viewing vistas never before seen, and most likely, never to be forgotten. Foreign lands have been discussed previously at great length I may add, however, never was our month's long vacation to the Western States with another married couple. The trip was taken two years before the coming of the glorious event, the birth of our son at a few minutes after 9 AM on May 7, 1986.

All the details prior to the trip were meticulously pre-planned six months before the actual departure including, among other things, the itinerary, car rental and hotel accommodations. On arriving at the San Francisco Airport and picking-up our luggage, we walked toward the brand new white Buick that had been reserved for us, and without a moments delay, drove directly to Yosemite National Park; at the National Park, we had reserved a log cabin for a night's lodging. A cabin in the middle of a forest having no heat or hot water may not be the ideal place to spend a cold night. Nonetheless, it was a new experience, and like some new experiences, huddled together under the skimpy blanket provided for us, the wife and I did enjoy that cold night in a log cabin in the midst of huge pine trees. The following day we encountered the inspirational nature sights Yosemite had to offer, the highest water falls in all of North America, one was named "The wedding veil" because of the fall's long and narrow length of water cascading down from high above a cliff. Tall pine trees over four hundred years old were everywhere, one of which was one of the world's largest trees, and had the named, "the grizzly giant." As a final added attraction before leaving the park, the four of us saw for the first time a real live wolf, of course not looking like the one in "Little Red Riding Hood," but this animal, except for its large bushy tail, had the appearance of a German Sheppard dog.

The next scheduled stop on our itinerary is Monterey, where the lady attending us at the tourist information cottage, much to my surprise, doesn't know Monterey means Kings Mountain in Spanish. Finding out it had been the capital of California until 1847, but little else of interest, we leave Monterey and drive directly to San Simeon. The one and only enormously popular tourist attraction in the town is the 165 rooms estate of the publishing magnate, William Randolph Hearst who aptly had named it "Casa Grande," or big house. The estate of San Simeon Castle as it's known was built during a period lasting over twenty eight years, and became somewhat of a playground for the Hollywood crowd, and dignitaries, two of whom were Winston Churchill and George Bernard Shaw. On viewing the estate for the first time, Shaw is said to have wryly remarked, "This is the way God would have done it if He had the money." "Casa Grande" is Mediterranean in architectural style having a gloomy atmosphere, or a large house spread in dimness and furnished with priceless works of arts and antiques. Most of the vast European collection Hearst purchased from New York auction houses, and had them shipped to San Simeon. The collection included entire dismantled rooms with their carved walls and ceilings originating from Italian Monasteries. As if this were not enough, there is a large private movie theatre to screen films. And for the grand finale, like adding icing to the cake, the estate has various lavish pools, one of which is the breath taking Roman inspired in-door pool surrounded with life size statues of Greek Goddesses.

Somewhat overwhelmed after the tour, with the spectacle of antiquities viewed in a house that, undoubtedly, was meant to be a museum, I had the ill-feeling that too much of a good thing no matter in what setting or situation one encounters it, can tend to become repetitive, dull and yes, downright boring. There was just too much to be seen so that after a while, over stimulated, one lost all appreciation for the priceless objects, which in effect, appeared to serve no practical purposes whatsoever, except specifically placed there most likely to impress an audience; and to impress might have been what Hearst had set his sights on by collecting whatever may have cast him in a better light with the public, or realistically speaking, a way of putting the spotlight on himself by the excessive display of art treasures in his "Casa Grande." Perhaps this was his method of compensating for the flaw in his character, for despite all his money, he was reported to have been an insecure man.

Leaving Hearst's art treasures for other tourists to view, the following day we drive along the spectacular rocky Pacific coastline that extends from San Simeon to Carmel and is known as "Big Sur." Destine for the City of the angels, Los Angeles, much to our surprise, an unforeseen accident occurs, and to everyone's relief not a serious one, and not to the car but to Linda, who with her husband Doug are our traveling companions. On the outskirts of Los Angeles, we drive by an in-door roller skating rink, and Linda suggests we go skating. In no rush to arrive in the City, we agree and the four of us outfitted with rental skates merrily skate on the oval shaped rink with background disco music adding to our enjoyment. Linda is skating in front of me, and in attempting to negotiate a sharp turn falls with her left arm striking the floor. Quickly skating to her aid, I see her wrist beginning to swell. Suspecting a fractured because of the rapid swelling, we drive to the nearest hospital where the x-rays taken indicate she has fractured a bone in her wrist. With her left arm in a cast for the remainder of the vacation, which in fact doesn't curtail in any manner our future activities, we head for our next destination.

Los Angeles is a big disappointment. A blighted City, particularly its downtown area where the Whites have obviously taken flight to the suburbs and left it to the Blacks and Mexicans. Also a big disappointment is the big tourists attraction, Sid Grauman's Chinese theatre, opened in 1927 and billed as one of the world's greatest movie palaces. Along the theatre's "entry Court" over one hundred and sixty movie stars have ser their signatures and hand and foot prints in slabs of cement. Most of the signatures have eroded badly with the passing of time and are barely legible. What in fact the four of us enjoy is the all-day tour to Universal Studios where we are treated to an actual shooting, or filming, of a scene for a motion picture. Among the many sets throughout the Studio's huge lot, and one of which has a lasting appeal for me is the set used in 1932 for the film, "King Kong." With its large platform surrounded by artificial trees and bushes, and two long poles in the middle of it, the gorgeous movie star, Fay Wray's outstretched arms were tied to them by the Island's natives as their offering for the mighty beast, Kong.

Our next stop is San Diego where my wife's sister lives, but first we take a detour by way of a day's visit to Catalina Island. There we witness the sight that appears to attract all the visitors, masses of Flamingo birds, most of which are not flying as one may have expected it, but instead, literally covering the Island's passageways meant for pedestrians, and performing a bird's version of pan handling for food. And to make matters worse, street vendor are everywhere creating a scene reminiscent of a summer street fair in Manhattan. The drive to San Diego is about two hours along the shores of the Pacific Ocean, the sight of which reminds me of a long ago era traveling on a Greyhound bus, and viewing in the distant landscape the now familiar scene of orange groves and oil well rigs. Arriving in San Diego there is still the familiar sight from World War II, people walking the City's streets, most of whom are sailors.

The visit to my sister-in-law is over, and because of its close proximity to San Diego, we decide to visit Mexico. Briefly passing through the crowded and dust filled border town of Tihuana, we drive to Encenada, which is about forty miles south of the U.S./Mexican border. With its traffic jams, masses of people trying to sell you something, and dust hovering everywhere, we leave Ensenada and head Northwest toward the Petrified Forest purposely bypassing the City of Phoenix in Arizona. However before getting to the Petrified Forest, and thereafter proceeding to what is to be the highlight of our vacation, the Grand Canyon, satisfying the urgent appeals of my wife, we stop at an unplanned visit to the Apache Indian Reservation.

How can the reservation best be described? To be quite frank, it's surely not a pleasant sight. The initial impression is that of a World War II German concentration camp without the guard towers. It's an arid landscape, parched, and an unfertile soil where nothing will grow, not even weeds. One-family cabins are surrounded, not with trees, shrubs or flowers, but with a lifeless ground where nothing is growing except for the dust above the dry soil that stirs occasionally with the help from the wind. The school house, which is actually a large cabin has children's desks that seem to have been made way back in the nineteen century, and an ancient blackboard that appears to be in dire need of replacing. Children are seen everywhere, skinny, and with their small bellies sticking out, which is a sure sign they are undernourished. And they are dressed, not exactly in rags, but in clothing obviously bought at a second hand store, or given to them, maybe by the Salvation Army, or the Red Cross. Men are seen tinkering with their old cars, and with facial features that tend to give away their high consumption of alcohol. And the women have set-up tables displaying hand made necklaces with beautiful turquoise stones attached to silver chains, men and women rings, and men's belt buckles set in silver. But despite the beautiful merchandize, it's a horribly sad scene with only the four of us as their customers.

CHAPTER 85

Reactions to an Action

At this very moment, which to be more exact, is the morning of September 13, 2001, I feel an urgent need to suspend all further writing related to my past experiences, temporarily at least, and react to a horrific disaster that happened two days ago of such magnitude that the media have declared it the biggest terrorists attack in the Country's history. This monstrous act, which has resulted in the untimely deaths of over two thousand people has aroused, not a loathing for the highjackers as might have been expected, who in all likelihood were carrying out a mission they strongly believed in, but rather, an insecure feeling, and an all-out disappointment in our Government for allowing it to happen. Granted, the catastrophic event has indeed revealed the deep hatred that most foreigners, in particular, the Arabs have for the Americans. The Government, nonetheless, has been aware of this fact that has been on-going for decades, yet has allowed the lack of insufficient security at airports by giving the airlines responsibility for maintaining security at all airports. This fact alone allowed for the incredible calamity to have happened causing the deaths of thousand of lives. Yes, a calamity that could have been averted had the government been in charge of security, instead of the airlines.

A key factor that arises is how and why did the security system at three major airports fail to detect nineteen Arab highjackers who managed successfully to board, almost simultaneously in fact, four commercial airline jets at Boston Dulles and Newark airports? Before proceeding further with the issue of why it happened, how and when the horrendous tragedy occurred should be described.

On Tuesday morning, September 11, 2001 at about 8:48 AM one of the highjacked jets, which had departed Boston and bound for Los Angeles rammed the north tower of the World Trade Center. Eighteen minutes later a second airline jet that had also departed Boston with its final destination Los Angeles plowed into the south tower of the 110 stories World Trade Center. At about 9:50 AM the south tower collapsed, and forty minutes later the north tower met the same fate. Almost at the times of these happenings, another large airline jet, which had departed Dulles Airport in Washington D.C. for San Francisco, diverted its course, and instead, plunged into the western part of the Pentagon Building. Finally, at about 9:45 AM, another highjacked plane, a United Airlines jet flying from Newark to San Francisco crashed near Pittsburgh killing all passengers and crew. According to voice recordings from the cockpit, the probable cause of the crash was due to the flight crew and passengers' attempts to subdue the highjackers. The aircraft's intended target is still unknown, however, based on speculations from the media and some high ranking officials, they have asserted that the most likely objective was to crash the plane into the capitol by utilizing the jet airliner as a missile weapon to destroy the building.

One may be justified now in asking the crucial question, how were nineteen highjackers able to commandeer four airline jets within a span of less than two hours? The obvious fact is that it had to be an operation long in the planning stages, and one ultimately well executed, which resulted in success for both the highjackers and their supporters. The aftermath of the violent events left the President vowing to seek-out and punish all those responsible for the vicious act. Not surprisingly, nothing has yet been said about the U.S. Government also being at fault for the tragedy, which at the risk of repeating it, should have never happened. But why hold the Government accountable for an act carried out to great success by nineteen Arab terrorists against this Country? Undoubtedly, the motive for the attack on these buildings was, as has previously been mentioned, the deeply imbedded grievances and hatred the Arab Nations harbor for the Americans' way of life that among others, are freedom, prosperity, religious plurality and national suffrage, which all go against the grain of their beliefs. But once again to be repetitive, how were the highjackers able to seize four airline jets and use three of them as missiles loaded with human cargo to destroy the World Trade Center and part of the Pentagon Building in Washington D.C.? And how did the security system at three major airports allowed it to happen? And who, if not the security system, can be held responsible for failing to prevent the highjackers from boarding the jets?

The first factor that needs to be mentioned is information associated with security personnel, and the equipment they use to detect passengers attempting to board aircraft with firearms in their possession. For starters, it's not the Government but the airlines that are, in effect, responsible for the security system at all airports, which may seem somewhat of a surprise to many people. The airlines hire and pay the people who manned the scanning machines and walk-thru portholes, and compensate them with the lowest wages, in accordance with the law, six dollars an hour, after training them for one or two weeks. These, in fact, are wages compatible to what an individual receives for flipping hamburgers at a McDonald's restaurant. By contrast, security workers performing the same identical work at European airports receive up to three months of training, and thereafter earn fifteen to sixteen dollars an hour. As a result, you have a large turnover of security workers at this Country's airports where the average tour of a worker amounts to about three months. A second factor worth highlighting is that the airlines are moneymaking enterprises, thus it's only natural that lowering their overhead by paying low wages to unskilled labor, for example the security workers, will increase the airlines' profits. In light of the fact that airlines tend to shave-off expenses in order to increase their profits, it's not surprising that a cost-saving strategy applied by them was the critical device that was the prime cause for the biggest terrorist attack in the Nation's history. One of the cost-saving strategies of the airlines is to use low-cost scanning machines that can only detect metal objects, instead of the more highly expensive ones that can detect both metal and plastic objects; this fact must have been known to the highjackers. But what prompts me to make this statement? Simply this, the weapons they used were not bombs or firearms, for instance, guns or rifles with sawed-off barrels, but plastic knives and cardboard box cutters.

The final question is why has security at airports been delegated to the airlines? Most likely, now that the horse has left the barn, as the saying goes, the Government will take over the responsibility of maintaining the security system at airports, not unlike the European countries where security is strictly enforced by Governments. However, what can in fact be done to deter terrorists form boarding airlines? First, and foremost, scanning machines that are able to detect not only metal objects but also plastic ones must be installed at all airports. Moreover, air marshals should be on board all commercial flights, and the cockpits of all airline aircraft should be equipped with special electronic locks to prevent any non-authorized person from entering them. In addition to this, and what may seem farfetched, but indeed can be an added defense against terrorists aboard planes, flight crews should be authorized to carry firearms. Frightening as it may sound, terrorists attacks are not always preventable, and we must be aware and on guard against them. The Government, in particular, should take heed of this fact. Let's ask ourselves this question, how often have we read newspaper headlines citing terrorists attacks on Israel by the Palestinians? Another question to dwell on, and one which may well be a lingering thought after the happenings on September 11, 2001, how can law enforcement people, or others for that matter, detect and prevent the individual who has the will to sacrifice his life for a cause he believes in by concealing explosives in his body with the intent of setting them off in the middle of the George Washington Bridge?

CHAPTER 86

The Vacation Ends

To get on with the writing project, or the memoirs might be a better way of expressing it, and resume describing our travels, after leaving the blighted environment witnessed at the Apache Indian Reservation, we set our course for East Central Arizona; our next stop will be the Petrified Forest. At the mention of the place, memories come to life of a young boy, perhaps no more than ten years old sitting in a dark and almost empty theatre viewing on a silver screen the opening scene of the film, "The Petrified Forest" in which the hero, the popular British actor Leslie Howard is walking briskly along the side of a highway, and oddly enough, with no cars in sight. Instead, what the young boy sees is sagebrush rumbling alongside the highway as though accompanying the walker. This is the same highway we're traveling on at the moment, and which has been described in Frommer's Travel Book as "The twenty seven miles scenic drive." The only scenic thing we see, however, is the ground literally covered with dull petrified wood in various sizes and forms, and much to our dismay, we're not permitted to pick-up any of it for souvenirs. To prevent this from happening, signs along the highway warn tourists that at the end of the drive, guards will randomly search cars for any petrified wood. "Stiff fines" are the consequences for tourists found with petrified wood in their cars. Naturally, after passing by the exit gate, there is the usual gift shop that enables us to purchase some small pieces, all of which have been polished so as to make the wood more appealing for the tourists.

Leaving the forest we drive North West to what promises to be the highlight of our vacation, the splendors of the majestic Grand

Canyon with its North and South Rims. The South Rim, in particular, is much more scenic than the North one. Rock formations of various shades of colors can be seen, depending on the sun's angle at the time of viewing them, present an unforgettable sight. All of the exciting photos taken of the Canyon attest to this fact. However, to fully appreciate one of nature's great wonders, it should be seen in person. By contrast, the North Rim predominantly has tall pine trees, which often obscure the rock formation. A notable experience that warrants a brief description is our mule trip to the bottom of the North Rim. We leave on our journey along with twenty four other tourists at eight o'clock in the morning and our guides, and all mounted on mules. The animals, one behind the other, amble down in single file along a rocky path, which appears to be terribly treacherous, yet made quite safe by the sure-footed mules. Not adding to our enjoyment of course, especially when riding in tandem, the animals are defecating constantly along the way. Arriving at the bottom of the Rim, much to everyone's surprise, a stifling heat greets us, and mosquitoes are everywhere. The effects of both the heat and the mosquitoes result in twenty five tourists eating their lunch in great discomfort, and longing to get on the mules and head back to the top of the Rim. Similar to the trip down to the bottom of the North Rim, the up-hill journey to the top is uneventful; that is, except for the following day when we're hobbling along with aches and pains in our bodies from the results of the previous day's ride on the mules.

Leaving the Grand Canyon, we travel west to Las Vegas before heading Northeast again for Bryce Canyon, and then on to Yellowstone National Park. Las Vegas does have its appeal for tourists, especially for gamblers, nonetheless, for us traveling on a tight budget, it allows no room for trying our luck on the ubiquitous slot machines. One of the City's offerings, if you can call it that, is the unbearable heat with surface temperatures hovering at 112 degrees Fahrenheit during noon hours. The swimming pool's water where we are staying is actually warm. The only enjoyment during our brief visit is the complimentary nightly shows at the casinos.

After the two days of relentless heat and restlessness, we have had enough of Las Vegas and drive to Bryce Canyon National Park in Utah.

Bryce Canyon's scenic attraction derives from its form, which is made-up of rocks intricately shaped and known as "Hoodoos." The origin of the name is unknown to us, nor anyone else we ask seems to know. The rock forms are colored in shades of red, brown, orange and yellow, which change and glow with the rising and setting sun. Continuing on with our travels, we stop at Jackson Hole in Wyoming before heading for Yellowstone National Park. Jackson Hole is a huge circular valley facing a tall rock formation known as The Grand Tetons. The name for the towering twin peaks reaching almost 14,000 feet was given to them by a Frenchman, who on first seeing the twin peaks appeared to him to resemble a woman's breast. Jackson hole's biggest attraction, in addition to the breathtaking scenic view of the snow capped twin peaks, are the horses. Horses are everywhere in sight, and the dude ranches, which seem to dot the landscape, are a haven for those who enjoy horseback riding. For the four of us, however, we had lost all enthusiasm for riding animals after the prolonged aches and pains due to our daylong experienced of riding mules down to the bottom and then to the top of the North Rim of the Grand Canyon. Instead, we simply enjoy the guided walking tours enjoying all the scenic views the Valley has to offer, its mountain peaks numerous small lakes, enchanting narrow roads, which are surrounded with trees of all sizes and shapes, and people watching, most of whom are tourists like us.

Rapidly our month's vacation is coming to an end, and we decide to proceed to Yellowstone National Park without any further delays so as to allow ourselves at least two days in San Francisco. The Park with its assortments of thermal geysers and hot springs have been cited in the Frommer guide book to exceed the number found on the rest of earth, and the Park's waterfalls are twice as tall as Niagara Falls. Some areas have large populations of wild life, most of which stay away from the hordes of tourists who visit Yellowstone during its brief summer season. Nonetheless, we see

Moose at far-off distances, and buffalos at close range, which make it possible to take close-up photos of the animals. Never do we realize until leaving the Park, when a forest ranger warns us of the dangerous risks of getting too close to buffalos because they're liable to charge at you at any moment if they become frightened. The tourists visit Yellowstone only during the short summer season, which is due to the fact that winter begins in September, and by October all roads are impassable because of the large snowfalls. Snowfalls are almost a daily occurrence from October until late May in Yellowstone National Park. After leaving the park, one brief stop is made at Salt Lake City where we visit the huge tabernacle, and thereafter, another brief stop at Reno, Nevada, which is more like a town than a small city, and very much like a miniature Las Vegas. Finally, we arrive in San Francisco, the starting point of our month long vacation.

San Francisco, unlike New York, is a City with steep hilly streets, cable trolley cars and the Golden Gate Bridge. The bridge is really painted orange, but when the sun's rays cast its rays on it, appears golden in color. The relatively small City with its population of less than a million inhabitants also has China town, which is about the cheapest place to shop, and their restaurants are significantly less expensive than the ones in New York City. A delicious Chinese dinner, including soup and fresh oranges for dessert, for example, is less than five dollars. Our three days accommodations are at the elegant St. Francis Drake Hotel off Union Square, and flowers and bowls of fresh fruit are in our rooms on our arrival. All are the complements, not of the hotel as we believe, but from the kindness of my mother-in-law who is in the hotel reservation business and has graciously made the arrangements for our stay at one third the original price of the rooms. The City, in a literal sense, charms the wife and me, primarily because of, among other appealing aspects, its small size, not densely populated, and its cleanliness, so much in fact that she and I devote time looking at an apartment that's for rent. No doubt, the thought of relocating is on our minds. This is not to happen once we find out the high cost of the rent, but of more importance, I also find out my employer, the Federal Aviation Administration, has no openings available at their San Francisco Facility. Our last day in the City prior to our departure, we drive north to the Napa Valley where we visit wineries, and sample some of the delicious wines offered to us. Finally, to revert to a saying often heard, all good things come to an end, ours most certainly did the following day when we boarded the flight and returned to Kennedy Airport. Dwelling on the saying a bit, the underlying circumstances surrounding a good thing are that, indeed, they must sooner or later come to their end like everything else in our lives; no matter how good a thing may be, for instance, a vacation, a performance at the opera, a theatre, a concert hall, or anything else for that matter, they always come to their end. And in light of our month's vacation, jaded from all the traveling by car, the many sights viewed, and physically exhausted, we were glad to return to our home in New York City, the Big Apple.

CHAPTER 87

Journey's End

It has indeed been a long journey along memory lane; and one that in fact began as a writing project and searching for a theme, which ultimately developed into the writer's memoirs. The journey has dealt with a life span that had its beginning sometime in the year 1929, with a young boy's happiness during his early childhood years in Puerto Rico. Gradually it unfolded to scenes in New York City, and the great depression of the 1930's, World War II, the post war years and the catastrophic terrorists attack on the World Trade Center on September 11, 2001. Finally three and a half months later, January 1, 2002, New Years Day, and it's almost the end of the journey.

A month ago the annual birthday arrived announcing my seventy seven years of life. Predictably, if one believes in lucky numbers, there will be many more years to come. Apart from me, there is of course the family, a wife and son who will be sixteen years old in five months. I must admit, his years have been good to him thus far, experiencing no hardships whatsoever, having all the essentials he needs, and also most of what he craves for. He does merit all that he has received, perhaps unaware he has rewarded his parents by earning good grades in school. Adding to the son's laurels, are his prowess for kicking a football, which for the boy's age is not surprising to the father. Not surprising I have said since even as an eight year old playing with his father in the park, he was able to kick the ball great distances. He has been selected as the regular kicker in the school's varsity team despite the fact he is only in his sophomore year; and he is also in the school's wrestling team. Obviously, this has all the earmarks a father boasting about his son's abilities both academically and in sports, and rightfully so I may add. This is a father who is very proud of his son, and will always love him, regardless of his academic or athletic achievements.

A year has just ended, and likewise, the writing project is almost at its end; however, where there is an end there is always a new beginning for the City's new Mayor and for the writer. With the end of Rudy Giuliani's last term in office, Michael Bloomberg was sworn in today as our new Mayor; but what about the writer? Quoting Robert Frost's memorable words from his poem, "Stopping by Woods on a Snowy Evening," hopefully, I will have " . . . miles to go before I sleep." And now to go forward, what events will most likely unfold in the new year? Naturally, we can speculate, nonetheless, time will reveal all that's in store for us in the coming year. More specifically, what objectives, or long term goals will be pursued? To be sure, the son and I, the mother is unable due to her work commitments, are embarking on twofold mission to Puerto Rico on February 18, 2002. The first is to acquaint my son with the Island where his father was born now that he is old enough to perhaps appreciate it, and to meet cousins he has never seen. Second is the longing desire to locate my father's grave, and to confirm the rumors that my father's father was a Jew from the Canary Islands who changed his name from Solomon to Solano when he emigrated to Puerto Rico. Thereafter, the son will return to school after his "winter break," and I will continue teaching English courses at Mercy College, and at the College of New Rochelle. The short term goal is to acquire a literary agent who applying his or her professional skills will attempt to get these words published. And at this final juncture, there is nothing else that remains to be said. Therefore, without further ado, adios, or goodbye to all those who have had the time and patience to read, Reflections of a New York Puerto Rican: A Memoir, I thank you.

BVG